כֶּרֶם לַנוֹטְרִים

From The Guardian's Vineyard

On Sefer B'reshith (the Book of Genesis)

Rabbi Dov Abraham iBen-Shorr

Beith David Yeshiva Publications

Har *Hebron*

ISBN 979-8-83997-400-5

For more information:

Beith David Yeshiva

US: 347-264-1764

Israel: 053-4605428

e-mail: publications@beithdavid.org

www.beithdavid.org

IN LOVING MEMORY

שלמה גדליה
בן
ביילע
Sanford Fleishman

לאה מרים
בת
פנינה
Lenore Fleishman

שמחה דוב
בן
יענטע ביילה
Samuel Bernard Fleishman

ביילע
בת
מרים
Beulah Spitz Fleishman

חייה לאה
בת
ביילע
Anita Helene Fleishman

חיים
בן
אסתר
Haim Jay Reece

In Loving Memory

פנינה

בת

רחל

Pauline Frank Reece

משה

בן

רחל

Morris Frank

רוז

בת

אסתר

Rose Rissin Penn

APPROBATION

בס"ד

Rabbi Sam Kassin, Dean
Rabbi Eliahou Shamoula, Director

Board of Directors
Alan Dweck
Leo Esses
Zac Gindi
Joey Habert
Morris A. Sutton
Richard A. Sutton
David R. Ades
Scott Shrem

י"ב סיון, תשס"ו עש"ק פר' 'בהעלותך' לסדר
"וַיְהִי בִּנְסֹעַ הָאָרֹן וַיֹּאמֶר מֹשֶׁה קוּמָה יְהֹוָה וְיָפֻצוּ אֹיְבֶיךָ
וְיָנֻסוּ מְשַׂנְאֶיךָ מִפָּנֶיךָ ...' (במדבר י:לה)

בא לפני האברך החשוב, תלמידי, ר' דוב אברהם בן שור שליט"א שלמד
בישיבתנו מספר שנים ועתה עוסק ביישובה של ארץ ישראל בגופו ממש
ומתגורר במעלה חבר, שמלאו ליבו לכתוב עיונים על פרשת השבוע. והביע
לעיוני עלים מספרו בנושא פרשת השבוע; עברתי על דפי הספר ומצאתי
שר' דוב אברהם בן שור כותב רעיונות שונים בצורה קלילה. וזאת על
מנת לקרב ללימוד פרשת השבוע ציבורים רחבים של לומדי תורה
המחפשים זיקה ליהדות דרך לימוד פרשת השבוע ומקבלים באמצעות
עיון בספר רעיונות חדשים ונשגבים.

וכבר לימדנו הנצי"ב שספר בראשית הוא: שורש כל התורה כולה ואם כן
ראוי שורש זה לחיזוק נוסף בדורנו והנני מברך את ר' דוב אברהם בן-שור
שיפוצו מעייניותיו החוצה ויזכה להגדיל תורה ולהאדירה.

בברכת התורה והחותם לכבודה,

שלמה ב"ר עזרא קצין
ראש הישיבה

Approbation

SSC shehebar sephardic center

Rabbi Sam Kassin, Dean
Rabbi Eliahou Shamoula, Director

בס"ד

(translated from the Hebrew)

12 *Sivan*, 5766
Erev Shabbat Qodesh parshath "B'ha'olathekh"

"וַיְהִי בִּנְסֹעַ הָאָרֹן וַיֹּאמֶר מֹשֶׁה קוּמָה יְהֹוָה וְיָפֻצוּ אֹיְבֶיךָ: (במדבר י:לה)
When the ark went for Moshe said, "Arise HaShem and scatter Your enemies,."
(*Bamidbar 10*)

The young scholar, Ribbi Dov Abraham Ben-Shorr, *shlita*, my student has come before me for this approbation. He had learned and taught in our yeshiva for many years and now, in addition to his learning, is engaged in settling the Land of *Erets Yisrael* in actuality living in the community of *Ma'aleh Hever* in *Har Hebron*. It now has filled his heart to write concerning the weekly Torah portions, and hs written them in this book. I have reviewed the pages of this book and have found that Ribi Dov Abraham Ben-Shorr has brought a variety of complex ideas and has presented them in simple clear language accessible to general public. He has done so in order that more people will merit the learning of the weekly Torah portion, and this book is an excellent vessel for facilitating that access.

We have already learned from the *Natsiv* that *Sefer Bereshith* [the Book of Genesis] is the root of the entire totality of Torah. And if so, it is most appropriate that this root should be strengthened in our generation, and I therefore offer Ribbi Dov Abraham Ben-Shorr my blessings that his ideas will go out and merit the growth and splendor of Torah.

With Blessings of Torah and Signed in its honor,

Shlomo ben HaRavi Ezra Kassin
Rosh Yeshiva

CONTENTS

ACKNOWLEDGMENTS

For:

HaShem, the Holy One of Blessing

Who has created and sustained me

And bestowed upon me blessings

Whose number cannot be counted

Yet, who in the course of my daily life I often fail to fully appreciate.

And To my parents:

Shlomo Gedaliah (Sanford)

And *Leah* Miriam (Lenore)

His partners in my creation.

May He bless them with a multitude of all of His Blessing

And Especially to my wife and family

Who have been His greatest blessing In my life.

FOREWORD

"Turn it and turn it again (delve deeply into it) for all is found within," teach our sages concerning the Torah (*Pirqe Avoth* 5:26). The Torah we are taught, is the blueprint for the entire universe, therefore its study connects one both with the Builder (God) and His Creation. As a blueprint, all can be found within - given enough study.

Our sages clearly are talking about much more than a superficial reading of the text. In fact, according to the Holy Zohar (*parshath b'Huqotekha*), the text we call "Torah," that is the stories of the Bible, is merely a garment for the Heavenly Torah. Just as *malakhim* [angels] do not come to this world in their pure form but "dress" as humans, for the world wouldn't suffer them if they didn't, so too the Torah, which created the *malakhim*, needs to dress in a form that gives it expression in this world. This is the narrative of the Torah. (This is not, God Forbid, to suggest that the stories are anything but factual. HaShem, the Architect of the world and Mover of history, caused the events in conjunction with the narrative.) The Zohar teaches that one who thinks that these stories are the essence of Torah, are not only foolish, but it would be better if they had never been born. Such a person will judge an individual by the clothes he wears, and not examine the person any further.

A good analogy would be a person receiving a precious gift, which, due to its importance, was wrapped in an impressive wrapping. Even though the wrapping itself is special, one would consider a person a fool if they simply kept the package wrapped up, without ever investigating its contents.

The Zohar continues that the body of the Torah is the *mitswoth* [the commandments], but one who stops his investigation there, also falls short of its essence, which, like with a person, is found within the soul of the Torah. The body is simply that which articulates the soul, and gives expression to its hidden depth.

"*Shelomo* had a vineyard at *Ba'al amon*, he gave the vineyard to guardians. For its fruit everyone was to bring a thousand silver. My vineyard, which is Mine, is before Me. A thousand for you, Shelomo, and two hundred for the guardians." (*Shir HaShirim* [Song of Songs] 8:11)

HaShem has planted a vineyard, the Torah, an expression His presence, and He has appointed guardians to guard it and delve into its midst, harvesting its fruit for His children to indulge. <u>The Guardian's Vineyard</u> offers a taste, a glimpse, into the fruits of HaShem's Holy Vineyard. May its fruit satiate our essence and give us continued strength for our journey in life.

PARSHATH B'RESHITH

Overview

The beginning, and yet as we learn, this beginning is a continuation of our "ending". When a Jew completes a cycle of reading Torah, he immediately begins again anew. It is related that the Torah begins with the Hebrew letter "*beth*" and ends with the Hebrew letter "*lamed*." If one reads the Torah from beginning to end, and stops – feeling that he's "completed" it, then his learning was on the level of "*beth-lamed*," a word meaning "*balu'i*," "shabby or worn out." "*Bal*" also means, "not" or it can mean "*b'lo*," meaning, "without." However, when one begins anew, effectively going from the "*lamed*" to the "*beth*," then one's learning is on the level of "*lev*," "heart," and the learning becomes a part of the person.

Further, the Oral Law, in the form of the Mishna, begins with the letter "*mim*," the letter that follows *lamed*, and ends with the last letter of the *aleph-beth*, the "*taw*." This suggests that Torah is not complete unless one has both the written and the Oral Torah. The Oral Torah is, among other things, the explanations and methodology for exegesis that *Moshe Rabbeinu* [Moses our Teacher] received on Mount Sinai and has been passed down from father to son and teacher to student to this day.

The Torah, and thus *Sefer Bereshith* [The Book of Genesis], begins with the Creation of the Universe. Many "*m'forshim*" [commentators on the *Tanakh*[1]] question why the Torah begins with the Creation of the world. This may seem like a strange question, but only because we are so conditions to begin the Torah with Creation. Learning Torah requires one to question even the most fundamental assumptions.

---

1 *Tanakh* is an acronym for *Torah* (the five Books of *Moshe*), *Nivi'im* (Prophets) and *K(h)'tuvim* (Writings)

Parshath B'reshith

Considering that Torah is really about the relationship between *HaShem*[2] and His people *Yisrael* [Israel], shouldn't the Torah start with *Sh'moth* [Exodus], which begins the story of *Yisrael*'s birth as a nation? Or, maybe it should begin with *Wayiqra* (Leviticus), which has the vast majority of laws and ritual?

Rashi (Rabbi Shlomo *YitsHaqi*, the foremost commentator on the entire *Tanakh* and Talmud, lived in Northern France during the 49th Century[3] (eleventh century C.E.)] points out that *Bereshith* establishes HaShem's ownership of the Universe. It is His creation. Therefore if the nations of the world were to say (as they so often do) to *Yisrael*, "You are bandits for you conquered the land of the seven (Canaanite) nations," then we will be able to respond that all of the earth is the property of the Holy One of Blessing. He created it and gave it to those whom He chose. It was His Will to give it to them, and it was His Will to take it from them and give it to His Chosen People, *Yisrael* as an eternal inheritance.

The story of Creation, which is a detailed account of the creation of the Universe and the development of human civilization, has caused many "modern" people a lot of difficulty. Wanting to believe in God, and the Truth of the Torah, they have difficulty reconciling *Bereshith* with modern science. How can one understand the literal meaning of the text, and, at the same time accept the seemingly incontrovertible evidence of science?

There are several answers to this difficulty. First, Torah cannot be understood without commentary. The written Torah that we received at Mount Sinai is only a part of the revealed Truth that we received. The written Torah (*l'havdil*- an expression that means there can be no real comparison here, we are only using it as a metaphor) can be compared to class notes of a lecture. Someone who wasn't in the lecture would have a hard time understanding the notes without some type of explanation or at least a basic understanding of the subject matter. The Oral tradition provides meaning to the Torah and helps us understand the "notes." *Moshe Rabbeinu* [our teacher] sat in the lecture for forty days on *Har* [Mount] Sinai, and when he descended, he taught the Torah, with its explanations to several groups of people, until the entire Nation of *Yisrael* learned the tradition. This was then passed down from parent to child and teacher to student for almost two hundred generations.

---

2 Literally, The Name, which designates the name of the God of Israel Who is beyond the limits and definition of a name.

3 Traditional Judaism has several methods for dating. The most common begins from the creation of Adam, thus 49th Century is equivalent to the 11th C.E. Century of the Christian calender.

So, understanding what is written is only a hint of the Truth, we can now take a more critical look at what seems to be a conflict between science and Torah. I will not argue that there aren't differences between the way each see the world, but as time progresses, science has slowly begun to understand the world in the same light as the Torah's understanding.

For instance, for close to two thousand years, the scientific understanding of the universe was based on the Greek philosopher Plato's understanding that the there wasn't a beginning. That the Universe always existed and has simply changed formed over time. In other words, until the Big Bang Theory, science believed that there was no beginning to the Universe, that there wasn't a Creation. In fact, this belief was so fundamental to science that it took over fifty years for science to accept the truth of the Big Bang. There were even notable scientists, including Albert Einstein, who changed results of their calculations (which would have suggested a beginning), because they were so indoctrinated in the Platonic concept of the world that they thought they had simply erred in their calculations.

The Torah has always maintained that there was a beginning to the universe and that God created it out of nothingness. The Qabbalist,[4] through the writings of Rabbi *Moshe ben* NaHman (known as the Ramban or Nachmonides), goes even further. He writes, in his commentary to *B'reshith*, that the entire universe began from an insignificant speck, which God created, and then exploded out into what we now know as the Universe. The Ramban postulated in his commentary, based on the Torah and his teachers' tradition, that this insignificant speck was a bundle of primordial light, pure energy, that as it expanded began to form matter, creating the universe we know today. In other words, the Ramban, based on a thorough understanding of the Torah, postulated the theory we call today, "the Big Bang." It is important to note, that the Ramban lived in the thirteenth century C.E. Spain, when most of Europe still thought the world was flat.

Further, the *Midrash* [Rabbinical stories based on or derived from the Biblical narrative] suggests that before this Universe was created, HaShem created and destroyed many other universes. Thus the sages preempted the concept of multiple universes, nine hundred years before the modern era.

According to one interpretation of the Seven Days of Creation, we can understand the dichotomy through the science of Albert Einstein and his theory of relativity. According to Dr. Gerald Schroeder, in his books, <u>Genesis and the Big Bang</u>, and <u>The Science of God</u>, the 'seven days' can be understood from the point of perspective. It is common for the Torah text to shift perspectives, helping the reader understand things from different angles.

---

4 For lack of a better term - Jewish Mysticism, though note that this is imprecise.

Parshath B'reshith

Here, according to Schroeder, the Torah begins from the perspective of the point of Creation. From that perspective, the Universe was created in seven, twenty-four hour Earth days (exactly what the reader understands a day to be). However, understanding time to be relative, those seven days are much longer from the perspective of the Earth itself. In fact, according to Schroeder, by calculating a known phenomenon of the physic of light called the Blue Shift, the age of the universe from the Earth's perspective should be approximately fifteen or sixteen billion years old. Further, Schroeder applies the Blue Shift to each of the six days of Creation and comes up with amazing results, wherein each day of Biblical Creation corresponds to the scientific understanding of the earth's formation. For further study, one should examine Dr. Schroeder's books.

There are also other interpretations of the seven days; interpretations which reconcile the apparent conflict between the Bible and science hundreds, and sometimes thousands, of years before there even seemed to be a conflict.

The sages in the Talmud suggest, for instance, that the seven days of Creation, as described in the Torah, are 'outside' of the Biblical time line.

And spectacularly, in his commentary *Sefer Yetsirah* [The Book of Formation attributed in part to the Patriarch Abraham], Ribbi *YitsHaq* of Akko, a student of the Ramban, calculates the age of the current universe as being approximately fifteen billion, three hundred and forty thousand. See his commentary on chapter four for his detailed calculation.

Parshath B'reshith describes the creation of the world and then the beginning of humanity. The Jewish calendar begins from the creation of *Adam ha-rishon* [literally the first human], or more precisely his expulsion from the Garden, which began 5,781 years ago (as of Fall of 2020 according to the Christian calendar). "*Parsha*" means section or chapter, and it is the traditional way the Torah is divided. Each *parsha* being publicly read each week on the *Shabath* [Sabbath], completing the cycle in a year.

In this first parsha. we read the story of Adam and *Havah* [often translated as Eve], their sin and expulsion from *Pardes*-the Garden. Then we learn about an argument between the brothers, *Kayin* and *Hevel,* which resulted in latter's murder. The generations of *Shet,* Adam's later son, are detailed, along with the various discoveries and developments throughout the generations.

Finally our parsha concludes with the Generation of the Flood, which became incredibly corrupt and distant from God. The end of the parsha introduces *NoaH* and describes God's exasperation at the behavior of his Creation, and His resolve to destroy (almost entirely) the world. *NoaH* is introduced to us as a righteous and simple man in his generation. We are told that *NoaH* walked with God. Already, at the end of this week's parsha, there is a foreshadowing of events to come. HaShem has begun to "regret" most of His creation, with the exception of *NoaH*.

In Detail: *A selection of some verses of interest:*

1:1 –   בְּרֵאשִׁית
"Bereshith ..."

The first word, as Rashi points out, screams, "Interpret me!" Grammatically the word is in *"smikhut"* form, meaning, the first noun in a compound noun pair (an English example would be schoolhouse ["school" and "house"]). In Hebrew this first noun takes a special grammatical form. However, *"Bereshith"* isn't followed by a second noun, but, instead, by a verbal phrase. This has led to a variety of interpretations.

The Ramban [Ribbi *Moshe ben* NaHman] interprets the verse, "In the beginning of time, God created the Heaven and the Earth" (see overview above).

Rashi [Ribbi Shlomo *YitsHaqi*]offers several interpretations.

Rashi offers a midrashic (Midrash is specific form of interpretation) interpretation found in *Bereshith Rabbah*, that the Torah is called *"reshith,"* based on the verse from *Mishley* [Proverbs], *"Reshit darko,"* "HaShem created me as the beginning of His way, the first of His works of old," which refers to Wisdom. This Midrash explains how God created the Torah first, as a blueprint for the Universe, and then, looked into the Torah, and created the world. Thus, the verse would be interpreted, "From *Reshith* (Torah), God created the Heavens and the Earth."

Offering another interpretation, more in line with the simple meaning of the text, Rashi interprets the entire predicate as the second noun in the smikhuth form, rendering the verse, "In the beginning of God's creating the Heaven and the Earth ..."

1:1 –   בְּרֵאשִׁית בָּרָא אֱלֹהִים אֵת הַשָּׁמַיִם וְאֵת הָאָרֶץ
"Bereshith bara El-him eth HaShamayim w'eth ha-Arets."
(in the beginning, G-d created the Heaven and the Earth)

It can not be stressed how mind blowing the nuanced and

multilayered text of the Torah can be. And it all starts with the first verse. For example (and the following is is really just a drop in the bucket): The final letters of the first three words of the Torah spell אמת *Emeth* – Not only does this word mean truth, they happen to be the first, middle an last letter of the Hebrew alphabet.

Added to that, the sum of the remaining final letters is the *gematria* (numerical equivalent – each letter has a fixed numerical value) of the expression בראשית טוב meaning "In the beginning of good". It is also the *gematria* of the verse [2:18]: "וַיֹּאמֶר יְהוָה אֱלֹהִים לֹא־טוֹב הֱיוֹת הָאָדָם לְבַדּוֹ". "It is not good that man should be alone." Or, if you prefer, the final verse of the Book of Tehillim (Psalms): כֹּל הַנְּשָׁמָה תְּהַלֵּל יָהּ which means, "Every soul will praise G-d".

Further, the sum of the first letters of this first verse is the *gematria* value of twenty-two, which *happens* to be the number of letters of the Hebrew alphabet, which the esoteric teachings of Torah consider to be the vessels of Creation.

The first verse has many other curiosities. Ivan Panin, a Russian mathematician, discovered that there are over fifty different permutations of the number seven in the first verse. Some examples are as follows:

There are seven words in the first verse, consisting of a total of twenty-eight (7x4) letters, fourteen (7x2) in the subject, and fourteen in the predicate. The *gematria*[5] of the only verb, "*bara*" [bet (2), resh (200), aleph (1)] is equal to 203 (7x29). The *gematria* of the three nouns (added together) is 777 (7x111). Also, the *gematria* of the first and last letters of every word (added together) equals 1393 (7x199).

Even more intriguing is that the number seven plays a significant role throughout the entire Creation story. The word for "God," "*Elhim*," appears thirty-five times (7x5) while the word for "earth" appears twenty-one times (7x3). Also, the words for day, heavens, good, flying, and crawling also appear in multiples of seven.

One more note of significance: Pinchas Zalman Hurwitz, from

---

5 Numerical value – each letter has both a sound and a numerical value. The first letter, *aleph* is "1," beth is equal to "2," and so on.

Cracow Poland, discovered that the name for God [spelled with a yud (10), and a *hey* (5) and a *waw* {sometimes pronounced vav} (6) and another *hey* (5) adding up to the *gematria* of 26] appeared 1,820 times in the Torah, which, coincidentally, is 70 x 26 (the *gematria* for the name).

Seven is a significant number for a number of reasons. It symbolizes natural completeness or the essence of things. Our world is three dimensional, meaning that all things have six sides (each dimension in both directions) and the seventh "side" in Jewish thought is the thing itself, the whole, or gestalt, which is greater than the sum of its parts.

It should be noted that just like the first verse of the Torah has twenty-eight letters, divided into two sets of fourteen (fourteen is the numerical equivalent of hand), the introductory verse for the receiving of the Ten Commandments also has twenty-eight letters, divided into two sets of fourteen. This reflects the concept that here, the Torah teaches about the external reality of the Universe, the physical, while the Revelation at Sinai reflects its inner reality.

1:1 –   בָּרָא אֱלֹהִים
"bara El-him"

Rashi points out that the word for God in the beginning of Creation is "*El-him*," and not God's more intimate name, written with the letters "*yod*" and "*hey*" and "*waw*" and "*hey*," and pronounced (though with the exception of blessings and other rituals it should not be casually pronounced) as "a-donuth," and refered to as "HaShem" (as spelled above with the *gematria* of 26). This name, *Elhim*, represents the attribute of Justice, in which God originally tried to create the world. However, God then "realized" that the world cannot exist under the dictates of strict Justice and thus continued the creation with the Attribute of Mercy.

Another explanation for the use of *Elhim* as opposed to HaShem, is that *Elhim* is the more general name for God, the name in which the entire world knows Him, while HaShem is the more intimate name that God uses with the Jewish People from the time of Sinai. It therefore makes sense that the more Universal name would be used in the Creation of the entire world.

1:2 – תֹ֙הוּ֙ וָבֹ֔הוּ

"tohu w'bohu"

Often translated as "without form and void," or "chaos," this expression is very difficult to understand. Translating *"tohu"* as unformed seems to be a good linguistic translation of the word, however, linguistically *"bohu"* does not seem related to void or chaos. Both the *Gemara* (Talmud *bnei Masekhet Hagigah* 12a) and the Ramban's commentary on this verse suggest something more powerful. They suggest that the word implies "the building blocks of Creation." According to Dr. Gerald Schroeder, an accurate translation might be, "the earth was in a state of chaos, but filled with the building blocks of matter."

1:2 – וְר֣וּחַ אֱלֹהִ֔ים מְרַחֶ֖פֶת עַל־פְּנֵ֥י הַמָּֽיִם

"...and the spirit of God hovered (*m'raHefeth*) over the surface of the waters ..."

The word, *"m'raHefeth"* is the same word used for a mother bird sitting on her children – with love and care—an apt metaphor for HaShem's concern for His Creation.

1:3 – וַיֹּ֥אמֶר אֱלֹהִ֖ים יְהִ֣י א֑וֹר וַֽיְהִי־אֽוֹר

"God said, 'Let there be light' and there was light."

It is important to note that "light" in the context of this verse isn't referring to the natural light of our environment. The sun, stars, and moon were not created until the fourth day. This is what the Qabbalists call the supernal light, that light which is God's essence, so to speak, in this world. This is the light of knowledge and understanding. This light is beyond our normal perception, and unlike natural light, hasn't any admixture of "darkness" within it. This helps us to understand the next verse.

1:4 – וַיַּ֧רְא אֱלֹהִ֛ים אֶת־הָא֖וֹר כִּי־ט֑וֹב וַיַּבְדֵּ֣ל אֱלֹהִ֔ים בֵּ֥ין הָא֖וֹר וּבֵ֥ין הַחֹֽשֶׁךְ

"God saw that the Light was good; God made a differentiation between the Light and the Darkness ..."

Rashi says that to understand this verse we need to learn the *Aggada* [the non-legal texts in the Talmud] from *Masekhet Hagigah*, where it states that God saw that the Light was so good, that it was not fitting for evil people to use it, so he separated it out for the Righteous in World to Come. Rashi declares something incredible here. He says that this is the simple meaning of the text and that which we call "light" today is a mixture of light and darkness called "day" and a night is also a mixture of light and darkness (though a different mixture obviously). Rashi, it should be noted makes a point of reading the simple, basic meaning of the text, what is called "*pshat*," and has dedicated his commentary to such an understanding.

It is thus important to understand what "*pshat*," is and what it isn't. It isn't necessarily the literal meaning of the text nor it's simplistic meaning, but rather a basic understanding using understandable terms (if you understand the terms). In other words, when the Torah uses an expression, one must understand it in context (and this is where the Oral Law helps). It's often not appropriate to reduce the expression to a literalistic meaning, for then it's real meaning would be lost, such as in the common expressions, "being large," or "head and shoulders above the rest," or a "chip off the old block." Taking literally these expressions would most often simply be silly.

1:5 –   וַיְהִי־עֶרֶב וַיְהִי־בֹקֶר יוֹם אֶחָד
"...there was evening; there was morning, one day (or Day One)."

Rashi points out that according to the order of the other days, we would expect to find the words, "the first day." Rashi brings a midrash from *Bereshith Rabbah*, which says that God did not create the *m'lakhim* [Angels] until the second day, and this is also a hint that for each *m'lakh* was appointed a specific day of the week.

I think another possibility might be that this wasn't the first day as such, because only with the creation of something called "a day," and thus the creation of time, would there be something of a linear progression of time. This anomaly may be pointing to the creation of time, and therefore, after one was created, we are able to call things, "second," or "third."

1:14 –   וְהָיוּ לְאֹתֹת וּלְמוֹעֲדִים וּלְיָמִים וְשָׁנִים
"...there were signs (*othoth*) and seasons and days and years."

The word "*othoth*" means signs, but is also closely related to the concept of seals, concerning covenants. For instance, the term is used for three different things in the Torah: *Shabbath*, *milah* [circumcision] and *tefillin* [phylacteries], which act as witnesses to the covenant between HaShem and *Yisrael* (This is why we don't wear *tefillin* on *Shabbat*, as contracts and covenants only require two witnesses).

From this we can see a hint of the sages teaching that from the very beginning of Creation, HaShem created the future signs and wonders that would later occur, as with Yehoshua causing the sun o be suspended in the sky so he would have enough time to destroy his enemy.

Through the help of Heaven, I also discovered that the word, *"othoth"* when written out in full as אותות, it has the *gematria* of the well known expression, meaning "Dawid, King of *Yisrael*, is alive and well." This phrase has become a 'sign' of faith among Jews in the eventual advent of redemption and the coming of the *MashiaH* [Messiah].

1:26 – וַיֹּאמֶר אֱלֹהִים נַעֲשֶׂה אָדָם בְּצַלְמֵנוּ כִּדְמוּתֵנוּ
"Let us make Man in our image, like our likeness …"

The obvious question that arises with this verse is, who is God talking to, and why does He ask permission? Rashi tells us that this verse teaches that humans are similar in many respects to the Hosts of Heavens, the *m'lakhim* [Angels], and that he consulted with them.

Others teach that God is teaching us a valuable moral lesson with this verse. Even though HaShem is vastly superior to the Heavenly Hosts (in fact they are His creation as well), he asks their opinion to show them respect.

It is taught that the *m'lakhim* were very jealous of the Creation of Man and in fact argued against Mankind's creation. However, God overruled them and established humanity.

Rashi interprets "in our image" to mean in understanding and wisdom.

1:27 – צֶלֶם אֱלֹהִים בָּרָא אֹתוֹ זָכָר וּנְקֵבָה בָּרָא אֹתָם
"…in the image of God, He created Him; male and female, He created them."

According to *Midrash Aggadah*, Man was created with two faces initially and only afterward was he divided into two. This is supported by the text wherein Man is called *"Adam"* [the more generic term for human] until after the creation of woman from his side, after which he is also called *"ish"* [the more specific term meaning man].

The reason "Man" was created male and female, back to back, was to protect him/her from the external forces. Since he was newly created, and hadn't any merits or good deeds, HaShem created them back to back, to guard that side from which the external forces tries to draw and suckle from the inherent holiness of their being.

1:28 – וַיְבָרֶךְ אֹתָם֮ אֱלֹהִים֒ וַיֹּאמֶר לָהֶם אֱלֹהִים פְּרוּ וּרְבוּ וּמִלְאוּ אֶת־הָאָרֶץ וְכִבְשֻׁהָ וּרְדוּ בִּדְגַת הַיָּם֙ וּבְעוֹף הַשָּׁמַיִם וּבְכָל־חַיָּה הָרֹמֶשֶׂת עַל־הָאָרֶץ

"God blessed and said to them, 'Be fruitful and multiply and fill the earth, conquer it, and rule over the fish of the sea, the birds of the sky, and every living thing that moves on the earth."

This is the first *mitswah* in the Torah. Immediately after God created Man, He blessed him and charged him. This *mitswah* is generally called *"p'ru ur'bu,"* 'to be fruitful and multiply.' This seems somewhat strange as a *mitswah*, a commandment, of God. Humans are built with natural inclination towards procreation and logically we shouldn't need to be commanded to engage in it.

Sefer HaHinukh, a compendium of the six hundred and thirteen Torah commandments, declares this to be a crucially important *mitswah*, without which, the other *mitswoth* can not be carried out. In other words, there needs to be people to follow God's will.

Yet, this still doesn't explain its necessity. I would suggest two possibilities. God understands that humans, unlike animals, might be inclined to divorce themselves from the natural world, particularly the world of marital relations in an effort to be "spiritual." We see this in many of the world's religions, which stress asceticism.

Often adherents will divorce themselves from the world, either permanently or for short periods of time. This is not a Jewish ideal. Instead, the Torah teaches us to imbue the mundane with the holy; that every day acts, when placed in the proper framework can be elevated to being "spiritual." "Spirituality" is not some "high" one can get from time to time, but rather, a way of living connected to the ultimate reality that is God.

There are ideas of asceticism within our tradition. The *nazir*, for example, was sworn from wine and other things for a period of time. Yet, this is not considered the ideal, as demonstrated by the fact that the *nazir* was required to bring a sin offering when his vow was completed. Torah stresses the elevation of life, not divorce from it.

The second reason, which may be more central, is that by making it a *mitswah*, God was able to frame this natural inclination and delineate its limitations. The *mitswah* is only incumbent upon men. Women are not required to take the initiative and strive to marry at all costs, and if they refuse to marry, they do not violate any *mitswoth* (though it is still considered good for them to do so). In this way, wives were given a certain amount of autonomy with regard to relations with their husband, which would not exist if they were equally obligated. In addition, it places the obligation of marriage with men who are naturally less inclined to marry, especially today when, to our sorrow, so many seek to taste the sweet fruit without taking on its responsibility.

According to our tradition, man becomes obligated to marry in his eighteenth year (i.e.; from his seventeenth birthday) and should strive to be married by his twentieth birthday. Some scholars suggest that it is meritorious for them to marry even younger (though not before fourteen). He may also delay fulfillment of this *mitswah*, if he is engaged in Torah study, and not otherwise distracted by his urges. The Talmud [*Masekhet Kiddushin* 29b] teaches that until the age of twenty, the Holy One of Blessing sits waiting in hope for a man, saying, "When will he take a wife?" Once he has reached twenty and is not married, He says, "May his bones rot!" This is brought to explain the difficulty of finding a suitable wife after the age of twenty.

A man fulfills his obligation of procreation when he has both a son and a daughter and they each have a son and a daughter (between them), but he is encouraged to have more.

It is an obligation incumbent upon men, remaining in force for all time, in every place. According to *Sefer HaHinukh*, anyone who fails to fulfill this *mitswah* (in his lifetime) disobeys an obligation of action for which his punishment will be very great, for "he shows personally that he does not want to fulfill the wish of the Eternal HaShem to settle His world."

A side note for modern times, wherein many people claim to be worried about the enormous population on the planet today. First, in truth, if (admittedly a big "if") we use the resources of the planet wisely, there is plenty for everyone, and there shouldn't be any danger to the planet or humanity as a whole. Secondly, I heard a very wise teaching once, that suggested that it is not seemly for Jews, at least, to worry about the population "problem" of the world, because, simply put, the world has continually decimated our numbers. At the present, Jews comprise approximately 0.2% of the world's population. At one point, we were approximately two percent of the world's peoples (right before the Holocaust we were 0.8%).

Also, another aspect of the phrase, פְּרוּ וּרְבוּ, is that it has the *gematria* [numerical equivalent] of five hundred, which is also the sum of the 'filled letters' of one of the names of God, the name Sha-day. 'Filled letters' or hidden letters are those which would complete the name of each letter. for instance, the first letter Aleph, is spelled out as אלף - the first letter being the actual letter, while the letters following tell us how to pronounce the letter. The filled letters of the name Sha-day, would be: *shin, yod, Nun — daleth, Lamed, taw — yod, waw, daleth* - (שׁ יּ *נ ד לת י וד*).

1:31 –   וְהִנֵּה־טוֹב מְאֹד
"…and it was very good…"

Unlike the other days where God declares them to be simply "good," here He calls His creation "very good." The sages interpret this to be referring to the "*Yetser haRa'*," often translated as the "evil inclination." According to our tradition, everyone has two inclination, one towards *tov* [good] and one towards *ra'* [translated as evil]. However, the sages see the *Yetser haRa'* as a positive force at its root, as everything from HaShem is ultimately good.

It is taught that the rabbis once sought to slaughter the *Yetser haRa'*, but were only able to confine it. However, the very next day, they noticed that the world had ceased to function: eggs were no longer being laid, buildings weren't being built. They were compelled to release the *Yetser haRa'* back into the world.

Our tradition teaches, that when the *Yetser haTov* [the inclination to good] can reign the *Yetser haRa'*, then the latter can be used to benefit the world. Therefore, it is not the inclinations of lust and ambition that are in themselves evil, rather, it is in the way we channel our energies and the object of our desires that define the good or evil outcome of our impulses.

2:3 – וַיְבָרֶךְ אֱלֹהִים אֶת־יוֹם הַשְּׁבִיעִי וַיְקַדֵּשׁ אֹתוֹ

"God blessed the seventh day and sanctified it …"

Shabbath is the object and goal of creation. It is the seventh side (the soul - see above) of the physical universe. In other words, on a very deep level, *Shabbath* is not the result of Creation, but Creation is the result of *Shabbath*, just as the body's existence is to house and sustain the soul (and clearly not an end in itself).

2:5 – כִּי לֹא הִמְטִיר יְהֹוָה אֱלֹהִים עַל הָאָרֶץ

"for HaShem had not caused it to rain upon the earth …"

Rain did not exist before the creation of Man. The purpose of rain is to help establish a relationship between humanity and God. Oftentimes man can toils the earth, planting, fertilizing, doing it all, but, as Rashi points out, without rain, his efforts will be for naught. Man needs rain, and thus must request it from God; it is beyond his control.

This explains why Israel has such a bounty of everything but receives rain with difficulty whereas, other places, like Egypt often have too much water. God wants us "to stay in touch."

There is the story of a king who had two sons, one was the apple of his eye while the other was constantly rebelling and caused the king great anguish. Finally, he bought the rebel his own castle and set him up an account that all of his needs would be provided for. The other son, however, had to come to the king for every little request. A servant was perplexed and asked the king, "If you love this son so much, why do you make him come to you for every little thing, while the one who vexed you is given everything he needs?" The king answered, "I love both of my sons and must provide for both of their needs, but my one son makes me so happy, I want him to be constantly around me, so therefore I arranged it that he would come to me for every little thing. That way we will always be in touch and I can revel in his goodness."

2:10 – וּמִשָּׁם יִפָּרֵד וְהָיָה לְאַרְבָּעָה רָאשִׁים

"… and from there it was parted and branched into four streams …"

We all assume that the world is the way it is because it had to be that way. In other words, that there is an imperative to the development of the world. However, this is not so. It is taught that there were four streams flowing out of Gan Eden, one stream was the lust for money, one stream was the lust for power, one stream was the lust for sex (as opposed to love), and one stream was the lust for Truth and Goodness. The world, our world, is the way it is because we choose those particular streams that lead away from Truth and Goodness. For instance, we, as a world, could have chosen to invest our resources in pursuits other than war and domination. It is also important that we are not stuck in any particular path, but can always choose to follow the stream in a different direction from the one we started on. Free choice is always an option, though we might have more difficulty trying to swimming upstream from our original path.

3:1 – וְהַנָּחָשׁ הָיָה עָרוּם מִכֹּל חַיַּת הַשָּׂדֶה
"The serpent was the most *Arum* (translated as crafty, but literally means naked) of all the beasts ..."

The serpent is called "*Arum*." Rashi understands this to mean that the serpent saw Man and Woman naked and thus devised a way to steal the woman from her husband.

I believe there is a very powerful message here. Our use of language suggests that nakedness is the opposite of craftiness; that to "expose oneself," one is not hiding anything. However, the opposite is in fact true. By exposing my physical being, by being naked or by dressing immodestly, I am suggesting that this physicality is who I really am and therefore, I am really hiding my true essence. However, if I dress modestly, I am inviting someone to get past the surface and get to know the real me, that is, my essence. This can be compared to a bright light being shone on a window. While I see the window very clearly, the reflection of the light actually hides what I might see through the window. Only when I turn off the light will I be able to peer inside.

3:3 – אָמַר אֱלֹהִים לֹא תֹאכְלוּ מִמֶּנּוּ וְלֹא תִגְּעוּ בּוֹ
"...God has said, neither shall you eat it nor shall you touch it ... "

How did the snake trick the woman? Our tradition teaches that she, or her husband, "added on" to the commandment of God, by saying, "neither shall you touch it," which God had not said. Therefore, the snake simply pushed *Hawa* [Eve-the Hebrew name can be translated as 'mother of all life'] into the tree. Once nothing happened, he was able to convince her that the entire warning was erroneous and convinced her to eat from the fruit.

3:5 – יֹדְעֵי טוֹב וָרָע

"… knowing good and evil …"

The first question one might ask is: what is wrong with knowing good and evil? Why is this problematic? According to our tradition, before Adam and *Hawah* ate from the tree, they were operating on the level of truth and falsehood, which is a higher level than good and evil. There isn't any ambiguity in truth and falsehood whereas good and evil are always seen through a prism of degrees, which include shades of gray, wherein one good is often played off anther good and one must choose between the most good. This is not always a clear choice.

In the language of the *Qabalah*, the Tree of Good and Evil was a level of existential being where both exist side by side. More specificly, it is good encapsulated in a shell of evil, where as the the Tree of Life is totally in the realm of good.

3:6 – כִּי טוֹב הָעֵץ לְמַאֲכָל וְכִי תַאֲוָה־הוּא לָעֵינַיִם וְנֶחְמָד הָעֵץ לְהַשְׂכִּיל וַתִּקַּח מִפִּרְיוֹ וַתֹּאכַל

"The woman saw…delight to the eyes … desired …she took … and she ate."

In this story of the woman and her husband listening to the snake and eating the fruit, all the senses (sight, hearing, taste, touch) are employed, with the sole exception of smell. Smell remained uncorrupted by the sin of the First Man, Adam.

My great great great grandfather, the saintly Ribbi Avraham Dayan, *z"l*, wrote in his commentary *Tuv Ta'am*, adds that it seems strange that the text would state that the fruit was good in her eyes, before she even tasted it. That normally people will first smell an unfamiliar fruit, as a foul smell might indicate that it is hazardous. He even brings support for his assertion from the Holy Zohar. He then contends that we are often enraptured by harmful things that appear attractive to our eyes, and in fact it is often through our eyes that we end up causing the most damage, especially spiritually, to ourselves, because harmful things are often disguised behind a beautiful image.

In this, we can understand the teaching of the sages that the *MashiaH*

[Messiah] will be able to sense truth and judge through faculty of smell [Talmud *Sanhedrin* 93b]. His sense of truth comes from an uncorrupted level. It is not based on "relative morality," but on the absolute truths of the Universe.

3:8 – וַיִּתְחַבֵּא הָאָדָם וְאִשְׁתּוֹ מִפְּנֵי יְהֹוָה אֱלֹהִים בְּתוֹךְ עֵץ הַגָּן

"And the man and his wife hid themselves from before God, amongst the trees of the Garden"

Rabbi Shlomo Carlebach, *z"l*, teaches that there are two kinds of hiding. "There is hiding from, and there is hiding with. Hiding is the most lonesome thing in the world, because a person is lonesome anyway. If you're hiding, this is heartbreaking aloneness, unbearable aloneness. This is the lowest existence there is – hiding from. The highest existence (not being in the aloneness) is when you are hiding with.

He teaches, "There's a hiding of hell, and hiding of heaven. In hell you're hiding from God, from the whole world, because you did so much wrong you don't know what to do with yourself. Heavenly hiding is hiding with.

"Adam and Eve didn't know what it means to hide together. They hadn't learned it yet. Their first connection to each other was that they were hiding from God. They learned a little bit; at least they were together. Eventually they learned how to hide together, not from, just together."

PARSHATH NOAH

Overview

The beginning of *Parshath NoaH* introduces us to *NoaH* as a righteous and simple man in his generation. We are told that *NoaH* walked with God. Already, at the end of last week's parsha, there was a foreshadowing of events to come. HaShem had begun to "regret" most of His creation, with the exception of *NoaH*.

The Torah tells us that the world was filled with violence and corruption. The Oral Tradition and commentators point to several principle sins of the Generation of the Flood: the sin of violent robbery ("*gezel*" implying the strong taking from the weak without shame), idolatry, and unnatural relations between men and beasts. God tells *NoaH* that He has decided to destroy humanity.

God commands *NoaH* to build an ark, giving him specific instructions as to its design. Our Oral Tradition tells us that the process of making of the ark was to give the generation an opportunity to repent from their ways. It took *NoaH* one hundred and twenty years to build so that people would be inclined to ask him its purpose and thus learn of God's plan to bring a Flood to the world.

NoaH is then commanded to bring his wife, his sons, and their wives, into the Ark. *NoaH* is told to collect a pair (male and female) of every animal, along with seven of every "clean beast" (either for sacrifice or for eating).

The fountains of the deep arc broken open, it begins to rain and HaShem seals *NoaH* and company into the Ark, Himself. It rains for forty days and forty nights wherein the waters flooded the earth, covering whole mountain ranges and drowning all living flesh.

The earth remained flooded for 150 days, before the waters began to recede. The Ark ended up resting on the top of Mount *Ararat*. The waters continued to recede for another three months, when *NoaH* begins seeing the mountaintops around him. *NoaH* sent out a raven that did not return (the raven stayed away from the ark flying back and forth until there was a place to rest). He then sent a dove that came back, being unable to find a place to rest. After another seven days, *NoaH* sent the dove again and this time she returned with an olive leaf (not a branch) in her mouth. This indicated to *NoaH* that the waters were receding. He waited another seven days, and sent the dove forth again. *NoaH* was now sure that the waters had receded so he removed the covering of the ark and saw that the ground was dry.

HaShem then tells *NoaH* to leave the Ark with his family and release all the animals. He does so, and builds an altar to HaShem and made an offering to Him.

HaShem makes a *brith* [covenant] with *NoaH*. He promises *NoaH* that He will not curse the ground for man's sake, nor destroy every living thing by flood waters, as He had done. HaShem promises that as long as the earth endures, there will be regularity to the seasons. After blessing him, HaShem commands *NoaH* and his descendents to replenish the earth. God designates the animals, fishes and plants that are to be suitable food for humanity, but forbids murder (and suicide according to the commentators), requiring the death of the murderer. The rainbow is set in the sky as an eternal symbol of this covenant. It should be pointed out that the rabbis see the appearance of the rainbow as a bad sign – meaning that the world was fit to be destroyed and it is only because of the brith that it is not.

Interestingly, the first thing *NoaH* does is plant a vineyard. He becomes drunk and was uncovered in his tent. Then *NoaH* had a shameful experience with his youngest son *Ham*. The sages offer several ideas as to what occurred. Some suggest that Ham simply saw his father in such a state and told him, embarrassing him. Others suggest that *Ham* castrated his father, making him impotent (a eunuch), while others say that *Ham* performed sodomy with his father. His other two sons cover up their father, walking backwards, making sure to guard his modesty. When *NoaH* wakes up, he realizes what occurred and curses *Ham* (the progenitor of the Canaanite nations) and blesses his other two sons.

We then learn the descendents of *NoaH* and the family tree of the world. The Torah then tells us that the world was one language and the nations of the world gathered together to rebel against the God. The commentators tell us that the sin of the Generation of the Division was worse that of the Generation of the Flood.

The Torah is more obscure as to what the sin of this generation was, so there is disagreement as to what the exact sin was. Some teach that the sin was that they tried to gather in one place and not "fill the earth" as had been commanded. Others suggest that they were so involved in the building of the tower; they ignored their wives and did not follow the commandment of procreation. Still another explanation is that they valued bricks more than human life, and built the tower at the expense of lives. All of these interpretations can be understood from hints in the verses.

The Ramban [Rabbi *Moshe ben* NaHman] teaches that the Generation of the Flood tried to throw off the yoke of Heaven saying, "God should rule in His world (Heaven), but we should do what we want in our world (Earth)." However, the Generation of the Division tried to, so to speak, rule over both the Earth and the Heaven, removing all traces holiness from the earth but still reaping all the good that Heaven could bestow.

The claim that they acted in unity is interesting, say our sages, for there is no unity when one is against HaShem. While they had the same objective, that is to break the yoke of Heaven, each did so for their own reason and their own benefit. This is not unity. One can only truly become unified when one submits one's will to a greater Will. (This is the message of Abraham, who was born in this generation and will be called upon to correct humanity's direction.)

Thus, HaShem scatters the people and confuses their speech, removing the illusion of unity. It is taught that the Generation of the Division lost their portion in the World to Come.

The parsha concludes with a listing of the generations of *Shem*, and the introduction of *Abraham Avinu* [Abraham our father].

There aren't any actual *mitswoth* [commandments] from *Parshath NoaH* - at least not directly for the Jewish people. However, the rabbis derived seven general laws from the Torah (referred to today as the Seven Laws of *NoaH*), which are binding on non-Jews. This obligation comes from the *brith* [covenant] that God makes with *NoaH*. Judaism does not teach that all of humanity must be Jewish in order to have a portion in Eternal Life, but it does define basic guidelines for all of humanity. These are much more general, and fewer, than the specific laws for Jews.

The Rambam [Rabbi *Moshe ben* Maimon] states that six precepts were commanded to the first Man, *Adam*. These are the prohibition against idol worship (or worship of false gods), the prohibition against cursing God, the prohibition against murder, the prohibition against incest and adultery, the prohibition against theft, and the obligation to establish civil law and courts of justice (specifically outside the land of Israel wherein Torah is suppose to be the "civil" law). The Rambam continues that for *NoaH*, God added the prohibition against eating flesh from a living animal (while at the same time allowing Man to eat slaughtered animals).

It should be noted that the civil laws of the non-Jewish nations do not have to be the same as that which exists for Jews. They are simply obligated to set up courts and judges in every major city and render judgment in accordance with the Seven Laws. They can enact rules and or*Dina*nces that fulfill these seven laws.

Also, the definition of incest and adultery is somewhat different for non-Jews than for Jews, according to the Rambam, who lists only six forbidden relationships (there are many more for Jews). A man is forbidden his mother, his father's wife, a married woman, his maternal sister, another man, and an animal. These prohibited relationships are learned from a close reading of *Bereshith* 2:24 and 20:23. According to the Rambam, divorce is also defined differently. A non-Jewish divorce does not require a bill of divorce as does Jewish divorce, but occurs whenever a man and woman simply separate and create separate residences. However, non-Jewish courts can always establish stricter rules (as most have).

In Detail: *A selection of some verses of interest:*

6:9 –   אֵלֶּה תּוֹלְדֹת

"Elah Tolodoth ..." [These are the Generations]

The word "*Tolodoth*" is a very interesting word, loaded with a lot of meaning. The word comes from the root whose meaning relates to giving birth. This is why most of the time, it is translated as "generations." Yet, this only touches on its meaning and leaves us wanting in many places, where such a translation does not quite fit. In addition, if this were the sole meaning of the word, then we would expect to find an immediate listing of the individual's progeny. This is not the case here, where the Torah continues to describe who *NoaH* was before introducing his sons.

Also, this meaning does not fit so well in *Bereshith* 2:4, we read, "*Elah Tolodoth HaShamayim w'HaArets*" [These are the "generations" of the Heaven and the Earth]. The word "generations" of course. does not fit, as neither the heaven nor the earth have progeny. There, Rashi explains its meaning as pointing to the previously mentioned Creation.

Here, in our verse, this can also be the understanding, as *NoaH* was actually introduced several verses earlier, in the end of last week's parsha. However, I think that there also may be more to the meaning of the word.

In keeping with its literal meaning, based on its root derivative, I think that "*Tolodoth*" is best translated, not as meaning what has come before, but what is yet to come. It prefaces or introduces a story, or more precisely, a history. Thus, in the second chapter of *Bereshith*, we can even reconcile Rashi's understanding and build on it with this added meaning. There, one might translated the verse to mean, "Now that [it was related how] the Heavens and the Earth were created, this is what happened next:"

With our verse, this understanding adds new meaning. Here the verse can be understood as, "This is the story of *NoaH* and how he effected the world."

6:9 – נֹחַ אִישׁ צַדִּיק
" *NoaH* was a righteous ..."

Rashi noting (as we mentioned above) that the children of *NoaH* are not immediately mentioned after the word "*Tolodoth*" (see the previous commentary) suggests that this is because the real "offspring" of righteous individuals is their good deeds.

6:9 – נֹחַ אִישׁ צַדִּיק תָּמִים הָיָה
"*NoaH* was righteous and perfect ("*tam*" or whole-hearted) ..."

The word "*tam*" is often translated as simple, naive, or honest. To be honest, or to be righteous seem both to be very similar in meaning. I learned that a righteous individual is simply one that follows the *mitswoth*. One that submits his will to God's Will. To be "*tam*" refers to one who lives his life in wholeness, wherein he acts in a way that reflects his concern for his fellow. Opposed to the modern understanding of naive, which is usually understood as one having less awareness, the Torah suggests the opposite. To be concerned about one's fellow requires a greater awareness that penetrates not only the immediate situation, but also the impact of one's actions on other individuals and the world at large.

This idea can be learned from the Hebrew word for "Aware," which is עֵר - `Er, spelled Ayin Resh, which is the opposite of the word for evil, רע R`a, spelled Resh Ayin. Evil occurs when we fail to be aware of our fellow, ouselves and our place and role in the world. Since the Torah sees evil, less as its own manifestation, but rather an absence of good, we can understand how our failure to be aware can result in evil. Clearly, this can be manifest in varying degrees and on varying levels, as small slights, failures of awareness, wouldn't be called 'evil," per se, particularly with all of the implications of the English word.

However, we must understand that even these small manifestations of our failure to be aware are rooted in the same concept. Living a Torah life requires us to continually be aware, and to grow in our awareness. It's not a goal, as much as it is a process, as we can never be fully aware, as that ultimately level is reserved for HaShem, of course. However, our goal is to continually strive to towards that goal, to continually grow in our awareness and emulation of the Holy One of Blessing.

6:9 – בְּדֹרֹתָיו
"in his generation ..."

Commentators disagree as to whether this is to *NoaH*'s credit or discredit. The disagreement is manifest in the Talmud, *Masekheth Sanhedrin*. Some suggest it means that to merit being called righteous in a generation that merited destruction is an incredible feat. Environment has a tremendous effect on the individual, and yet he was able to remain righteous. As Hillel says [*Pirke Avoth*], "In a place where there are not human beings [that is people acting in a way that merits being called "human"], strive to be a man [act in such a way that is worthy of the name, "man" or "human"]."

Others suggest that this means that *NoaH* was only righteous when compared to his generation, however, compared to another time, such as the generation of *Abraham*, he would not have been noteworthy. It seems to me that both meanings can both be true simultaneously, and this is the simple meaning of the verse.

6:9 – אֶת־הָאֱלֹהִים הִתְהַלֶּךְ־נֹחַ
"With God, walked *NoaH* ..."

Rashi compares this verse with 24:40, which, concerning *Abraham*, it states, "HaShem, before whom I walked." This, I think, supports those who argue that "in his generation," limits *NoaH*'s righteousness compared with *Abraham*. *NoaH* maintained a relationship with God, following His Will, but nothing more (not that one should belittle such a tremendous feat). However, *Abraham* became God's standard-bearer. He ran in front of HaShem; he was proactive. *NoaH* was more passive.

Rashi understands this differently though. The difference in "with" and "before," he says, is that *NoaH* required God's support to uphold him in righteousness, but *Abraham*, walked in his righteousness by his own efforts.

6:11 – תִּשָּׁחֵת הָאָרֶץ לִפְנֵי הָאֱלֹהִים וַתִּמָּלֵא הָאָרֶץ חָמָס:
"...And the land was corrupted before God, and the land was filled with violence ..."

The land being "corrupted" is, according to the Talmud [*Sanhedrin* 57], an expression of sexual immorality and idol worship. We learn that the Generation of the Flood engaged in unnatural and forbidden relationships including bestiality, incest, homosexuality, and wanton rape.

That this is linked to violence (and our commentators specify that this refers to violent robbery) should not be surprising to anyone living in our generation where the sexual immorality and wanton violence are a both a part of daily living. Intrinsically they seem to be linked for the focus on on the individual's needs, and not his communal or heavenly responsibility.

6:12 – כִּי־הִשְׁחִית כָּל־בָּשָׂר
"For all flesh is corrupt ..."

Rashi comments that this means that even cattle, beasts and fowl consorted with that which was not its own species. It has been taught that Man's actions in this world have an effect on the very nature of the world. Therefore when humanity begins to act unnaturally, the animal world around him mimics his actions.

6:14 – עֲשֵׂה לְךָ תֵּבַת
"Make yourself an ark [*tevah*] ..."

The word *tevah* is a very interesting word. It only appears in one other place in Torah. It is used for the basket or box in which *Moshe Rabbeinu* was placed in as a baby, and where Pharaoh's daughter found him on the River Nile [*Sh'moth* 2]. Both stories conjure the image of being carried on the back (floating) of water in hopes of salvation. In both instances, as well, the salvation of the individual (or individual family) inside the "*tevah*" has far-reaching implications for the salvation and redemption of others: Humanity in the case of *NoaH*, and the Jewish people in the case of *Moshe*.

The word "*tevah*" can also means, "word," creating an interesting range of possible meanings on a more esoteric level, such as being saved through a Heavenly word or decree.

6:14 – עֲשֵׂה לְךָ֙ תֵּבַ֣ת

"Make yourself an ark [*tevah*] ..."

Rashi asks the question, why did God command the building of the ark? Aren't there other, less complex methods of salvation? The answer, says Rashi, is that the construction of the ark (which took 120 years) was intended to give the people of the generation an opportunity to inquire as to its purpose and meaning, in hopes that they would repent.

6:14 – בַּכֹּֽפֶר

"with pitch [*b'kofer*] ..."

It is striking that the word for pitch, "*kofer*," is very similar for the word for atonement. Perhaps it is an allusion to the idea that the ark or the flood would atone for the sins of humanity and the world would have a chance to begin a new.

Additionally, the pronunciation of the word is the same as that meaning, "heretic." This offers many interesting possible meanings on an esoteric level. The ark was made necessary because of the wanton denial of God in the world.

6:15 – וְזֶ֕ה אֲשֶׁ֥ר תַּעֲשֶׂ֖ה אֹתָ֑הּ שְׁלֹ֧שׁ מֵא֣וֹת אַמָּ֗ה אֹ֚רֶךְ הַתֵּבָ֔ה חֲמִשִּׁ֥ים אַמָּ֖ה רָחְבָּ֑הּ וּשְׁלֹשִׁ֥ים אַמָּ֖ה קוֹמָתָֽהּ:

"...300 *Amah* in length ...50 *Amah* in width and 30 *Amah* in height."

It is no coincidence that the total of the measurements is equal to the *gematria* of the word "*pash* [פ *peh* (80)- ש *shin* (300)]." "*Pash*" means, "he rested." The word comes from the word, "*nefesh*," meaning, "soul."

6:16 – צֹהַר ׀ תַּעֲשֶׂה לַתֵּבָה

"A light [*tsohar*], you will make in the Ark ..."

Bereshit Rabbah suggests that this was a precious stone that emitted light for them. I am not aware of any stone found today, that emits light of any real value for so many days. However it conjures up the image of the stone tablets later received on Sinai, which contained Heavenly light.

Others suggest that this means, "a window." Rashi brings both possibilities, and the *Gur Ariyeh* explains that Rashi had dificulty with defining the term as window, because it that is what it was, why wouldn't the test simply say window.For we do see that when *NoaH* opens the window after the rains ceased, the word used there [8:6] is "*Halon*" which is the standard word for window. In addition, a window does not provide much light during a storm, especially one of this magnitude.

It seems striking to me that *NoaH* is commanded to make a "light," in the Ark. The *Tsror HaMor* says that this was commanded so *NoaH* would understand that even though the world was plunged into total darkness, HaShem preserved one Light to illuminate the world after the devestation, and this was *NoaH* and his sons. It should be noted that Light was the first thing that HaShem created on the first day of Creation. Therefore, it is important that even at a time of its destruction, Light was preserved for the world. Because the devastation was only perpetrated in order to rebuild. It was a re-breaking of the vessels, in order to repair the breach.

Further, more than anything else, Light is a symbol of HaShem's Presence in the world. After God created the original Light, He hid it, because he "foresaw" that there would be evil in the world. Our tradition teaches that this brilliant light would be reserved for the Righteous in the World to Come. It may be that *NoaH* was commanded to prepare a place in the Ark to receive and "store" this "brilliant" light of Creation since the world would be returned to chaos temporarily. It should be noted that the normal use of *tsohar* is that of "brilliant light," and is the root for the term used to describe midday.

6:17 – וַאֲנִ֗י הִנְנִי֩ מֵבִ֨יא אֶת־הַמַּבּ֥וּל מַ֙יִם֙

"And I, Behold I, bring the flood of water ..."

The simple meaning suggests that HaShem meted out punishment personally and did not delegate it to an attending angel or some other agent. This is in juxtaposition to the courtesy God extended the attending angels when He said, "Let Us make man in our image." [*Bereshith* 1:26] There it is taught that God's intent was to teach the ethical lesson of including one's subordinates in one's decisions. Here, too we learn an ethical lesson: that difficult task should be performed by oneself, taking full responsibility for one's actions, no matter how difficult they might be.

6:18 – וּבָאתָ֙ אֶל־הַתֵּבָ֔ה אַתָּ֕ה וּבָנֶ֛יךָ וְאִשְׁתְּךָ֥ וּנְשֵֽׁי־בָנֶ֖יךָ אִתָּֽךְ

"You shall come into the ark, you and your sons, and your wife and the wives or your sons ..."

Rashi explains the unique structure of this verse. It is written describing the men's entrance separately from the description of the women's entry. This hints at the teaching of *Bereshit Rabba* which states that marital relations (also between the animals) was forbidden in the Ark due to the great tragedy taking place outside of it. This concept is, in fact, the *Halakhah* [Jewish Law]. In times of great tragedy, famine, or war marital relations are forbidden.

7:1 – כִּֽי־אֹתְךָ֥ רָאִ֛יתִי צַדִּ֥יק לְפָנַ֖י בַּדּ֥וֹר הַזֶּֽה

"For in you have I seen righteousness before Me in this generation ..."

Here, *NoaH* is only referred to as "righteous," and not also "*tam*," or perfect. Rashi understand this to teach that one should mention only some of a person's good qualities while in his presence, but all of them when not in his presence.

The *Hatam Sofer* offers another possibility for the missing characteristic. Citing the sacrifice that *NoaH* does after he leaves the Ark, the *Hatam Sofer* suggests the omission was because *NoaH* sinned. He adds that the sacrifice was brought to atone for his sin. When God revealed His plan to destroy the world, a righteous and perfect man should have yelled against the decree, as *Abraham* did for the people of *S'dom*. *Abraham* understood the level of corruption in the city of *S'dom*, but he still fought for its survival.

7:4 – כִּי לְיָמִים עוֹד שִׁבְעָ֔ה אָנֹכִי֙ מַמְטִיר עַל־הָאָ֔רֶץ

"For in another seven days, I will cause it to rain..."

According to the Talmud [*Masekheth Sanhedrin* 108], God delayed the flood for seven days out of respect for the honor *MetushalaH* the Righteous, who died on the day of the flood.

It is possible that God also delayed to offer another opportunity for repentance. Maybe, *MetushalaH*'s death would spurn people to reflect on their lives and repent.

7:13 – בְּעֶ֙צֶם הַיּוֹם הַזֶּה֙

"On that very day ..."

God brought *NoaH* into the ark at midday before the eyes of the entire world. We learn that the people of *NoaH*'s generation threatened to kill him if he entered the Ark, therefore God brought him in before everyone, as if to say, "We will see whose word will prevail."

7:16 – וַיִּסְגֹּר יְהֹוָה בַּעֲדוֹ

"And HaShem shut him in (the ark) ..."

This conveys the idea of HaShem's protection. *Bereshith Rabba* suggests that HaShem surrounded the Ark with bears and lions so that the people of *NoaH*'s generation shouldn't try to destroy the Ark. However, as Rashi states, the simple meaning is that HaShem closed the door securely, protecting *NoaH* from the flood.

8:1 – וַיִּזְכֹּר אֱלֹהִים֙

"And God remembered ..."

Remembered is not written here in the sense that HaShem forgets, God forbid, but that he noted or acknowledged him. That is, He took note.

8:1 – וַיַּעֲבֵר אֱלֹהִים רוּחַ֙ עַל־הָאָ֔רֶץ

"And God made a wind (or spirit) pass over the earth ..."

Compare this with *Bereshith* 1:2, "And the spirit (or wind) of God hovered over the surface of the waters ..." It seems that this is a suggestion that the world was thrown into a state of chaos, returning it to it's primal form. Then God reformed the world anew. In verse 13, we learn that the waters dried up in the first month. Ribbi Elieazer teaches that this was the month of *Tishre* or *Rosh HaShanah*, the date of the Creation of the world.

Rashi however says that this is a spirit of consolation.

8:7 – יָצוֹא וָשׁוֹב
"to and fro ..."

It did not set out on its mission but circled the Ark. We learn in the Talmud [*Sanhedrin* 108] that the raven was suspicious of *NoaH* concerning its mate (Remember, one of the reasons for the flood was unnatural unions).

8:7 – עַד־יְבֹשֶׁת הַמָּיִם
"Until the waters were dried up ..."

According to our tradition, this is a hint (also) to the time when *Eliyahu HaNavi* caused the rains to be withheld (*Melekhim* I 17:6). He was forced to go into hiding from King *AHav* and the ravens brought him meat and bread to sustain him.

8:16 – צֵא מִן־הַתֵּבָה אַתָּה וְאִשְׁתְּךָ וּבָנֶיךָ וּנְשֵׁי־בָנֶיךָ אִתָּךְ:
"Leave the Ark, you and your wife, and your sons and their wives ..."

In this verse, *NoaH* is paired with his wife, and likewise his sons with their wives, implying that marital relations are now permitted to them.

8:17 – הַיְצֵא אִתָּךְ וְשָׁרְצוּ בָאָרֶץ וּפָרוּ וְרָבוּ עַל־הָאָרֶץ
"Bring them out of the Ark ... that they may be fruitful and multiply ..."

Implying that the animals were also forbidden to cohabit while inside the Ark.

9:3 – לָכֶם יִהְיֶה לְאָכְלָה
"shall be for you food ..."

The Talmud [*Sanhedrin* 57] teaches that the first man (*Adam*) was only given vegetation to eat, but was not permitted to eat meat, but *NoaH* was given permission to eat both vegetation and meat.

It seems that the relationship between man and beast changed after the flood, for here we see that man was given permission to eat meat and in verse two we learn that God place fear and dread of people on the beasts. This distance might have been created in order to protect against the unnatural unions that led to the flood. This distance is also important, it seems to me, to remind us that we are not animals, but rather potentially much more.

9:6 – כִּי בְּצֶלֶם אֱלֹהִים עָשָׂה אֶת־הָאָדָם
"for in the image of God, He made Man ..."

In other words, removing a person from the world is like removing [the reflection of] HaShem in the world, God forbid. Rabbi Ya'aqov Peretz, *shlit"a* says that idea of being created "*Tselem Elokim*" (in the image of God) means with "*Derekh Erets*," that man (should) behave with respect and honor for his fellow.

9:21 – אָהֳלֹה
"his tent ..."

The word for tent is not written normally, but its last letter is the letter "*hey*" instead of the letter "*waw*." This is an allusion to the ten northern tribes of *Yisrael* who were called by the name "*Shomron*," which was called "*Oholah*" (spelled the same way). [*Yehezkel* 23:4] According to the prophet *`Amos*, the ten tribes were exiled because of wine. [*`Amos* 6]

9:22 – וַיַּרְא חָם אֲבִי כְנַעַן אֵת עֶרְוַת אָבִיו
"And *Ham*, the father of Canaan, saw the nakedness of his father ..."

The sages offer several ideas as to what actually occurred. Some suggest that *Ham* simply saw his father in such a immodest state and told him, embarrassing him. Others suggest that *Ham* castrated his father, making him impotent (a eunuch), because he didn't want any more siblings with whom to share the inheritance. While others say that *Ham* performed sodomy with his father. [Talmud, *Masekhet Sanhedrin*, 70]

10:9 – גִּבֹּר־צַיִד

"a mighty hunter..."

Rashi teaches that Nimrod was a mighty hunter in the sense that he was able to capture men's minds with his mouth and lead them astray against God.

10:32 – אֵלֶּה מִשְׁפְּחֹת בְּנֵי־נֹחַ לְתוֹלְדֹתָם בְּגוֹיֵהֶם

"These are the families of the sons of *NoaH*, for the generations (*tolodoth*) in their nations..."

Reflecting on the meaning for *Tolodoth* above, the meaning here might be, "These are the families of the children of *NoaH*, and this (the following) is the story of their nations and how these nations were divided upon the earth after the flood."

11:1 – וַיְהִי כָל־הָאָרֶץ שָׂפָה אֶחָת וּדְבָרִים אֲחָדִים

"And the whole land was one language and united speech ..."

Bereshith Rabbah teaches that they said, "Once every thousand, six hundred and fifty six years the firmament totters, just as it did during the days of the Flood. Come let us make a support for the firmament."

Rashi brings another interpretation. Namely, they came with one counsel and said, "Not all depends on Him. He had no right to choose for Himself the Heavens, let us ascend to the firmament and wage war with Him."

Another interpretation of this phrase is they spoke against the one God of the world. This can be understood by the phrase itself, rendering "*sfath eHad*" as language for one, meaning "the One," God.

The Ramban has another interpretation that they tried to change the nature of the universe, so that they could reap the benefits of heaven while acting as they wished.

11:4 – פֶּן־נָפוּץ עַל־פְּנֵי כָל־הָאָרֶץ

"Lest we be scattered abroad ..."

This became a self-fulfilling prophesy, as it is written in *Mishle* "The fear of the wicked, it shall come upon him."

11:5 – וַיֵּרֶד יְהֹוָה לִרְאֹת
"And HaShem came down to see ..."

This does not mean that HaShem, God forbid, is physical and needs to come closer to examine a situation. Instead, *Midrash TanHuma* teaches HaShem acted thus to teach us that we should not condemn an offender until one has made sure to see and understand everything involved.

11:6 – הֵן עַם אֶחָד ... וְעַתָּה לֹא־יִבָּצֵר מֵהֶם כֹּל אֲשֶׁר יָזְמוּ לַעֲשׂוֹת
"And behold, they are one people ... and now it will happen that it can not be withheld from them, anything that they attempt to do ..."

This is a very startling statement, for it seems to imply that HaShem was worried about this group of people who thought that they could wage a war against heaven. The Ramban brings an interesting understanding to this. In short, it involves the power of language. HaShem built the universe through language and, in doing so left within the blueprints, the ability, so to speak, for humans to manipulate Creation with the right combination of letters and words. While this ability may ultimately be illusory, for it is impossible to "conquer God," it teaches us a lesson about the gift of Free Will. Included within it is the potential for choosing wrongly, and bringing self-destruction upon oneself.

11:28 – וַיָּמָת הָרָן עַל־פְּנֵי תֶּרַח אָבִיו בְּאֶרֶץ מוֹלַדְתּוֹ בְּאוּר כַּשְׂדִּים
"And *Haran* died in the presence of his father, *TeraH* ...in *Ur Kasdim* ..."

"*Al pnei*" can mean " in the presence of," or "on account of." The Midrash teaches that *TeraH* complained before *Nimrod* against his son, *Abram*, because he had smashed his idols. *Nimrod* and *Abram* had a mighty debate on the nature of the universe. In the end, *Nimrod* decreed that he would throw *Abram* into the furnace (because *Nimrod* was bested in the debate). His brother was also required to stand trial at the time. *Haran* said to himself, if *Abram* wins I'll side with him, but if *Nimrod* wins, I'll declare my loyalty to him. *Abram* was thrown in first and was miraculously saved from the flames. *Haran* was then asked on whose side was he, *Abram*'s or *Nimrod*. *Haran* saw that *Abraham* was saved and so he said *Abram*. They cast him into the furnace and he was burned. Since his faith was contingent on the outcome, he didn't merit being saved.

11:29 – יִסְכָּה
"Yiskah ..."

According to Rashi, this is Sarah (*Abraham*'s wife), which also makes her *Abraham*'s niece. This was not uncommon, and the sages tell us that such a match is even desirable.

PARSHATH LEKH L'KHA

Overview

HaShem commands *Abram* to leave his native land and journey to a place that "He will show him," which is *Kena`an* [Canaan], or the land of Israel. *Abram* makes the journey with his wife, his household, and his brother's son *LoT*. Once there, he travels the length and breadth of the land in a symbolic act of possession.

After arriving in *Kena`an*, there is a famine in the land. According to tradition, this is the first time that the world has suffered famine. *Abram* is forced to journey to *Mitsrayim* (Egypt), which is known for its lewd and licentious nature. He presents his wife, *Saray*, as his sister instead of as his wife, to protect himself from those that would be interested in murdering him in order to posses her.

Pharaoh takes *Saray* into his house as a wife, but is prevented from having relations with her due to a plague that God sends. After it becomes revealed that she is Abram's wife, they are sent away from *Mitsrayim*, laden with wealth.

They return to *Kena`an*, where *Abram* and *LoT* decide to divide and go their separate ways. *LoT* moves to *S'dom* and settles there.

There is a war between the four kings and the five kings. *LoT* is taken captive in the course of the war. *Abram* sets out with his servant(s) to rescue *LoT* and defeat the four kings, after which the Priest of *Salem*, *Malki-Tsedek*, blesses him.

After this war, *Abram* has a vision in which HaShem reveals to him that he will not remain childless. HaShem and *Abram* make a covenant symbolized by animals split in half. *Abram* has a vision concerning the future of his seed, their enslavement and eventual fre*Edom* from *Mitsrayim*.

Saray give *Abram* her handmaiden, *Hagar*, to wed, and she conceives and bears him a child, *Yishma'el*. An angel of God promises that *Yishma'el* will become a nation in his own right.

Abram's name is changed to *Abraham*, and *Saray*'s to *Sarah*. HaShem affirms the covenant and commands that *Abraham* circumcise himself and his household as a symbol of the covenant. HaShem informs *Abraham* that *Sarah* will bear *Abraham*'s heir and his name will be *YitsHaq*.

In Detail: *A selection of some verses of interest*:

12:1 – לֶךְ־לְךָ

"Lekh L'kha [literally: Go for you]"

This is a very curious expression. Rashi suggests that it means, "Go, for your own benefit." That HaShem is addressing *Abram*, saying, "Go for there (*Kena`an*), I'll make you a great nation, but here (*Haran*) you aren't worthy to have children, and further, there I'll make your nature known to the world.

I would suggests that maybe this phrase is related to the end of last week's parsha, wherein we see that *Abram*'s father, *TeraH* began the journey to land of *Kena`an*, "And *TeraH* took *Abram*, his son … and they went out from *Ur-Kasdim*, to go to the land of *Kena`an* …" Here, HaShem is telling *Abram* to finish the journey without his father, that this journey is for *Abram* and *Abram* alone.

12:1 – מֵאַרְצְךָ וּמִמּוֹלַדְתְּךָ וּמִבֵּית אָבִיךָ אֶל־הָאָרֶץ אֲשֶׁר אַרְאֶךָּ:

"…from your country, from your birthplace, from your father's house, to the land that I will show you."

We find a number of times in the *parshioth* dealing with *Abraham*, a listing of things from more general to more specific. Also with the `*Akedah*, in *parshath Vayyera*, for instance, *Abraham* is told there, to take his "son, his only one (special one), the one in which you love, *YitsHaq*." The progression always takes place when HaShem requests (or rather commands) something that carries an expectation of emotional difficulty for *Abraham*. The latter talks about the offering of *YitsHaq* as a sacrifice to HaShem, the former concerns leaving one's familiar surroundings and one's family.

Throughout the story of *Abraham*, HaShem acts as a perfect example as to how we humans are supposed to relate to one another. HaShem visits *Abraham* when he is ill, he consults him, and allows him to voice his opinion when HaShem is about to judge *S'dom*. It seems to me that here too, HaShem teaches us a lesson. Even when we are in a position to, and have to command one of our charge with a difficult task, etiquette demands that we be cognizant of their feelings.

Further, it seems to me that one can hear a dialogue between HaShem and *Abraham* taking place, similar to the one described in the Midrash concerning the *Akedah* (see *Parshath Wayera*). HaShem tells *Abraham* to leave his country. *Abraham* answers that he has already left his country. HaShem tells him to leave his birthplace. *Abraham* points out that he is now in *Haran*, and he was born in *Ur-Kasdim* (or alternatively that he has already abandoned the environment in which he was born into). HaShem commands him to leave his father's house, and *Abraham* responds that he has already left his father's ways. Then HaShem tells *Abraham* that he must go to a new place, one that HaShem will show the patriarch, and with that, *Abraham* begins his journey.

12:1 – מֵאַרְצְךָ

"...from your country..."

The simple meaning is from *Ur-Kasdim*. It should be noted though, that *Abram* had already left *Ur-Kasdim* with his father (see above) and was now in *Haran*.

Rashi says that this means, "Remove yourself even further from there."

However, I think that there might be an additional meaning to this. Connected to the phrase, "*Lekh L'kha*" (Go for you), that he must travel for himself, *Abraham* is being told that he must remove himself from the destructive and corrupting environment of his past.

Oftentimes immigrants leave their country, their homeland, but only physically. In fact, the transplanted immigrant often feels more connected to his homeland once he has left it. For instance, today in Israel, many immigrants identify themselves according to their country of origin, even though in that country they never felt at home and identified with the Land of Israel much more strongly.

There may be a similar connotation here, for it is important that *Abraham* start anew, and not dwell on where he came from but where he is going towards. Not only must he remove himself from his country, but he must remove his country from his self.

12:1 –　וּמִמּוֹלַדְתְּךָ

"...from your birthplace..."

This is also *Ur-Kasdim*, so why has the Torah seemingly repeated itself? I think this is referring to *Abram's* upbringing and birthright. HaShem does not simply want *Abram* to relocate, rather he wants him to uproot himself, remove himself from the influences of his community, and start anew. Why should HaShem be concerned about this? After all, we are familiar with *Abram's* faith in HaShem, and in his war against the idolatry of his environment.

I believe, like every good idealist, we might assume that *Abram* thought that he could change his environment, that he could bring the knowledge of HaShem to this corrupt community and environment. After all we are told that he made souls (see below) in *Haran*. HaShem answers *Abram*, saying that for *Abram's* mission to work, he must relocate, both physically and mentally. Before he can transform the world, he must create a safe haven to transform himself and demonstrate to the world the power of HaShem. This is a powerful message: One can only be a universalist, through the concentration on the particular.

12:1 –　וּמִבֵּית אָבִיךָ

"...from your father's house..."

Despite the fact that the Torah reports the death of Abraham's father (verse 11:32), our oral tradition teaches that *TeraH* did not die at that moment, but sixty years after Abraham had moved to *Kena`an*. Rashi explains that this is for Abraham's honor, that people would not say that "Abram did not fulfill the obligation of honoring his father, for he left an old man and went away."

12:1 –　אֶל־הָאָרֶץ אֲשֶׁר אַרְאֶךָּ׃

"...to the land that I will show you."

Rashi tells us that HaShem did not reveal the land to him immediately for two reason, to make the gift of the land more beloved in *Abraham*'s eyes and to give him a greater reward. Why would this bring him a greater reward? *Abraham* would have to show a greater faith to go to an unnamed place. He would be totally dependent upon HaShem.

It seems to me, that this is might be referring to a prophetic vision of the land of *Kena`an*. HaShem will show *Abraham* the land of *Kena`an*, not as it is, filled with idol worship and paganism, but as is can be, the center for monotheism and the homeland of a nation that comes from his seed. HaShem will show *Abraham* a new way of perceiving the world. This is the answer to all those who claim that they don't want to come to Israel because of all of its problems. Our obligation as Jews is to come to the Land that HaShem will show us and then help transform it into that vision. We can draw a parallel with our sojourn in the desert, wherein HaShem showed us a vision of the *Mishqan* [HaShem's dwelling place] and only then did we proceed to build it.

I heard that the Kotsker Rebbe's grandson teaches, concerning this verse, that there isn't any *mitswah*, which is as unclear as the *mitswah* of living in the Land of *Yisrael* [Israel]. This is because HaShem said to *Abraham*, "Go to the land that I will show you," and this means that you can only go to *Yisrael* when HaShem reveals it to you," that is, until He opens your heart to its holiness.

12:2-3 – וְאֶעֶשְׂךָ לְגוֹי גָּדוֹל וַאֲבָרֶכְךָ וַאֲגַדְּלָה שְׁמֶךָ וֶהְיֵה בְּרָכָה: וַאֲבָרֲכָה מְבָרֲכֶיךָ וּמְקַלֶּלְךָ אָאֹר וְנִבְרְכוּ בְךָ כֹּל מִשְׁפְּחֹת הָאֲדָמָה:

"And I will make you a great nation; I will bless you; and make your name great; and you shall be a blessing. I will bless them that bless you, and cures him that curses you; in you, all the families of the earth will be blessed."

There are seven blessings here, indicating physical perfection. The three-dimensional world has six physical directions or sides. Judaism (Maharal) teaches that there is actually a seventh side that is, the object itself; its essence. Thus the seven blessings represent that Abraham received a full measure, a complete blessing.

12:5 – וְאֶת־הַנֶּפֶשׁ אֲשֶׁר־עָשׂוּ בְחָרָן

"...and the soul(s) that they had made in *Haran*..."

Rashi tells us that the simple meaning is the slaves and handmaidens that they had acquired in *Haran*.

However, this does not seem completely right as slaves and handmaidens would be considered property and not "souls." Therefore, the text, says Rashi, indicates that *Abraham* and *Sarah* had brought proselytes to the idea of "One God" and are credited with actually having "made" the souls.

Another possibility, noting the word "*nefesh*," soul, is singular, is that it refers to the soul of *Abraham*. In other words, he brought his elevated self with him.

In either case, it seems curious that the text say "in *Haran*" and not in *Ur-Kasdim*, where *Abraham* spent the majority of his life. The reason for this is that he had fled *Ur-Kasdim* and thus, any proselytes he had influenced would have remained there. Alternatively, if we follow the suggestion that it was his own enlightened self he brought with him, we could understand that after the crisis of *Ur-Kasdim*, losing a brother, being thrown into and surviving a fire pit, and being forced to flee, he gained new insight into the nature of the world, and was able to further develop in *Haran*. Thus, the *nefesh* he made in *Haran*.

12:6 – וְהַכְּנַעֲנִי אָז בָּאָרֶץ

"...and the Kena`an'im were then in the land ..."

Rashi tells us that the *Kena`an'im* [Canaanites] were in the process of conquering the land from the seed of *Shem*, who inherited the land when *NoaH* apportioned the earth to his sons.

An added meaning is that, the land being inhabited, required greater faith on the part of *Abraham*, for it defies "common sense," when compared with the next verse that indicates that HaShem will give this land to *Abraham*'s seed.

Alternatively, this reflects back to the phrase, "the land that I will show you," as meaning the potential of the Land and not its current state.

12:9 – וַיִּסַּע אַבְרָם הָלוֹךְ וְנָסוֹעַ הַנֶּגְבָּה:
"Abram journeyed on, he went and he traveled southward…"

Through his travels *Abram* "took possession" of the land for his descendents. While the Land was promised to *Abram*, the promise was not realized until he performed an act of acquisition. After he traveled the Land the promise when from potential to actual. From this we learn that every four *amoth* [cubit] one walks (of new territory) in *Erets Yisrael* [the land of Israel] is considered the fulfillment of *mitswah* (meaning, waling eight *amoth* is considered fulfillment of the *mitswah* twice.

12:10 – כִּי־כָבֵד הָרָעָב בָּאָרֶץ:
"…and there was a famine in the land…"

The Midrash tells us that this was the first time there was a famine in the world. Rashi says it was a test for *Abraham*, for first HaShem told him to go to the Land and now he was inducing him to leave it.

12:11 – וַיֹּאמֶר אֶל־שָׂרַי אִשְׁתּוֹ הִנֵּה־נָא יָדַעְתִּי כִּי אִשָּׁה יְפַת־מַרְאֶה אָתְּ
"…he said to Saray his wife, 'Behold, I now know that you are a pretty woman to look at.'"

It seems unlikely that Abraham did not look at his wife previously, nor that he was unaware that she was attractive. Rashi offers several interpretations to try and understand this verse, including a Midrash that talks about their modesty, but I don't think that this is the text's intention.

Rather, I think, similar to one of the understandings brought by Rashi, that the simply meaning of the verse is that "Now, I have to worry about your physical beauty, because we are going to an immoral place, wherein they inhabitants might covet you."

However, it is also clear that there is a deeper meaning to this verse. Until this point Abraham had only related to his wife through her sublime spiritual beauty and had not focused on her physical beauty. Until now, Abraham had completely mastered his desires. Now, that he would be journeying to *Mitsrayim*, which was notorious for their lewdness, he realized that they would relate to his wife solely in a physical manner. One reason for descent into *Mitsrayim*, it seems, was to dwell amongst their licentious nature and yet emerge unscathed from the ubiquitous temptations that would surround him.

12:12 – וְאָמְרוּ אִשְׁתּוֹ זֹאת וְהָרְגוּ אֹתִי

"...that they will say, 'This is his wife, and they will kill me...'"

This verse begs a question for me. Why does Abraham assume that the Egyptians would not commit adultery, when he thinks they are capable of murder? And further, if their morals are so lax, why would they bother with Abraham at all, brother or husband, and not simply take Sarah, regardless of Abraham's presence.

The second question seems easiest. We see it evident in society today. Even the Mafia offers money or other enticement before resorting to threats and violence. It's easier to buy someone than to kill him, is their purported expression. From this, we might understand the first question also. To take a man's wife was not beyond the moral bounds of the Egypt, but it would have proven easier, and more efficient, to eliminate any potential threat, i.e., Abraham, and then take the widow.

Yet there may be another aspect to this. For, while ultimately people might be driven to extremes, most of us want the air of respectability. Taking a man's wife, while he is still a live was considered beyond the pale for most Egyptians, while conquering him (murder) and then taking possession of his wife was acceptable. While this is contrary to the "morals" of western society (where adultery is only considered mildly taboo - a "slip" or a mistake), it shows the emptiness of a moral code based on something other than Torah, wherein something as evil as murder (or adultery) can be considered morally acceptable.

12:17 – וַיְנַגַּע יְהֹוָה ׀ אֶת־פַּרְעֹה נְגָעִים גְּדֹלִים וְאֶת־בֵּיתוֹ

"And HaShem plagued Pharaoh with great plagues and his house ..."

God plagued Pharaoh so that he was unable to have intercourse. A Midrash tells us that the plague spread to the walls and pillars of the Pharaoh's house as well. One should note that Abraham's descent and redemption from *Mitsrayim* parallels that of his descendents'.

12:17 – עַל־דְּבַר שָׂרַי אֵשֶׁת אַבְרָם

"...because of (literally on the word of) *Saray*..."

The literal meaning of this verse is "by the word (command) of *Saray*. Rashi tells us that *Saray* would say "Hit!" and the angel would hit.

12:19 – קַח וָלֵךְ
"…Take (her) and Go!"

These words, and this entire incident (as noted above) eerily foreshadow the descent into and escape from *Mitsrayim* (literally, the narrow place - Egypt) of the whole Jewish people. A famine hits *Kena`an*, forcing the Children of *Ya`aqob* [Jacob] to descend into *Mitsrayim*, where at first they are honored and rewarded, then the Egyptians are plagued, and Pharaoh sends the Jews out of *Mitsrayim* laden with much reward.

13:1 – הַנֶּגְבָּה
"*HaNegbah*"

The term *HaNegbah* literally means towards the South. This is difficult, because *Mitsrayim* [Egypt] is to the south of the Land of *Yisrael*, and therefore one must travel north to go from Egypt to Israel. Rashi tries to reconcile this difficulty by suggesting it means that Abraham travels to the south of the *Land of Yisrael*. Yet, such an understanding takes liberty with the literal, simple meaning of the verse, and requires reading in the larger context of the story to make it work, though awkwardly.

The phrase also can literally mean, "towards the *Negev*." *Negev*, which is a desert in the south of the Land of *Yisrael*. Yet, nowhere else in the *Tanakh* is this region called that.

I think the solution to this difficulty, lies in fact that there were two basic routes between Egyt and Israel—the northern *P'lishti* route, and the southern, desert route. It seems to me that text is telling us that Abraham took the southern route. This would also be compatible with Rashi's understanding.

There is an echo to this journey. When the Children of *Yisrael* leave *Mitsrayim* they are told not to go by way of the *P'lisht'im*, which requires them to travel the southern route, and this might be the simple meaning here.

13:7 – וַיְהִי־רִיב בֵּין רֹעֵי מִקְנֵה־אַבְרָם וּבֵין רֹעֵי מִקְנֵה־לוֹט
"And there was strife between the herdsmen…"

The entire episode of *LoT* and Abraham separating after their stay in *Mitsrayim* is explained in the *Zohar HaQadosh*. *LoT*'s strength, and that which makes him the ideal progenitor of the *MashiaH* [King David, through Ruth the *Moabiah*, is descended from him] was his ability to submit his will to Abraham's. Abraham's "mission" in *Mitsrayim* was to enter into the corrupt and lewd atmosphere and leave unaffected, unscathed. This he accomplished, and it was a *"Tiqun"* [a fixing, a *qabalistic* expression denoting the reparation of spiritual forces] for the "cardinal sin" of *Giluiy `ariyot* [illicit relationships]

However, the corrupt and lewdness of *Mitsrayim* had left their mark on *LoT*. In fact, it should be noted that *LoT*'s name means "spoiled" in Aramaic. In *Mitsrayim*, *LoT* became enticed and now he chaffed at being subservient to Abraham. In the language of the *Qabbalah*, his *Yetser Har`a* [Evil inclination] was awakened and he was now pulled towards the lewdness. This is why he chose to dwell in *S'dom*.

13:10 – וַיִּשָּׂא־לוֹט אֶת־עֵינָיו וַיַּרְא ... כְּגַן־יְהוָה כְּאֶרֶץ מִצְרַיִם
"*LoT* lifted his eyes and saw ... like the Garden of HaShem, like the Land of *Mitsrayim* [Egypt]"

As we have discussed previously, 'lifting up the eyes' is an expression that suggests seeing beyond the physical. Here, *Lot* sees the JordanValley as resembling *Mitsrayim*. Unfortunately, as we will see in the rest of his story, Lot did not emerge from the descent into Egypt unscathed. He was affected, not completely, but enough that it effected his judgment and righteousness. We will visit this theme again in discussing his interaction with the messengers of God and the men of *S'dom* at the time of its destruction. But, the seeds of his corruption are already hinted at here.

13:11 – וַיִּסַּע לוֹט מִקֶּדֶם
"...and *LoT* journeyed (from) east..."

The Midrash interprets this as *LoT* removed himself from the Creator of the world (the word for east, *qedem*, is similar to the word for Originator, *Qadmon*). *LoT* said, "I do not want either *Abram* or his God," according to the Midrashic text.

Rashi brings this midrash as well. It seems strange for the simple meaning of "from east" should be sufficient, except when one looks at a map and sees that *S'dom* is eastward (meaning he would have traveled from the west to the east). Many interpret this simply to mean "eastward" instead of from the east, but it is difficult. Rashi himself says that it means from the east to the west, which, while literally correct, does not correspond with what we know of their locations respectively. This is why the midrash is brought, to suggest that *LoT* journeyed from before HaShem (or his servant Abraham) towards the west (the word for which has a connotation of ambiguity (dusk), both physically and morally).

Additionally, Abraham phrased the choice as between north and south (literally right and left). For *LoT* to choose east seems confusing. North and south represent the qualities of judgment versus grace and kindness respectively.

It seems to me that Abraham's offer was not to split up, but to divide roles, as in the left and right arms of a person (the literal meaning of the words used for north and south). Abraham recognized that both his and *LoT*'s characteristic, as well as their progeny would be need for the redemption (see below) and to avoid strife, was trying to divide their roles. Instead, *LoT* removes himself from the partnership and heads forward (towards *qedem*) removing himself from submission to Abraham and his mission.

13:13 – וְאַנְשֵׁי סְדֹם רָעִים וְחַטָּאִים לַיהוָה מְאֹד:
"Now the men of *S'dom* were wicked, and sinners, against HaShem continually."

Commentators note that the crimes of *S'dom* are listed in triplet. We learn in various places how each previous generation was guilty of one of the three cardinal sins. The generation of *Enosh* was guilty of `*Avodah Zarah* [literally strange worship, meaning paganism or idol worship], the generation of the flood was guilty of illicit relations, and the generation of the Division [*Bavel*] was guilty of the spilling of blood (murder). However, from this verse, commentators learn that *S'dom*'s crime was a combination of all three sins.

Rashi brings another interpretation. They were wicked – with their bodies, and sinners – with their money, against HaShem – they knew their Master and rebelled against Him.

It should be noted that all of the *midrashim* [extra-biblical stories revolving around the story in the Torah] regarding *S'dom* do not paint them as the "cartoon evil" like that typically portrayed in a modern story or movie. The men of *S'dom* had a logic and rationale behind all their actions. They saw themselves as "good." For instance, there is a story of the girl who offered kindness to a stranger, which is a direct violation of their law. The girl (some *midrashim* say it was *LoT*'s daughter who learned this *mitswah* from her father) was strapped to a bed and honey was spread all over her body and she was left to be devoured by bees.

They said to her, "According to your ideas, why should you limit your kindness to people, you should also help the animals and the insects. And further, why shouldn't you help feed these insects with your very body, if you feel it is right to give to the hungry?" The girl protested and said, "But I'll die from this, they'll devour me!" They said, "It is the same with us. Each stranger comes and takes a little bit. It is true, each one does not do too much damage, but collectively, like the bees that devour your body; they will destroy us." Their "rules" against charity were for the "greater good."

Another of the cardinal rules of *S'dom* was that everyone should be treated equally, exactly the same, that no one should be given special treatment, for that would be unfair. As a result they made beds only one size; if one was too short for the bed, they put the man on the rack, if he was too tall, the chopped off his legs.

These examples might seem cartoonish and exaggerated, but they are offered as exaggerated as they are, in order to understand and pay close attention to the underlying message. That is, the men of *S'dom* saw themselves as moral and wholly good people (As, I'm sure, all other evil people, like the Nazis, saw themselves).

The evil that exists in the world is never spread by those that see themselves as evil, yet, their idea of "good" conceals HaShem's Light in this world (the source of all goodness). In fact, any "good" that is not connected to the Word of HaShem, that is the Torah, should be suspect in our eyes. We can not be better or more moral than the Source of Morality.

14:12 – וַיִּקְחוּ אֶת־לוֹט וְאֶת־רְכֻשׁוֹ בֶּן־אֲחִי אַבְרָם וַיֵּלֵכוּ

"And they took *LoT* and his goods, *Abram*'s brother's son, and they departed..."

The war was fought primarily to attack and defeat *Abram*. Rashi tells us in the first verse of this chapter that the king *Amrafel* is really *Nimrod*. This is a continuation of the battle between *Nimrod* and *Abram* according to the Midrash. When the armies captured *LoT*, they were satisfied because, in the language of the Midrash, he "resembled" *Abram. Nimrod*'s purpose in the world was to separate the physical world from HaShem, concealing His Light. *Nimrod*'s enemy, ultimately, was the seed of Abraham whose role is to bring the Light of HaShem to the world. *LoT* "resembled" Abraham because it is through his seed (*Moab and Ruth*) that the Redeemer of *Yisrael* will come and elevate *Yisrael* to its full potential as a Light (of God) unto the Nations. By capturing *LoT*, *Nimrod* felt that he had successfully thwarted the future redemption.

14:12 – וְהוּא יֹשֵׁב בִּסְדֹם
"...and he [*LoT*] dwelt in *S'dom*."

It was his living in *S'dom* that caused him to be captured. This can be interpreted both physically and spiritually. It is interesting to note that the *gematria* [numerical equivalent] of *S'dom* is equal to the word *"daq,"* meaning "precise." One of the ways in which they demonstrated their evil was in the very precise and uncompromising way in which they executed their law.

14:13 – לְאַבְרָם הָעִבְרִי
"...*Abram* the *Ivri* [Hebrew]..."

According to *Bereshith Rabba*, he is called "`*Ivri*" because he came [`*avar*] from the other side of the river.

Another interpretation of `*ivri* might be because he passed over from the "norms of society. He transformed his belief and left the world of evil to walk before HaShem.

14:14 – וַיָּרֶק אֶת־חֲנִיכָיו
"...those whom he educated..."

Actually, the written text reflects the singular; who he had trained. Some say this refers to *Eli`ezer, Abram*'s servant (see below). Rashi says this refers to the instruction of *mitswoth*.

14:14 – שְׁמֹנָה עָשָׂר וּשְׁלֹשׁ מֵאוֹת
"...three hundred and eighteen..."

This is the *gematria* [numerical equivalent] of *Eli`ezer*'s name. The Talmud teaches that Abraham took only his servant to battle the kings.

14:17 – עֵמֶק הַמֶּלֶךְ
"...the king's valley ..."

The Midrash tells us that it was so named because there, the kings came to an agreement and crowned *Abram* over them as a Prince of God and as a leader.

14:18 – וּמַלְכִּי־צֶדֶק
"And *Malki-Tsedeq* ..."

The *Gemarah* (*Masekhet Nederim*) teaches that this was *Shem*, the son of *NoaH*.

14:18 – הוֹצִיא לֶחֶם וָיַיִן
"brought forth bread and wine..."

Rashi teaches us two things from this verse. The first is that, to bring out bread and wine is customary for people tired from war. The second is that this was a gesture to indicate that *Malki-Tsedeq* did not bear any hatred in his heart against *Abram* for the killing of his sons, for all the kings listed were descendents of *Shem*.

One should also note the linguistic relationship between bread, "*leHem*" and war, *m'lHamah*."

14:19-20 – וַיְבָרְכֵהוּ וַיֹּאמַר בָּרוּךְ אַבְרָם לְאֵל עֶלְיוֹן קֹנֵה שָׁמַיִם וָאָרֶץ: וּבָרוּךְ אֵל עֶלְיוֹן אֲשֶׁר־מִגֵּן צָרֶיךָ בְּיָדֶךָ וַיִּתֶּן־לוֹ מַעֲשֵׂר מִכֹּל:
"Blessed is *Abram* of the God Most High, Maker of Heaven and Earth and blessed is the God Most High, Who has delivered your enemies you're your hands ..."

The Midrash teaches that *Malki-Tsedeq* offended HaShem's honor with this blessing, for he named *Abram* first, and as a result lost the priesthood for his descendents (instead they were given to the descendents of Abraham). In another instance, we see how showing proper honor can have great merit even for someone who was wicked. The *Gemarah* (*Sanhedrin* 94) teaches that *Nebukanezer* chased after a messenger when he learned that his king had sent a message to King *Hezkiyahu* and had listed King *Hezkiyahu* before HaShem. This gave him the "merit" to be God's agent in the destruction of the First Temple several years later.

14:24 – עָנֵר אֶשְׁכֹּל וּמַמְרֵא הֵם יִקְחוּ חֶלְקָם

"... `Oner, Eshkol, and Mamre', let them take their portion ..."

According to our tradition, these men did not engage in the battle, as the verses states only *Abram* and his servant did so. However, we learn that in the time of *Dawidh HaMelekh* [King David], that even those that stay with the baggage get an equal share. There, it is stated that *Dawidh* learned this rule from Abraham in accordance with this verse [*Shmuel* I 30:24ff].

15:2 – דַּמֶּשֶׂק אֱלִיעֶזֶר

"the *Damaseq, Eli `ezer* ..."

The simple meaning of this is that *Eli `ezer* came from Damascus, however the *Gemarah* interprets "*damaseq*" as meaning, "he drew [*dal*] and gave to drink [*mashaq*] of his master's teachings to others.

According to the sages, even though the People *Yisrael*, are free from the determination of *mazaloth* [astrological signs] when they fulfill the Torah, as a people, the Nation's 'natural' sign is that of the *dli* [bucket from *dal* -Aquarius], because we draw water, which is the symbol Torah, and offer it to the world to drink. The sages connect this to *Eli `ezer*. This is how *Eli `ezer*, by clinging to the righteous Abraham, was able to change his *mazal*, and follow the teachings of Abraham.

This connection to the sign of dli explains many other matters in the Torah, such as the test *Eli `ezer* does to find a wife for *YitsHaq*, *Moshe* being drawn from the Nile, and him later drawing water for the daughters of *Yithro*, as well many of the episodes during the wandering in the dessert.

15:6 – וְהֶאֱמִן בַּיהוָה וַיַּחְשְׁבֶהָ לּוֹ צְדָקָה:

"He was faithful to HaShem and H/he regarded (for) him for righteousness..."

The traditional meaning of this verse is that HaShem counted *Abram*'s belief (in HaShem) for *Abram*'s righteousness. However, one could understand the verse to mean that "*Abram* had faith in HaShem and regarded Him as righteous." Even though he was unable to perceive HaShem's plan, *Abram* accepted that his suffering was for the good, and that there was a reason why he had remained childless and his wife barren.

15:19-21 – אֶת־הַקֵּינִי וְאֶת־הַקְּנִזִּי וְאֵת הַקַּדְמֹנִי: וְאֶת־הַחִתִּי וְאֶת־הַפְּרִזִּי וְאֶת־הָרְפָאִים: וְאֶת־הָאֱמֹרִי וְאֶת־הַכְּנַעֲנִי וְאֶת־הַגִּרְגָּשִׁי וְאֶת־הַיְבוּסִי:

"the *qeni* and the *q'nizi* and the *qadhmoni* and the *Hiti* and the *p'rizi* and the *r'faim*, and the *emori*, and the *k'na`ani*, and the *gir'gashi* and the *y'vusi*."

Ten nations are listed here, who are the current residents of the Promised Land. The series follows and interesting pattern, where the initial letters of the words repeat ten times "*hey-waw*. (or nine times, *waw-hey*, with a leading definite article of *hey*)." These two letters represent the last two letters of HaShem ineffable Name. In the *Qabbalah*, these two letters represent the 'lower aspects' of the Infinite, while the first two letters (*yod-hey*) represent the higher aspects.

It seems to me that this might be a hint that the descendents of Abraham, that is, the Children of Israel, are meant to be the head of the Nation of Israel, whose body contains a multitude of other peoples who choose to follow the path of HaShem and His Torah. The Children of Israel are designated to be the *kohan'im*, priests, of the nation (just as the descendents of *Aharon* are designated to be the *kohan'im* of the Children of Israel).

16:1 – שִׁפְחָה מִצְרִית
"...a handmaiden, an Egyptian ..."

Our tradition teaches that she was the daughter of Pharaoh. When he saw the miracles, which HaShem wrought for *Sarah*, he said it is better that my daughter be a handmaiden in *Abram*'s house, than a princess in another house.

16:5 – וַתֹּאמֶר שָׂרַי אֶל־אַבְרָם חֲמָסִי עָלֶיךָ
"...my wrong (the wrong done to me) is upon you ..."

Sarah told Abraham that when he prayed to HaShem, he only prayed for himself, but he should have prayed for both of them.

16:16 – וְאַבְרָם בֶּן־שְׁמֹנִים שָׁנָה וְשֵׁשׁ שָׁנִים בְּלֶדֶת־הָגָר אֶת־יִשְׁמָעֵאל לְאַבְרָם

"And *Abram* was eighty-six years old when *Hagar* bore *Yishma`el* ..."

Rashi tells us that this is written in praise of *Yishma`el*, for it informs us that he was thirteen when he was circumcised, yet did not prevent his circumcision. In fact, in many places in our tradition, we learn that the Muslims are given great merit because they circumcise themselves. This includes the merit of sitting on *Har Habayit* [Mount Moriah] until right before the *MashiaH* comes to build the third Temple. May he come soon.

Eighty-six is the *gematria* for "*El-ohim*, which while usually is translated as meaning "God" or "gods," it can also mean "great one," "leader," or "judge." This may be a hint to Abraham's growing status amongst his neighbors.

17:1 – אֲנִי־אֵל שַׁדַּי

"...I am *El Shadai*..."

One interpretation of this name is from the word "*Shoded*," to conquer. Another is that it means, "that which (*sh'*) is sufficient (*dai*).

17:1 – הִתְהַלֵּךְ לְפָנַי וֶהְיֵה תָמִים

"...walk before Me and be *tamim* [perfect, whole hearted]..."

Targum Onkelos translates this to mean, worship (pray) before Me. Another interpretation offered is that it refers to the commandment of circumcision, without which *Abram* is imperfect and is considered to have a defect.

I understand this differently. When compared with *NoaH* [6:9], who walked with God, we understood that *NoaH* had to rely on God to be righteous. We also noted that immediately before the flood, he is no longer called "*tamim*" but instead only "righteous." Here, HaShem is telling *Abram* to take the lead, and act on his righteousness, which *Abram* does in fact do throughout his life. He acts in the world, instead of closing himself off and away from sin. As noted in last week's parsha, to remove oneself from the evil influences of one's environment is a noble undertaking, but the next step is to change one's environment and society.

17:10 – זֹאת בְּרִיתִי אֲשֶׁר תִּשְׁמְרוּ בֵּינִי וּבֵינֵיכֶם וּבֵין זַרְעֲךָ אַחֲרֶיךָ הִמּוֹל לָכֶם כָּל־זָכָר:

"This is my *brith* [covenant] which you shall keep, between Me and you and your descendents, after you; every male among you shall be circumcised."

This is the *mitswah* of circumcision. It is repeated to the entire people of *Yisrael* in the Book of *Wayikra* [Leviticus] (12:3).

Through *brith milah*, the Jew attains perfection of the human form, for the foreskin is considered abhorrent before HaShem. According to our tradition, *Adam* did not have a foreskin until after his sin, when he descended towards the level of animals. This idea is further expressed by the preceding verses, where HaShem says, "Walk before me and become whole."

The reason that HaShem did not create us complete and perfect from the womb is to hint to us that, just as the perfection of our physical form is in our hands, so too, is the perfection of our spiritual essence, through the worthiness of our actions.

The *brith milah* [the circumcision] becomes the sign and signature of the *brith* [covenant] between HaShem and Abraham's descendents. We are taught that the Jew is surrounded by two "witnesses" of this covenant continually. During the week, the *tefillin* [phylacteries] act as the second witness (along with the *brith milah*), and on the *Shabbath* (when Jews do not wear *tefillin*), the day itself becomes a witness. All three of these, *milah*, *tefillin*, and *Shabbath* (and only these three), are called "*oth*," or "sign" in the Torah.

According to the *Gemarah* [Talmud, *Masekheth Kiddushin*], the *mitswah* of circumcision is an obligation incumbent upon the father of every male child (and the master of purchased slaves). The father can appoint an agent to perform the circumcision on his behalf. If the father is unavailable or refuses to perform circumcision, then the obligation falls to the *Beth Din* [courts]. Women do not have the direct obligation to circumcise their sons. If one is not circumcised upon reaching the age of majority (13), then the obligation falls to him to perform, or have it performed on him.

If one dies without being circumcised (except if he is prevented from doing so against his will, or if it is delayed for medical concerns and the like), then he suffers the punishment of *Karet* [excising or spiritual cutting off], and his soul is cut off from his people and from eternal life.

It seems to me that this "punishment" is evident, even before one dies. An uncircumcised Jew will often experience spiritual blindness because of his physical state.

I have a friend who grew up the son of Jewish parents in the then Soviet Union. As such, he was uncircumcised, for to perform the *brith milah* was against the law. (Like many repressive regimes, the Soviet Union did not outlaw Judaism per se, but rather the symbols of the faith). Growing up however, he had always had a spiritual dimension, so much so, that when he reach maturity he told his parent that he wanted to join a Christian monastery. His parents, although unable to express their Judaism because of the repressive policies of the Soviet Union, identified strongly with their People and were very upset.

This was the time of Perestroika and Habad had already established themselves in Moscow. His parents hurriedly sent him to Moscow hoping that the Habad House could 'cure' him. He went willingly, spent some considerable time there but came home more convinced than ever that his destiny lay with the Russian orthodox church. His parents, in a last desperate attempt, sent him back to Moscow.

This time, as he entered the Habad House, he witnessed an extraordinary event. Many people were there to fulfill the *mitswah* of *brith milah*, having been heretofore unable to do so. He was asked if he wanted to join them as well. Something, even today he's not sure what, inspired him to agree. He relates that as soon as the foreskin was removed he had a revelation as if clouds covering his mind suddenly parted and he knew that he was Jewish. He continued his spiritual quest, but this time as a Jew. He is now a rabbi and a *mohel* (one who performs *brith milah*) for a burgeoning community in Russia.

A *brith milah* ceremony today consists of two parts. The actual circumcision and the naming event. The circumcision must be performed by the father or a *mohel* acting as an agent on his behalf. A *mohel* is an observant Jew trained in the legal, spiritual, ritual, and practical aspects of *milah*. He is often, but not necessarily, a rabbi.

The ceremony begins with the child being delivered to the "Chair of *Eliyahu HaNavi*," who according to our tradition is present at every *brith milah*. The child is then transferred to the lap of the *Sandaq*, upon which the *brit milah* is performed. It is considered a great honor to be a *Sandaq*. He is compared to being the *mizbaH* [Temple altar] in the *Beth HaMiqdash* [the holy Temple]. The father, or the *mohel* acting on his behalf, then places a *magen* [shield] on the foreskin, protecting the organ. A special knife, shaped like a double edged sword is then used to cut off the foreskin. Then the *mohel*, using his fingernails, tears the thin membrane under the foreskin and pulls it back. This is called *p'riya*. The *mohel* then takes a mouthful of wine, dribbles it on the place of the cut and then sucks wine and blood from the *milah* (spitting it into a cup afterward). This is called *metsitsah*. All three of these actions are initially necessary for a kosher *brith milah*. The *mohel* then cleans and dresses the organ. At the same time blessings are recited over a cup of wine. During these blessings, the child is given his name. Afterward, there is a *se'udath mitswah* [a festive meal in honor of the performance of the *mitswah*].

17:12 – וּבֶן־שְׁמֹנַת יָמִים
"...eight days old ..."

As noted in *Parshat Bereshith*, seven is symbolic of physical perfection. The number eight represented by the letter *Heth*, signifies a level above physical perfection, that which is beyond nature and natural phenomenon. It should be noted that when Abraham is told to journey to *Erets Yisrael*, he is given seven blessings. We discussed earlier how this symbolizes physical completion and perfection. Now, with the transformation of his name, and the establishment of the *brith* [covenant], Abraham's blessings extend beyond the normal bonds of nature.

17:16 – וּבֵרַכְתִּי אֹתָהּ וְגַם נָתַתִּי מִמֶּנָּה לְךָ בֵּן וּבֵרַכְתִּיהָ וְהָיְתָה לְגוֹיִם מַלְכֵי עַמִּים מִמֶּנָּה יִהְיוּ:
"...and I will bless her ... and I will bless her ..."

We are forced to ask the question: What is the reason for the second blessing? Rashi tells us that she will be blessed with breast-feeding so that people will not say that they brought a foundling from the streets.

17:23 – בְּעֶצֶם הַיּוֹם הַזֶּה
"...on the very day ..."

Abraham did not delay in performing the *mitswah* and he performed it at midday before the entire world.

Because of this, there are some who have the custom to perform the *brith milah*, in the afternoon, though the best time is considered to be immediately after morning prayers, "not delaying" as like our father Abraham, and performing the *mitswah* at the first possible opportunity.

PARSHATH WAYERA

Overview

Our parsha begins as a continuation of events of last week. Abraham is sitting in the opening of his tent, recovering from the circumcision, when HaShem visits him; along with (or through) three travelers who we learn are really three *malakhim* [angels]. Each of the *malakhim* has a separate mission: one has come to heal Abraham, another has come to announce the birth of *YitsHaq* and the third is designated to destroy the cities of *S'dom* and *`Ammorah*. Abraham greets his guest and demonstrates the *mitswah* of "Welcoming a Stranger."

After the *malakhim* depart, God reveals his plan to Abraham to destroy the cities. Abraham argues with God in hopes to save the cities. He suggests that if there are found at least ten righteous, God should save the city on their behalf. HaShem agrees, but even this does not suffice to save the cities.

Two of the *malakhim* continue on to *S'dom*, where they are greeted by *LoT*, who in the manner of his uncle Abraham welcomes them into his house. The men of *S'dom* display their wickedness and demand that *LoT* turn over his guests so they might "know" them, implying that they wished to sexually assault them. *LoT* offers his daughters instead. The men at the door are blinded by the *malakhim*, and *LoT* is told that he must prepare to flee. He, his wife, and his two unmarried daughters are led out of the city by the *malakhim*. His other daughters and their husbands are left behind because *LoT*'s sons-in-law did not believe *LoT* when he warned them to escape. *LoT*'s wife looks back and becomes a pillar of salt. *LoT* decides to flee to the mountains instead of to another city, even though he requested to go to that city explicitly.

After the destruction of the cities, *LoT*'s daughters think that the entire world is destroyed and they get their father drunk and lie carnally with him. From this union, come two nations, including the nation of *Moav*, from which Ruth and eventually *Melekh Dawidh* [King David], (and soon, God Willing, the *MashiaH*) emerge.

Abraham travels to the land of the Philistines where a similar incident occurs as that which occurred in *Mitsrayim* [Egypt]. However, the king in this incident, *AbiMelekh*, proves to be more righteous and develops good relations with Abraham later.

HaShem "remembers" Sarah, and *YitsHaq* is born to the couple. Abraham circumcises him, as he was commanded, on the eighth day and holds a feast when he is weaned. Sarah throws *Hagar* and her son, *Yishma`e'l*, out of their home when she sees how he was relating to her son *YitsHaq*. *Yishma`e'l* is saved by an angel in the desert. We then learn about his marriage and how the establishment of a nation through him.

Abraham encounters *AbiMelekh* again, and they make a covenant. After this, Abraham is tested by God and told to bring his son up to Mount Moriah and offer him up to God. When he arrives, he finds a ram and is told to offer him in *YitsHaq*'s stead.

Finally, Abraham is told of the birth of *Rivqah*, *YitsHaq*'s future wife, and the other children born to his brother.

We do not learn any of the six hundred and thirteen *mitswoth* from this parsha directly, though some of them are supported through the examples of the ethical actions of HaShem, Abraham, and Sarah.

In Detail: *A selection of some verses of interest:*

18:1 – וַיֵּרָא אֵלָיו יְהֹוָה

"*Wayera elaw* HaShem [HaShem appeared] to him…"

The first time HaShem "appeared" (specifically the use of the Hebrew word, "*Wayera*") was a few verses earlier, preceding the instructions for Abraham to circumcise himself [*Parshath Lekh L'kha*, 17:1]. There, Abraham falls to his face at the appearance of HaShem. Rashi tells us, concerning the verse, that he fell because he hadn't the strength to stand before God prior to his circumcision. In our verse, Abraham does not fall to his face, and in fact, desired to stand before

HaShem (see below). This reflects the spiritual power of circumcision, which allows the Jew to stand before his Creator.

Commentators disagree with the meaning of this verse. The Rashba suggests that this introduces the entire episode and that this refers, actually, to the three travelers that appear. Ramban writes that this is a separate event, and that HaShem's appearance before Abraham was a "reward" for Abraham's undertaking of the *brith milah* (circumcision). The Ramban suggests that Abraham was given a taste of the World to Come, and God's Presence came to rest on him.

It seems to me that there is a relationship between the expression, "*wayera*," "He appeared" and "*wayi'sa `eynaw*," "he lifted up his eyes." Both imply an extra-normal perception of the world; the first initiated by HaShem and the latter by man. This parsha is replete with such references (this might be a contributing factor in the Rambam's understanding (see below) that the entire episode is one vision), and yet within this same parsha, there are many references to blindness.

It seems to me that a message of our parsha concerns this dichotomy between 'true vision,' and 'spiritual blindness;' the earlier leading towards true leadership and accomplishment, and the latter bringing destruction and distortion to the world.

18:1 – וַיֵּרָא אֵלָיו֙ יְהֹוָה בְּאֵלֹנֵי מַמְרֵא
"HaShem appeared to him by the tents of *Mamre*..."

Rashi comments simply, "to visit the sick." The *Gemara* [Talmud] in *Masekhet* [Tractate] *Baba Matsia* [86] teaches in the name of Rabbi Hama bar Hanina, that it was the third day of his circumcision, when it is the most painful, and HaShem came to inquire after Abraham's welfare.

Through HaShem's example we learn the importance of the visiting the sick. The Torah teaches, "You who have attached yourselves to HaShem, your God, are all alive today [D'varim 4:4]," indicates that we should strive to emulate HaShem's ways (since literally, physical attachment is not possible). Our verse here teaches that God visits the sick, to provide us one example of how to emulate Him. No matter how important a person is, he must visit the lowliest of men; in performing acts of kindness, personal status is ignored.

When a person becomes ill, his relatives and close associates should visit him immediately. Others should not visit until after three days have passed, but if he is seriously ill, these distinctions are not made, and everyone must visit on the first day. One should visit as often as possible and inquire after his condition, however, one should be careful not to overwhelm the sick person. It is best to visit a person in the late morning to early afternoon. This is because in the early morning, symptoms tend to subside and one might not be inclined to pray for his health, and in the evening one's health seems to worsen, and one might become despondent about the person's condition and chances for recovery.

When visiting the sick, one should sit in his presence. One should not sit near his head since the Divine Presence is there, nor at his feet, but at the patient's side. One should dress in nice clothing when visiting the sick out of respect for the patient and the *mitswah* for which he is performing. One should offer a prayer or blessing for the patient in his presence. This can be done in any language and preferably it should be in a language understood by the patient. When one prays elsewhere, it is preferable that the blessing or prayer for the patient be in Hebrew as it is more effective. Upon praying for him, one should include all the other sick of *Yisrael*, as through the merit of many he will better be able to recover.

If he is in danger, it is a *mitswah* to help him take care of his affairs and attend to his debts so that his mind will be clear and if he leaves this world, he will be at rest in the next world. If his time draws near he should be encouraged to confess his sins in a *widu'i* (alternatively pronounced *vidu'i*) [confessional] before God, and repent of all his transgressions. Before the *widu'i* it should be explained to him that many people confess and do not die, but it is important that if it in fact occurs, he will be ready for the event. It has been my experience that reciting the *widu'i*, and sincerely resolving to repair one's misdeeds can have a restorative effect on the patient. Many people hesitate to remind the patient to say the *widu'i* fearing that it will cause them to lose hope, however, this should not be the case as one who encourages him to say it is considered a messenger of HaShem, and has done a great service to the patient, for one who dies unrepentant might undergo severe trials. Further, it is also possible that confession and true repentance might cause Heaven to issue a reprieve, and bring healing to the person.

18:1 – וְהוּא יֹשֵׁב

"…and he sat…"

Rashi notes that the writing of the verb is not the expected form. This indicates that Abraham desired to stand in the presence of HaShem but God told him to remain seated and He would "stand," so to speak.

18:1 – וְהוּא יֹשֵׁב פֶּתַח־הָאֹהֶל

"…and he sat in the opening of the tent…"

Abraham had a special constructed tent that was open in all four directions. He would sit in the opening all day, waiting for travelers whom he would invite into his tent as guests. This was the way in which he would teach the world about the one true God. He would invite them into his home for a meal, and then teach them about the Provider of the World.

We learn from this verse, that even in his weakened state, Abraham continued to search for passersby in order to extend his hospitality.

18:1 – וְהוּא יֹשֵׁב פֶּתַח־הָאֹהֶל

"…and he sat in the opening of the tent…"

The "tent" has special significance in the Torah. It implies being in HaShem's presence; it carries the meaning of being one with HaShem. As great as Abraham was, we read here that he was only in the tent's opening. Sarah, however, was actually in the tent [verse 18:9]. In the metaphoric language of the *Qabbalah*, Abraham was in the process of fixing his soul, while Sarah was already able to hide within the presence of HaShem; she was already "fixed." From this, we learn that Sarah was on an even higher spiritual plane than Abraham. This is further supported in the following episode involving *Yishma`e'l* and *YitsHaq* [21:10ff], in which Sarah orders *Hagar* and her son out of the camp. Abraham distressed, turns to God Who tells him to heed the voice of his wife. Abraham, in the language of the *Qabbalah* exemplified unbridled *Hesed* [grace - loving kindness], which is not the ideal state, whereas Sarah had attained a level of *Hesed* within *g'vurah*, that is, loving kindness within its proper limits. She knew where to draw the line. Abraham would not learn this until the `*Aqeidah*.

18:1 – כְּחֹם הַיּוֹם:

"…during the heat of the day."

The simple meaning of this verse is that this episode occurred during midday. However, the *Gemara* [*Baba Matsia* 86] teaches that God made the day hotter than usual (literally took the sun from its container) in order to discourage travelers, so that Abraham would not be burdened with guests. However, HaShem saw that this grieved Abraham, so He brought three angels to him in human form (see below).

18:2 – וַיִּשָּׂא עֵינָיו

"He lifted up his eyes…"

As discussed earlier, the use of this phrase through the Torah (and the rest of the *Tanakh*) seems to imply something other than conventional looking. It implies an awareness and a perception of things beyond normal perception, or at least beyond the perception that most people normally employ. For example, in *T'hillim*, we read, "I will lift up my eyes to the mountain of HaShem, from where my help will come," implying a looking beyond the material plane of existence. This is most evident, at the conclusion of the `*Aqeidah*, wherein Abraham suddenly "sees" the ram caught in the thicket. This ram, according to our tradition had been there since the dawn of time, and yet, only at that moment of spiritual awareness did Abraham "see" it. It is clear that he was able to see its spiritual essence, its purpose for existence.

18:2 – וְהִנֵּה שְׁלֹשָׁה אֲנָשִׁים

"And behold, three men …"

It is common for the *Tanakh* to refer to *malakhim* [angels] simply as "men." That they were messengers of HaShem is hinted at by their sudden appearance.

Bereshit Rabbah teaches that each *melakh* is assigned only one errand or mission. To support this, Rashi points out that throughout this episode, it is written in the plural, "they ate," and "they said to him," but regarding the announcement of *YitsHaq's* birth, it is written, "I shall return to you," and regarding the destruction of *S'dom*, it is written, "I am unable to do anything not to overthrow…"

The three missions of the three were, to announce the birth of

YitsHaq to Sarah (Abraham was already told earlier), to destroy *S'dom*, and to heal Abraham. It is taught that the *malakh* [literally messenger; meaning angel] that healed Abraham was *R'fael*, and that he went from there to rescue *LoT* (After he fulfilled his mission to Abraham he was given this new one, and accompanied the destroying *malakh* to *S'dom*. The third *malakh* having fulfilled his mission did not journey to *S'dom*, but returned to his place in heaven

18:2 – נִצָּבִים עָלָיו

"…stood over him…"

Rashi tells us that this simply means, "stood in his presence." However, it seems to me that the expression might also carry the impression of immediacy. "Suddenly, three men stood before Abraham."

Or, maybe, it was as if they stood over him, for Abraham saw the *mitswah* of welcoming the guest as imperative, compelling to act as if one had a taskmaster standing over him.

Alternatively, he recognized their purpose and its importance loomed over him.

18:2 – וַיַּרְא

"…and when he saw them…"

Twice within the same verse, we are told that Abraham saw them. The first instance we can understand as the initial visual perception of these three, however, the second one must imply that Abraham understood their nature. This can mean that he understood that they were *malakhim*, or that he recognized their purpose.

Rashi explains the second "saw" as that of understanding as well. He understands that Abraham understood that these three did not want to trouble him.

According to the *Gemara* [*Baba Matsia*], they saw Abraham unbinding and binding his bandages so the *malakhim* departed from him, not wishing to disturb him. So, Abraham ran after them. Through this reference, our sages are hinting about the *MashiaH*, who we are told is sitting at the gates of the City, amongst the lepers, unbinding and binding his bandages [*Sanhedrin* 98a.]

18:3 – אֲדֹנָי

"My Lord ..."

The grammar of this expression is puzzling. The vowelization of the word, with a *"qamats"* beneath the letter *"nun"* indicates the common usage when referring to God. If it he was referring to one person, there would be a *"hiriq"* under the *"nun,"* and to several people (my lords) a *"pataH"* is called for. Several possibilities are offered by commentators:

The Rambam assumes that the entire episode, including the appearance of HaShem is all one inclusive vision and Abraham is addressing HaShem.

The Ramban see the two visions as separate. However, he concurs with the Rambam, that Abraham is addressing HaShem, only he does so because he recognizes the true nature of the three "men" and therefore addresses the one that sent them, namely, HaShem.

There is a difficulty with both of these explanations, for Abraham does not behave towards the men as if they are *malakhim* [angels], for such beings do not eat nor drink, and if Abraham had recognized them as such, he would not have hurriedly prepared them meals.

The Rambam would argue, in keeping with his belief that the whole episode was a dream-like vision and not real, that this was simply a part of the vision and does not indicate to whom Abraham was addressing himself. I still find this difficult though.

Rashi says that the word should be interpreted as "lords," that is, in the plural, and not "Lord" the vocalization reserved for HaShem. Even though this is not the common vowelization for the plural it is plausible grammatically.

I think instead, though, that the second explanation of Rashi is the most comprehensible. Rashi suggests that Abraham is indeed addressing HaShem, but not because he recognized the nature of the men, but rather to request that HaShem excuse him, and wait for him while he ran to welcome the guests.

The only difficulty with this is this request; "My Lord, ... Do not pass by..." is written after the verse saying that Abraham ran to meet the guest. Rashi addresses this difficulty suggesting that it is common for verses to be written out of order in the *Tanakh*.

To support Rashi, it seems to me that the reason that this phenomenon occurs here might be to emphasize Abraham's quick response to perform the *mitswah* and welcome the guests.

18:5 – לִבְּכֶם

"...your hearts [*libkhem*]..."

Ribbi *H*ama teaches that that "your hearts" is written with only one '*beth*' (in other places it is written with two of the letter *beth*) to indicate that angels to not have a *yester har`a* [evil inclination].

18:6 – וַיְמַהֵר אַבְרָהָם הָאֹהֱלָה אֶל־שָׂרָה וַיֹּאמֶר מַהֲרִי

"Abraham quickly went to Sarah's tent and said quickly prepare..."

The word for haste or quickly is repeated twice in this verse teaching us a very valuable lesson. It is incumbent upon a host not to delay his guest unduly. Abraham, aware that his guests have a mission, does his best to prepare and serve them as quickly as possible.

This principle is also enshrined in the *halakhah* [Jewish Law]. Most people are probably unaware, but there are times when the *halakhah* mandates that one take the more expedient route, forsaking certain stringencies for the sake of brevity. For instance it is forbidden for a *shali'aH tsibor* [the communal prayer leader] to add extra prayers and praises within the main part of the service, for this might delay some of the pray-ers, making them late for work and the like.

The best illustration of this principle is found in the laws for salting meat. After an animal or foul is ritually slaughtered, and cut up into its various parts, one is required to salt the meat to draw out its blood in compliance with a Biblical verse. The accepted custom is to leave the meat in the salt for an hour, however, the *halakhah* states explicitly that if one has an important guest, such as a great rabbi, waiting, one should be stringent and only salt the meat for the required eighteen minutes. This is an important law, for one might have thought that for a great rabbi, the stringency would be to leave the meat in the salt the full hour. However, we learn the opposite, that the honor of guests is more important than a customary stringency, and that to delay serving them for such a custom, even though they themselves follow such a custom, would be a violation of the law.

18:7 – וַיִּתֵּן אֶל־הַנַּעַר
"and gave it to the young man …"

The lad is, according to *Bereshith Rabbah*, *Yishma`e'l*. Abraham gave him this chore in order to instruct him in the *mitswah* of welcoming guests. It is important to note that there are two *mitswoth* that the Torah describes Abraham teaching *Yishma`e'l*, namely circumcision and the welcoming of guests. It seems to me far from a coincidence that these two *mitswoth* are an integral part of Arab culture. Their fastidiousness with these *mitswoth* should be a banner for *Yisrael* who is the First Born of HaShem, in regards to our obligations.

18:8 – וַיֹּאכֵלוּ
"…and they ate"

Rashi points out that they only appeared to eat, for *malakhim* cannot eat. From this we learn, says the *Gemara*, that we are not permitted to change from the accepted customs.

18:9 – אֵלָיו
"…to him …"

Tradition places dots (in the Torah manuscript) above the *aleph*, the *yud*, and the *waw* of the word "*eilaw*" (to him). Rashi teaches that they also inquired of Sarah, "Where (*ayo- aleph-yud waw*) is Abraham?" to teach that one should always inquire in his lodging, of a man after his wife and a woman after her husband.

Another possibility stems from the *gematria* [numerical equivalent] of the three letters, which equals seventeen, the *gematria* of the word "*tov*," meaning "good." They asked after Sarah for her (or for his) good, to make known that she was "in the tent" (see below).

18:9 – הִנֵּה בָאֹהֶל
"…Here, in the tent…"

Rashi interprets this to demonstrate Sarah's modesty. I have already explained previously the understanding that Sarah was in the tent, while Abraham sat in the opening of the tent.

18:13 – לָמָּה זֶּה צָחֲקָה שָׂרָה לֵאמֹר הַאַף אֻמְנָם אֵלֵד וַאֲנִי זָקַנְתִּי

"Why did Sarah laugh, saying 'Will I really bear a child being that I am old?"

Rashi points out that HaShem altered Sarah's jest in the interest of family peace, for she really said, "my husband is old."

18:16 – וְאַבְרָהָם הֹלֵךְ עִמָּם לְשַׁלְּחָם

"…Abraham went with them on their way."

The *mitswah* of escorting guests on their way is an essential part of the *mitswah* of welcoming guests. This is hinted at with the word for "room and board," *eshel*. It's three letters, *aleph*, *shin*, and *lamed*, are said to stand for food (*okhel* which begins with an *aleph*,) drink [*sht'yah*], and escorting [*liwayah*].

It is told that the house of a prominent man burned down. He went to the rabbi inquiring why, declaring that his house, as it should be, was a place full of guests and hospitality. The rabbi asked the man if he escorted his guests when they left, and the man admitted that he hadn't. The rabbi then responded that this was the reason.

The *mitswah* of welcoming guests includes three parts, *'okhel* [food, the Hebrew word begins with the letter *Alef*], *shti'yah* [drink, the Hebrew word begins with a *shin*], and *l'wayah* [escorting, the Hebrew word begins with a lamed]. When one fails to do the third part, explained the rabbi, one is left with *'esh* [*alef – shin*], which means fire. The man saw the errors of his ways and rebuilt his home, transforming it into a place full of guests once again. Further, from that day onward, he always escorted his guests at least four *amoth* [a distance of six to eight feet] on their journey.

When someone is about to embark on a long journey, it is common custom to give him tsedaqah [charity] to give to the poor when they arrive at their destination. This transforms the person into an emissary of a *mitswah*, which offers them special protection.

There is another tradition that unfortunately has grown into disuse, which involves a ritual "script" between the traveler and the escort.

First the escort repeats thirty times "Your salvation, I hope for HaShem; I hope, HaShem, for your salvation; HaShem, for your salvation, I hope. Then he quotes verses thirty-five and six from chapter ten in *B'midbar* [Numbers] six times, followed by chapter six, verses twenty-four through six ten times. Afterwards he says *Bereshith* chapter forty-eight verse sixteen five times.

Then the traveler responds with *T'hillim* [Psalms] 90:17 and 90:1-2 seven times.

The escort responds with *T'hillim* 91:3-8.

The Traveler then says *T'hillim* 91:9.

The escort says *T'hillim* 91:9-16 and then *Y'sha'yahu* [Isiah] 26:4 forward and backwards (the words in reverse order) three times. This is followed by *T'hillim* 29:11 in the same manner three times, *T'hillim* 46:8 three times, *T'hillim* 84:13 three times, *T'hillim* 20:10 three times.

The traveler says, *T'hillim* 121:1-2 seven times.

The escort says, *T'hillim* 121:3-8 followed by *Bereshith* 32:2 three times. Finally the escort says, "*Lekh l'Shalom*" "Go in Peace," and the traveler then turns and proceeds on his way. (see Appendix for full script in Hebrew).

18:17 – וַיהוָה אָמָר הַמְכַסֶּה אֲנִי מֵאַבְרָהָם אֲשֶׁר אֲנִי עֹשֶׂה:
"And HaShem said, 'How can I hide from Abraham that which I am doing?'"

This question must be understood as an interrogative, for HaShem reasoned that He had given Abraham the entire land, including these cities, therefore, he should inform him what was about to happen. Rashi states, HaShem says, "I have called him Abraham, the father of a multitude of nations, can I destroy the children without informing the father."

Another reason why HaShem found it necessary to inform Abraham of this decision is because Abraham is His representative in the world and people would inquire as to how this God of Justice Abraham continually teaches about could do such an act.

It seems to me that another, subtler, reason is also possible. It may be that HaShem informs Abraham of the destruction of *S'dom* in order to spur Abraham into action. Evidence of this is the fact that after its destruction, Abraham journeys to the land of the *P'lisht'im* [Philistines] and stays there "a very long time." It is known, particularly through Abraham's behavior when encountering them, that he considers them a corrupt nation. He treats them as he treats the people of *Mitsrayim* [Egypt], who were known to be corrupt. Further, there doesn't seem to be any other reason to move there other than to try and elevate and redeem the people. We are not informed of a famine as with the journey to *Mitsrayim*. Abraham, it seems, as father of the nations, learns that he must reach out and educate his charges, the nations of the world.

One of the principle roles of the Nation of Israel is to educate the families of the world in basic morality and the existence of the one True God. We have an obligation to be a "Light unto the Nations" and encourage the nations of the world to adopt and follow the brith [covenant] of *NoaH*, which consists of seven basic *mitswoth* incumbent upon all of humanity.

18:21 – אֵרְדָה־נָּא וְאֶרְאֶה
"I will now descend and see…"

This teaches that judges should not decided cases wherein lives are at stake unless the evidence is very clear and they see it for themselves.

Another possible understanding is that He will see if there is a possibility for them to repent of their evil.

18:21 – הַכְּצַעֲקָתָהּ הַבָּאָה אֵלַי
"…according to the cry that has reached Me …"

In *Masekhet Sanhedrin* the rabbis interpret this cry as being that of the girl who was tortured for giving food to a poor stranger. Some say this was *LoT*'s daughter, as I have explained elsewhere [*Parshat Lekh L'kha*].

18:23 – וַיִּגַּשׁ אַבְרָהָם
"And Abraham drew near…"

There are several connotations of the phrase to draw near in *Tanakh*. It carries the meaning regarding war [*Shmuel* II 10:13], regarding conciliation [*Bereshith* 44], and regarding prayer [*Melakhim* I 18] and all of these meanings exist in Abraham's approach of HaShem here. He drew near to do battle for justice, he sought conciliation, and he prayed for the lives of the citizens of *S'dom*.

18:23 – הַאַף תִּסְפֶּה

"HaAf Tispeh ..."

"Af" can be the conjunctive, "also" meaning "Will you also destroy (the righteous with the evil)? However, it also carries the meaning "wrath" so Onkelos translates this question as "Will wrath persuade You ..."

18:25 – חָלִלָה לְךָ

"...Far be it from You ..."

That it is "foreign to Your nature to do such, and so that people will not say that this is how God operates, that He destroys indiscriminately. Otherwise, humanity might think that God also did so with the Generation of the Flood, etc.

18:32 – אוּלַי יִמָּצְאוּן שָׁם עֲשָׂרָה

"...maybe there will be found there ten ..."

It has been suggested (see *Parshath NoaH*) that the singular difference between Abraham and *NoaH*, is that Abraham argued for his generation. This is why he was crowned with the honor of being the "first Jew," as opposed to the *NoaH*.

Abraham finishes his argument at ten. It is possible that he thought any less than ten would be insufficient to save the cities. On the one hand, there were eight people within the Ark of *NoaH*; presumably they were all righteous, yet they were unable to prevent the destruction of the world.

We learn that ten is the minimum number of people allowing for God's presence to rest amongst a group (praying in a quorum of ten for example). We also learn in *Masekhet Megillah*, that a "city" is defined as such when ten people learn Torah there, full time. It seems logical that Abraham would assume that this would be the minimum number required to save a city, as if HaShem's presence is there, the city should be considered worthy.

Yet, if this was Abraham's reasoning, he might have been able to reduce the minimal requirement to two, for we learn that wh*Erev*er two people engage in Torah study, the *SheHinah*, God's Divine

Presence, dwells between them.

Further, it might be suggested that the episode of the `*Aqeida* (the Binding of *YitsHaq*) was a moral lesson, intended to teach Abraham of each and every soul, and that he should not have concluded his arguments at ten, but rather press, "if there is but one righteous …"

18:33 – וַיֵּ֣לֶךְ יְהֹוָ֔ה כַּאֲשֶׁ֣ר כִּלָּ֔ה לְדַבֵּ֖ר אֶל־אַבְרָהָ֑ם
"And HaShem went His way as soon has He had left off speaking to Abraham…"

Rashi states, "Since the defender became silent, the Judge went His way." I believe that this means, that the Abraham's silence suggested agreement with the final decree.

19:1 – וַ֠יָּבֹ֠אוּ שְׁנֵ֨י הַמַּלְאָכִ֤ים סְדֹ֙מָה֙
"And two *malakhim* came to *S'dom*…"

One was designated to destroy the city, while the second was there to save *LoT* and his family. The second one, according to tradition, was *R'fael*, the same one who was designated to heal Abraham. The Ramban points out that this is not a contradiction with the dictum that each *malakh* can have only one role, one mission. This mission was acquired by the *malakh* after he had already executed his first mission. In other words, says the Ramban, this rule is only operative for a particular place and time, but once the location has changed, a new mission can be given to the *malakh*. Another possibility is that Salvation and healing are considered the same "function."

The third *malakh*, who had come to announce the birth of *YitsHaq* had fulfilled his errand and was no longer needed, so he departed.

Another possibility is that Abraham was granted an audience of three *malakhim* and *LoT* only two, due to the difference in each of their spiritual status.

Bereshith Rabba notes that they are called "*malakhim*" here, but in the earlier episode they are called men. This is to teach that in the presence of Abraham they were "like men," but besides *LoT* they are called *malakhim*.

19:1 – בָּעֶ֖רֶב

"…in the evening …"

Rashi points out that the distance between Abraham's tent and *S'dom* does not warrant half a day's travel, particularly for *malakhim* (they were at Abraham's tent at midday). However, he teaches that they were *malakhai raHamim* [angels of mercy] and delayed in hopes that Abraham would be able to argue in defense of the city.

19:1 – וַיַּרְא־לוֹט֙

"…And *LoT* saw …"

Rashi comments that *LoT* saw and learned how to welcome guests from the house of Abraham.

19:2 – וְלִ֙ינוּ֙ וְרַחֲצ֣וּ רַגְלֵיכֶ֔ם

"…and stay the night and wash your feet…"

Rashi asks why "washing their feet" is written after staying the night, when logically it should be written in reverse. *LoT* reasoned, we learn from this, that if they washed their feet first, the men of *S'dom* would accuse *LoT* of harboring the travelers for several days, whereas if they spent the night with the dust of the road still on their feet, it would appear as if they had just arrived.

19:4 – טֶ֘רֶם֘ יִשְׁכָּבוּ֒ וְאַנְשֵׁ֨י הָעִ֜יר אַנְשֵׁ֤י סְדֹם֙

"Before they lay down the men of the city; the men of *S'dom* …"

Bereshit Rabba explains this repetition that before they retired the *malakhim* questioned *LoT* about the nature of the men of the city. *LoT* replied that that in every city there are good and bad, but here, the overwhelming majority of them are evil. Rashi, however, explains the repetition to be a description of the men of the city. Using the earlier verse, which describes the men of *S'dom* as evil and full of sin, here he suggests that "Men of *S'dom*" is a euphemism for evil men. He would read the verse, "Before they lay down, the men of the city, evil men, surrounded…"

19:5 – וְנֵדְעָ֖ה אֹתָ֑ם

"…that we may know them…"

That is, sexually. Rabbi Y'hoshua *ben* Levi said in the name of Rabbi

Padia, that *LoT* had been praying for mercy on behalf of the city the whole night, and the *malakhim* would have heeded him, until the men of *S'dom* demanded this. The *malakhim* said to *LoT*, "from now on, you do not have any right to plead for them."

19:8 – רַק לָאֲנָשִׁים הָאֵל

"…only to [these] men [*Anashim HaEl*] …"

Rashi interprets the word "*HaEl*" as similar to "*HaEleh*," meaning "these." However, another way of understanding the phrase, and to my mind the more simple meaning, would be "only to the men of [the] God," for "El" can mean "God." From his sojourn with Abraham, *LoT* may have come to recognize messengers of the One True God. *Bereshith Rabba* seems to confirm my understanding, offering also, "men of strength" or "godly men," as possibilities.

19:8 – כִּי־עַל־כֵּן בָּאוּ בְּצֵל קֹרָתִי

"…as they have come under the shadow of my roof …"

Targum Onkelos translates the phrase "shadow of my rafter" based on the midrash, which suggests that *LoT*'s wife would not let the *malakhim* under her portions of the house, but they were relegated to the part of the house that was *LoT*'s.

Another understanding of "shadow of my roof," is that this is a reference to Abraham, wherein "shadow" is an often a metaphor for protector. *LoT* tries to persuade the mob, that these men have the protection of Abraham, who, it was known, helped *S'dom* recover their losses from the war of the kings.

19:17 – אַל־תַּבִּיט אַחֲרֶיךָ

"…Do not look back …"

Rashi suggests that *LoT* was not worthy to see their punishment while he was being saved, because he was infected by the evil of *S'dom*, and only the merit of Abraham has saved him.

I have difficulty with this because *LoT*'s behavior towards the strangers demonstrates that he was not of the same character of the men of *S'dom*, albeit, he was clearly not righteous in all of his actions (his offering of his daughters for instance).

In regards to being saved only because of Abraham's merit, this seems correct, for we can understand that all of our good deeds are based on the merit of those who raised and educated us. In the sense that *LoT* learned righteousness from the years of living with his uncle, then clearly this is based on Abraham's merit.

Further, as was demonstrated with the restrictions placed on *NoaH* during the Flood, it seems that no one should be considered worthy to observe the destruction of his fellow, no matter how evil they are. We are not to revel in the destruction of evil people, nor even pray for their downfall, rather, we are enjoined to pray for their repentance and help them return to God.

19:18 – אַל־נָא אֲדֹנָי
"...please no, my Lord ..."

"My Lord," presents a difficulty because here, as earlier, its vowelization denotes a restricted use of the term for God. Ibn Ezra, however, suggests that this rule does not apply to the end of a verse, where often vowelization changes denoting the verse's end.

19:18 – אַל־נָא אֲדֹנָי
"...please no, my Lord ..."

Bereshit Rabba teaches that *LoT* did not want to flee to the mountain (Abraham) because when *LoT* lived with Abraham he had good deeds to his own merit. And while living in *S'dom*, *LoT* had good deeds to his credit compared to the people of *S'dom* so he would appear righteous before HaShem, but if he returns to live with Abraham, he will no longer had good deeds to his credit, and he will, in comparison, appear before God as a wicked man.

19:26 – וַתְּהִי נְצִיב מֶלַח
"...became a pillar of salt ..."

We learn that "by salt she sinned, and by salt she was punished." The Midrash offers two versions of her sin through salt. When the *malakhim* came, *LoT* told her to give them salt, as is the custom, and she chastised him, saying "This is an evil custom that you are trying to institute in this place!" Another version says, that when the guests came she went to her neighbors asking for salt because they had guests, in hopes that the townspeople would become aware of their presence.

19:29 – וַיִּזְכֹּר אֱלֹהִים אֶת־אַבְרָהָם

"…and God remembered Abraham …"

According to *Bereshith Rabba*, *LoT* was saved because of what he had done for Abraham. It is taught that God remembered that *LoT* knew that Sarah was Abraham's wife, but when Abraham said, "She is my sister," to the *Mitsrim* [Egyptians], he did not reveal the matter and he had compassion on Abraham.

This seems strange, for why would we have assumed that *LoT* would have exposed Abraham? We should remember that in fact, *LoT* was Sarah's sister, and even though he saw the wealth that was showered upon Abraham as Sarah's brother, *LoT* remained silent. He could have very easily become upset, for he was in fact Sarah's true brother, and therefore, he would have been justified in thinking that all that wealth rightfully belonged to him. Yet, he remained silent about the matter.

19:32 – וּנְחַיֶּה מֵאָבִינוּ זָרַע

"…we will preserve the seed of our father …"

Oftentimes, we find ourselves and other to be "hidden prophets," that is, we say things, not realizing the full impact or implications of what we say, only to be surprised later when events "follow our mouths." Our sages often found these hidden pearls in the words of the Torah. In regards to *LoT*'s daughters statement about preserving their father's seed, Rabbi Tan*H*um said in the name of *Shmuel*, who noted that their choice of the term "seed" instead of "child," is powerfully significant, for like a seed, whose power and potential is hidden, sometimes for many seasons, the benefit of their act would remain hidden for many generations, until the crowning of *Dawidh HaMelekh* [King David]. They also planted the seeds for the future redemption as the *m'shiaH* [messiah] will descend from them as well (through *Dawidh*). May he be revealed soon.

19:33 – וַתִּשְׁכַּב אֶת־אָבִיהָ

"…and lay with her father …"

Rabbi Levi said (some places say that Rabbi Na*H*man *ben H*anin said), "Whoever is eager for illicit sexual passion, in the end will be made to eat from his own flesh."

After being exposed to the immorality of *Mitsrayim*, *LoT* separated himself from the righteous Abraham and ran to depravity of *S'dom*.

Our own excess, become the downfall of our children.

20:1 – וַיִּסַּ֨ע מִשָּׁ֤ם אַבְרָהָם֙
"Abraham journeyed ..."

Rashi tells us that after the destruction of the cities, Abraham saw that traffic had ceased near him, so he moved to a different location. Another interpretation is that he moved to separate himself from *LoT*, for a bad name had gone forth concerning his relations with his daughters.

20:7 – כִּֽי־נָבִ֣יא ה֔וּא
"...for he is a prophet ..."

We learn in *Masekhet Baba Kama* [92] HaShem assures *AbiMelekh* that Abraham will know that he did not touch Sarah, so *AbiMelekh* should not think that she would become disgraceful in his eyes and that Abraham would not receive her. Nor will Abraham have hatred for *AbiMelekh* and he will pray for him.

20:11 – רַ֚ק אֵין־יִרְאַ֣ת אֱלֹהִ֔ים בַּמָּק֖וֹם הַזֶּ֑ה
"...surely there isn't any fear of God here ..."

Abraham argued that it is not common for a guest, when he comes into a city, to be asked concerning his wife, "is she your wife or your sister?" Therefore, he assumed that when they asked it was evidence of their godlessness (*Buba Kama*).

20:12 – וְגַם־אָמְנָ֗ה אֲחֹתִ֤י
"...she is, in fact, my sister ..."

Rashi explains a general rule of Biblical exegesis that "grandsons are like sons," so, since, Sarah was the daughter of Abraham's father's son, she was considered as a sister to him. We learn elsewhere (verse 13:8), that Abraham says, regarding *LoT*, "We are brothers."

It seems to me that we can understand the Biblical term brother and sister as kinsman, to distinguish between marrying outside of one's tribal family. The concept of family was much large and more complex than our modern understanding, and in this context both Sarah and *LoT* were kinsmen of Abraham. As, we will see later, *YitsHaq* would be able to honestly claim the same about *Rivqah*.

20:17 – וַיִּתְפַּלֵּל אַבְרָהָם אֶל־הָאֱלֹהִים
"…Abraham prayed to God …"

There are some commentators who suggest that this episode precedes, chronologically, the visit of the *malakhim*. They suggest that it was through Abraham and Sarah's praying for *AbiMelekh* that gave them the merit to receive *YitsHaq*. It is a general rule that praying for others, selflessly, helps in the answering of one's own prayers. We learn this explicitly is the *Gemara, Masekhet Baba Kama* [92a].

21:2 – בֶּן לִזְקֻנָיו
"…in his old age …"

Twice in this section it talks about the child being born in Abraham's "old age," yet it does not refer to Sarah's age. It seems curious, as it is more of a miracle for a child to be born to an older woman, whom we had already learned that her time of menstruation had stopped that to be born from an old man. This might be written such, out of modesty for Sarah, or as a reminder of Sarah's laughter at the announcement, which is where *YitsHaq*'s name is derived. *YitsHaq*'s name is derived from the word for laughter.

21:9 – וַתֵּרֶא שָׂרָה אֶת־בֶּן־הָגָר הַמִּצְרִית אֲשֶׁר־יָלְדָה לְאַבְרָהָם מְצַחֵק
"Sarah saw the son of *Hagar* the Egyptian whom she had born to Abraham "*mitsaHeq*" [playing]…"

The verb "*mitsaHeq*" comes from the root meaning "to play," or "to make sport." Rashi suggests several possible meanings based on its use elsewhere in *Tanakh*. Citing its use in *Sh'moth* (chapter 32:6), he says it can denotes idol worship, In *Bereshith* 39:17 it carries the meaning of "uncovering one's nakedness," or incest. The word also can mean "murder," as we learn in Second *Shmuel* 2:14. Rashi seems to favor the last meaning, for he provides a midrash, in which *Yishma`e'l* and *YitsHaq* were arguing over the inheritance, wherein *Yishma`e'l* proceeded to shoot arrows at *YitsHaq*.

Yet, I heard another interpretation of how *Yishma`e'l* tried to murder *YitsHaq* and the events that led to the expulsion of *Hagar* and *Yishma`e'l* which touch on all the above meanings of the word.

What Sarah saw was *Yishma`e'l* talking to *YitsHaq* and she overheard him saying that *YitsHaq* was not Abraham's son, but rather he was

AbiMelekh's son. *Yishma`el* related the entire episode and told his brother that he was, in effect, a *mamzer* [often translated as bastard, but specifically a child born from a forbidden union, such as adultery or incest]. To tell someone, especially someone whose father is *Abraham Avinu*, that he's illegitimate, that he is not the heir to Abraham's righteousness, is tantamount to murder, murder of the soul. As for the meaning of "idol worship," this becomes clearer in verse fourteen after they are cast out.

21:10 – גָּרֵשׁ הָאָמָה הַזֹּאת וְאֶת־בְּנָהּ

"…cast out this bondwoman and her son …"

The word *"garesh,"* meaning, "cast out," implies total separation and a severing or cutting off of all contact, as opposed to simply distancing one from the other (it's the same word for divorce).

21:12 – שְׁמַע בְּקֹלָהּ

"…listen to her voice …"

Rashi tells us that it is from this verse that we learn that Sarah was superior to Abraham in prophecy. That HaShem told Abraham to heed the voice of his wife, proves that Sarah did not act out of cruelty towards *Hagar* and *Yishma`el* but rather the justified protective nature of a mother who saw them as a danger to *YitsHaq*.

21:14 – וַתֵּלֶךְ וַתֵּתַע

"…she departed and strayed …"

Pirqe D'Rabbi Eliezer (chapter 30) tells us that this means that she returned to her idolatrous ways of her father's house.

21:17 – כִּי־שָׁמַע אֱלֹהִים אֶל־קוֹל הַנַּעַר בַּאֲשֶׁר הוּא־שָׁם

"…for God had heard the voice of the youth where he was there …"

We learn [in *Masekhet Rosh HaShanah*] that at this time the *malakhei haSharet* complained and pressed HaShem not to aid *Yishma`el*, reminding Him that *Yishma`el*'s seed is destined to kill His Children (*Yisrael*). HaShem asked them, "At the present, is he righteous or evil?" They were forced to answer that he was righteous. So God told them that He judges in accordance with one's present deeds and not their potential to do harm.

From this, my teacher taught that we can learn a valuable lesson, on how it is appropriate to approach every individual "where he is at—there." This is especially applicable in education, wherein it is the duty of the teacher to approach his students where they are at, and bring them to where they need to be. This, says my teacher, is hinted at in the following verse, for *Yishma`el* is want for thirst, and water is a symbol of Torah. "And God opened her eyes and she saw a well of water." She saw the beauty of Torah. "…and gave the youth to drink." She instructed him in Torah. "…And God was with the youth and he grew." He became knowledgeable in Torah; he matured and developed through his learning. This understanding is in harmony with *Yishma`el*'s age, for at this time, he had already reached the age of majority, and it would not seem likely for the Torah to be suggesting his physical maturation.

However, the simple meaning is his physical growth, and Rashi teaches that *Yishma`el* became a robber of wayfarers. Yet, if this is so, one must ask, how does the Torah state, "God was with the youth?"

22:1 – וַיְהִי אַחַר הַדְּבָרִים הָאֵלֶּה
"And it came to pass, after these things…"

There is a disagreement among the commentators as to when this episode, called `*Aqeidath YitsHaq* [the binding of *YitsHaq*/Isaac] took place. There is a general guideline in learning the Torah, that we can not assume that everything is written chronologically, and in fact some sections that are found later textually, actually occurred earlier. Anytime this occurs, it is for an educational purpose and the rabbis learn meaning from the placement of a particular section. This is especially true, when the text itself declares a connection, as, for example, in our verse here which states, "After these things …"

Masekhet Sanhedrin [89] teaches that this means, "after the words of *Satan*[6], who denounced Abraham." According to the *Gemara, Satan* accused Abraham of making a feast without making an (sacrificial) offering to HaShem at the same time. HaShem responds that Abraham would offer his own son if asked. Therefore, the "test" of the `*Aqeida* took place.

---

6   *Satan* literally means the accuser, the prosecutor, and he is an heavenly being that fulfills the role of foil. He is, like any other heavenly being, completely subservient to the Will of HaShem, and does not, as other religions suggest, have any independent role in the world.

Other commentators suggest that this takes place, "After the words of *Yishma`el*" who taunted *YitsHaq*, boasting that he was circumcised at the age of thirteen and did not protest, but *YitsHaq* had not choice. *YitsHaq* retorted, "With one organ you intimidate me? If God said to me, "Sacrifice your whole self," I would not refrain from doing so!"

Another possible interpretation is after Abraham argued for *S'dom* and desisted his defense at ten righteous individuals. God brought this experience to teach Abraham the value of every soul, and he should have continued his argument until God conceded that he would not destroy even one righteous in order to punish the wicked. There is a hint of this in the end of the argument when it says, "And HaShem went his way …" Rashi adds, "Since the defender became silent, the Judge went His way." I can understand from this that it was Abraham that ended the argumentation, and had he continued, HaShem might have conceded further.

Another possibility, presented in the *Qabalah*, is that this entire episode was designed to "fix" a deficiency in Abraham. We have already discussed that he represented "unbridled" *Hesed* as opposed to his wife Sarah whom was able to define her kindness in well-defined borders. Unbridled *Hesed* can be self-destructive. It is a characteristic we find in many Jews, who offer kindness to the enemy of our people, which ultimately causes our very own people to suffer. Sarah was not willing to sacrifice the well being of her son for the sake of "kindness" shown to *Hagar* and her son. In such a situation, one must steel oneself against unwarranted compassion for the other. Abraham had not yet learned this lesson. Therefore, the *`Aqeida* was brought to combine *YitsHaq*'s characteristic of *g'vurah* [restraint] with Abraham's *Hesed*, the result being their descendent, *Ya`aqov*.

22:1 – וְהָאֱלֹהִים נִסָּה אֶת־אַבְרָהָם
"…and God "*nisah*" [see below for meaning] Abraham…"

The common understanding of this is, "God tested Abraham." The word "*nisah*" can mean "to prove," "to cause to experience," or even "to publicly display (from "*nes*" meaning miracle of flag).

The Rambam understands the word to mean "test." He adds that it has the power to absolve punishment, such as in a trial.

Others understand this to mean, "HaShem made a public demonstration of Abraham's fidelity." To take the potential, as it were, and make it real; that is, to demonstrate the limits, or in this case, that there weren't any limits to Abraham's belief of HaShem and His goodness. For here, God was telling Abraham to sacrifice, not only his beloved son, but in effect the promise that God had made to Him, which would be fulfilled through this son.

22:2 – אֶת־בִּנְךָ אֶת־יְחִידְךָ אֲשֶׁר־אָהַבְתָּ אֶת־יִצְחָק

"...your son, your unique and only one, which you love, *YitsHaq*..."

Masekhet Sanhedrin teaches that this is only HaShem's half of a conversation, which displays the depths of Abraham's righteousness. God says, "Take your son," and Abraham responds, "I have two sons." HaShem says, "Your unique and only one," and Abraham responds, "This one is unique to his mother, and this one to his mother." God says, "The one you love," and Abraham responds, "I love them both." Finally, HaShem said to him, "*YitsHaq*."

Rashi teaches that Abraham received a reward for each word.

22:2 – אֶרֶץ הַמֹּרִיָּה

"...the Land of *Moriah* ..."

That is, *Yerushalayim* [Jerusalem]. It is called *Moriah*, according to the sages because Torah instruction was given there. *Moriah* seems to come from the same root as Hora-ah, instruction. Also, incidentally, the words for teacher, *moreh* or *morah*, and parent, *horeh*, come from the same root.

The Targum Onkelos suggests that the name comes from the incense offered in the Temple, namely *mor* [myrrh].

Abraham himself (verse 14) relate the word to the same root for "*ro-eh*," "sees," as in "the mount where HaShem is seen (or possibly appears or is revealed)."

One can reconcile the two meanings by understanding that parents and teachers give the child and student the ability to see and recognized the truth.

22:2 – וְהַעֲלֵהוּ שָׁם לְעֹלָה

"...and offer him up there for an *Olah* ..."

Rashi states that HaSham never tells Abraham to slaughter *YitsHaq*, but rather offer him up as an "*Olah*." However, an *Olah*, at least in the terms of Temple ritual means a "whole burnt offering." Rashi suggests that HaShem only wanted Abraham to prepare *YitsHaq* as an *Olah*, but not to actually offer him up.

Yet, there is a difficulty with this, for when someone receives prophecy he also receives its explanation. Our tradition does not allow for a prophet to misunderstand his prophesy.

22:3 – אֶת־שְׁנֵי נְעָרָיו

"...two of his young men ..."

Our tradition teaches that this was *Yishma`e'l* and *Eli`ezer*. Of course, *Eli`ezer* was not a young man, but we learn that the Torah often calls subordinates, "young men," no matter their age.

It is taught that both of them where excited at the prospect of *YitsHaq* being slaughtered and the two argued as to who would inherit Abraham after *YitsHaq* was killed.

22:4 – וַיַּרְא אֶת־הַמָּקוֹם

"...and he saw the place ..."

Our sages teach that Abraham saw a cloud attached to the top of a mountain. When he asked *YitsHaq*, he answered that he saw the same phenomena, but when Abraham asked the two young men, they said they only saw desert. *Pirqe D' Rabbi Eliezer* says that this is why the two men were designated to stay with the ass, though he renders it "as the ass." In other words, they were no more spiritually elevated than the ass.

22:5 – וְנָשׁוּבָה אֲלֵיכֶם

"...and come back to you ..."

Rashi teaches that Abraham prophesized that they would both return, yet if this were so, one could ask, what type of test is this really? Therefore, it is taught by others that Abraham believed that he would indeed sacrifice his son, and this would be such a public sanctification of HaShem's name, that the entire world would understand that everything is truly HaShem's and the Redemption would come immediately. When this happened, *YitsHaq* would be restored to life, for in the time of redemption, we know that the dead will yet live again [The concept of *MiHiyat HaMetim*] for the final Judgment.

22:6 – וַיֵּלְכוּ שְׁנֵיהֶם יַחְדָּו

"…and they went, both of them, together …"

Abraham who knew that he was about to slaughter his son and *YitsHaq* who was also prepared to sanctify God's name, both went together with a singularity of purpose.

22:9 – וַיַּעֲקֹד אֶת־יִצְחָק בְּנוֹ

"…and bound *YitsHaq* his son…"

Our tradition teaches that *YitsHaq* was thirty-seven years old (though there are other opinions). Therefore, it is clear that he could have struggled if he chose. Rather, our sages teach that *YitsHaq* begged his father to secure him tightly, so that he wouldn't involuntarily flinch and ruing the offering.

22:11 – אַבְרָהָם | אַבְרָהָם

"…Abraham, Abraham …"

Rashi teaches that this was an expression of love, while Ibn Ezra suggests that this was an expression of haste.

22:12 – כִּי | עַתָּה יָדַעְתִּי

"…for now I know …"

Rashi teaches in the name of Rabbi Abba who said, "Abraham said to Him, "I will now tell You my complaint: Yesterday, You said to me, 'For by *YitsHaq*, your seed shall be called.' Then You retracted and said, "Take now your son." Now You say, "Do not lay a hand on him.'" HaShem said to Abraham, "…I did not say to kill him, but 'Bring him up.' You have brought him up, now bring him back down."

22:13 – וַיִּשָּׂא אַבְרָהָם אֶת־עֵינָיו וַיַּרְא וְהִנֵּה־אַיִל אַחַר

"...And Abraham lifted up his eyes and looked, and here, there was a ram afterwords ..."

According to *Pirqe Avoth*, this ram was prepared for this on the evening of the sixth day of creation, but it was only revealed to Abraham when he was spiritually able to perceive it. This is the meaning of "he lifted up his eyes," that he perceived beyond the normal realm of seeing. This occurred "afterward." After he had achieved a level of closeness with HaShem from his act of faith, or, as Rashi renders it, after the words of the *malakh*.

22:20 – וַיְהִי אַחֲרֵי הַדְּבָרִים הָאֵלֶּה

"And it came to pass, after these things ..."

This is another test/trial for Abraham. After returning from the *`Aqeidath YitsHaq*, it occurred to him that if he had indeed slaughtered his son, then he would have died childless. Abraham realized his obligation to find his son a wife. At that point, HaShem announced to him the birth off *Rivqah*, says Rashi.

22:20 – הִנֵּה יָלְדָה מִלְכָּה גַם־הִוא בָּנִים לְנָחוֹר אָחִיךָ

"...behold, *Milkah* also bore children to your brother *Nahor*..."

There are a total of twelve children in all, eight from wives and four from concubines. The similarity with *Ya`aqov* is clear, yet the two families were opposites in regards to values and character. This is discussed in depth when in the upcoming chapters.

PARSHATH *HAYE* SARAH

Overview

Our parsha, called "The life of Sarah," ironically begins with her death. Abraham approaches the Children of *Het* and purchases, after brief negotiations, the Cave of the *Makhpelah* and the surrounding field from *Efron*, for four hundred silver shekels. He buries Sarah and mourns her.

Abraham then sends *Eli`ezer*, his servant, to find a wife for *YitsHaq* from among his father's family. *Eli`ezer* brings ten camels full of riches as a dowry. He arrives in the city of *Nahor*, and waits by the well. He prays to God that He should send a girl from Abraham's family, and that she should show kindness to him and his camels.

Rivqah immediately appears and give *Eli`ezer* to drink and then she waters all the camels. *Eli`ezer* is sure she is *YitsHaq*'s mate and gives her a ring and two bracelets before even asking her who her family was. She confirms his faith that she is indeed of Abraham's kin and then he reveals that he is Abraham's servant. Upon seeing the ring and bracelets, *Lavan*, her brother runs out to greet the man and welcomes him into their home. *Eli`ezer* reveals his mission and request for *Rivqah* to marry *YitsHaq*. The family agrees, but request that she not journey to *YitsHaq* for a year. *Eli`ezer* disagrees and they ask *Rivqah* herself, who states that she will go with *Eli`ezer* immediately.

She returns with him and marries *YitsHaq* and takeing the role of matriarch, coming to reside in Sarah's tent and providing comfort for the loss of Sarah.

Abraham remarries *Hagar*, now called *Qetorah*, and has many children through her. He, however, sends them away, to the east, with gifts before his own death, so that they will not contend with *YitsHaq* for the inheritance.

Abraham passes away, and *Yishm`a'el* and *YitsHaq* reconcile at the funeral, with *Yishm`a'el* accepting *YitsHaq*'s primacy. Finally, the parsha ends with the generations of *Yishm`a'el* detailed.

While there aren't any *mitswoth* directly learned from this parsha, however, the Rabbis learn several important principles. For instance, it is learned from this parsha, that a woman cannot be wed against her will. We also learn the important qualities one should consider in seeking a mate, being the inner beauty of compassion and modesty.

We learn the primacy of burying and eulogizing one's dead. One is exempt from *mitswoth* of action ("doing" type *mitswoth*) until one buries his close relatives. A close relative is considered a parent, sibling, child, or spouse. We are enjoined to participate in the mourning of any great sage, *tsadiq*, or other important figure in Judaism. The death of a *tsadiq* [saint] is considered to help atone for the sins of a generation, however, if he (or she) is not properly mourned by the community, then HaShem will bring the community to judgment. Anytime a major Rabbi dies, it is imperative that businesses be closed and the entire community try to attend the funeral. He should be eulogized by the leaders of the community and honored in death. In addition, any Jew, especially a God-fearing individual who kept the *mitswoth*, should be shown proper respect when he dies. If one encounters a funeral procession of a Jew, one is obligated to join the procession for a minimum of four amoth, which are approximately six to eight feet. Also, we are encouraged to participate and honor the dead of non-Jews who were leaders of the community, especially if they were friendly to the Jewish community.

In Detail: *A selection of some verses of interest:*

23:1 – וַיִּהְיוּ חַיֵּי שָׂרָה מֵאָה שָׁנָה וְעֶשְׂרִים שָׁנָה וְשֶׁבַע שָׁנִים שְׁנֵי חַיֵּי שָׂרָה
"And the life of Sarah was a hundred years, and twenty years and seven years..."

Rashi tells us that "years" is repeated after every unit of time to alert us that each term needs to be interpreted individually.

23:1 – מֵאָה שָׁנָה
"...was a hundred years ..."

According to Rashi this means, that at the age of one hundred, she was regarded as innocent as a twenty-year old in sin. To the modern ear this might sounds quite strange, for we don't tend to assume today that a twenty-year old woman is further away from sin than a hundred year old (in fact we might suspect the opposite - to our distress, May

God have Mercy on us). Instead of understanding this though in the context of the desire or "pull" one has to sin, Rashi seems to be explaining this in the context of the Heavenly Court which does not punish one for (certain) sins committed before the age of twenty. Thus, Rashi is suggesting that, just as at the age of twenty, Sarah was innocent in the eyes of the court, she also was so when she reached one hundred.

However the Maharal emends Rashi, suggesting that at one hundred she was like a twenty year old in beauty (and a seven year old in regard to sin). This of course seems more logical to the modern ear as well, and implies, not culpability but innocence. As far as her being a beauty at one hundred, there is support for this within the text of the Torah. When Abraham and Sarah visited *Mitsrayim* (Egypt) and the kingdom of *AbiMelekh*, Sarah was considered to be a very beautiful and sought after woman despite her advanced years.

Another possible interpretation can be that at the age of one hundred she was as a twenty year old, because she gave birth to her firstborn. The age of twenty is an appropriate age for one's first child.

23:1 – וְעֶשְׂרִים שָׁנָה וְשֶׁבַע שָׁנִים
"...and twenty years and seven years..."

Rashi says that this is in regards to beauty, that she had the beauty and innocence of a seven year old. However, as stated above, the Maharal emended this to read that at twenty she was as a seven year old in regards to sin.

23:1 – שְׁנֵי חַיֵּי שָׂרָה
"...the years of the life of Sarah."

The phrase seems to be a repetition. Midrash *Rabba* suggests that this is to indicate that all of the years of the righteous are precious before HaShem. Rashi suggests that they were all "equally good."

23:2 – וַתָּמָת שָׂרָה בְּקִרְיַת אַרְבַּע
"Sarah died in *Kir'yath Arb`a* ..."

The Midrash tells us that *Kir'yath Arb`a* (the City of Four), is called such for several reasons. The first is that is that it had four names: *Eshkol, Mamre, Kir'yat Arb`a*, and *Hebron*. Also, four righteous men dwelt there: *Abraham, Avner, Eshkol*, and *Mamre*. There are also four righteous men buried there: *Adam, Abraham, YitsHaq,* and *Yaaqov.* Again, there are four righteous women buried there: *Hawa* (Eve), *Sarah, Rivqah,* and *Leah.* Further it had four rulers: *Anaq* and his three sons. Also, Abraham went out from there to pursue the four kings.

23:2 – הִוא חֶבְרוֹן

"...which is *Hebron*..."

It has become a custom here in *Yisrael* to make a pilgrimage to *Hebron* during the *Shabbath* in which this parsha is read. Aside from the merit of visiting the graves of the righteous, it is a very good way "to make the Torah come alive." It also reminds those who would deny our inheritance of the land that our father Abraham purchased the land and passed its deed to us. It is our inheritance. Today, *Hebron* is under heavy attack. Daily, our enemies rain bullets and stones – and even more vicious, malicious lies suggesting that the land is not ours - on the Jewish residents of the city. May HaShem protect them and grant us the privilege to enjoy our inheritance in true peace.

23:2 – וַיָּבֹא אַבְרָהָם לִסְפֹּד לְשָׂרָה

"...And Abraham came to mourn Sarah..."

This verse seems strange. Where was Abraham that he had to come to mourn his wife? We read in the parsha immediately preceding this that Abraham returned from the `*Aqeida* and went to *Beersheba*. Rashi tells us simply that he came from *Beersheba*. Is it possible that he was not in the same place as his wife?

In the Midrash, Ribbi Levi teaches that he came from *TeraH*'s funeral to that of Sarah's. However, Ribbi Yose say that that is not possible for *TeraH*'s death preceded Sarah's by two years (see our study on *Lekh L'kha*). He thus determines that he came from *Har Moriah* where the `*Aqeida* (Binding of *YitsHaq*) took place. It is taught that Sarah died from shock, for while Abraham and *YitsHaq* were on the mountain, *Satan* visited her in disguise to bring her the "news" that *YitsHaq* had indeed been sacrificed. When, in another disguise, he revealed that "the other man" had lied, she was so overcome with joy that she died from shock.

23:2 – וְלִבְכֹּתָהּ

"...and he cried for her."

In the Torah the word "*w'l'bkotah*," and to cry for her, is written with a small letter *kaf.* Baal HaTurim suggests that this is to teach that he only cried a little, for Abraham knew that Sarah had lived a full live and was righteous so would attain a share in the World-To Come.

It seems to me that there might be another way to understand this. If one removes the letter *kaf* altogether, one is left with the word, "*l'batah*" for her daughter. What can this mean? Just as a son is often a reflection of his father, a daughter is often a close reflection of the mother. Sarah and Abraham succeeded in having a son, but she did not have a daughter; Abraham had someone to inherit him, but Sarah did not. Abraham cried for the reflection of Sarah, her daughter, which the world was deprived. This is might explain why immediately after Abraham buried Sarah he set about finding a wife for *YitsHaq* so that he could "bring her into her mother's tent" [*Bereshith* 24:67]. By acquiring a wife for his son, Abraham also acquired a daughter, one that could dwell within his wife's tent and, becoming a reflection of Sarah, bring comfort to his son and to the world.

It should be noted that there is a debate between Ribbi Meir and Ribbi Yehuda in *Masekhet Baba Batra* [Talmud - 16b], concerning the verse, "…HaShem blessed Abraham with all things, [*Bereshith* 24:1]" as to whether or not Abraham had a daughter. Regardless, we do not find explicit reference in the Torah that Abraham had a daughter, and if if that verse does hint at it, we know that Sarah did not have a daughter, yet *Rivqah* certainly became a true "daughter" in continuing Sarah's role.

23:3 – וַיָּ֙קָם֙ אַבְרָהָ֔ם מֵעַ֖ל פְּנֵ֣י מֵת֑וֹ וַיְדַבֵּ֥ר
"And he rose up before his dead and spoke …"

According to the *Gemara* [*Brakhot* 17b], this teaches that one is exempt from reciting the *Shem`a* when one's deal lies before him, for Abraham "rose up … and spoke."

In fact, one is exempt form all *mitswoth* of action (as opposed to prohibitions) when one is attending to the *mitswah* of burying a close relative (parents, siblings, or children) or another Jew who hasn't anyone to attend to his funeral needs. Such a person is classified as an `*onen* and can not be counted for a *minyan* [prayer quorum] or the like, until the deceased is buried. From that time onwards, as a mourner, his obligations are also curtailed for various periods of time, (lessening in stringency for each period) from one week, one month and one year from the time of the burial.

23:4 – גֵּר־וְתוֹשָׁב אָנֹכִי עִמָּכֶם

"A stranger and a resident, I am with you ..."

This is a curious expression for both terms are mutually exclusive. Rashi offers an explanation from the Midrash, wherein Abraham said to the men of *Hebron*, "If you will, I am a stranger, but if not the I will be a settler and will take it legally for the Holy One of Blessing has already promised me this land."

23:4 – אֲחֻזַּת־קֶבֶר

"...a*Huzath-qever* [a possession of a burial place]..."

The word "a*Huzah* implies inheritance as well. Abraham wanted to insure that this would become an inheritance for descendents.

23:6 – נְשִׂיא אֱלֹהִים אַתָּה

"...mighty prince..."

This can also be read as "Prince of God." This is evidence that the promise of God to Abraham was fulfilled in his lifetime. He was already acknowledged as a "prince" of God.

23:7 – וַיָּקָם אַבְרָהָם וַיִּשְׁתַּחוּ

"...And Abraham rose up and bowed down..."

The Talmud *Yerushalmi* says that Abraham bowed down to HaShem in front of the people of the land, He wanted to render thanks to Him for the gift, and publicly demonstrate that all of his blessings come from God.

23:9 – אֶת־מְעָרַת הַמַּכְפֵּלָה

"...*Makhpelah*..."

Literally the word means doubled. Rashi explains that it is a structure with an upper and a lower chamber. This is in fact its structure today. The burial tombs are below the current structure, which is a building built, and later added to over time, as a memorial for those buried below. There are legends about individuals that descended into the actual cave chambers to find the actual graves. They never returned.

Another interpretation for the name is found in *Masekhet Eruvin*, which says it represents that the chamber is called "doubled" because righteous couples are buried there. After the liberation of *Hebron*, the underground burial chambers were explored somewhat, and discovered that it is in fact built like a double chamber.

23:10 – וְעֶפְרוֹן יֹשֵׁב

"...Efron was sitting..."

The word for sitting is written without the letter *waw* (*vav*), indicating that men of *Het* appointed *Efron* to rule over them that day, so that a great man like Abraham would not have to purchase from one of humble rank.

23:10 – לְכֹל בָּאֵי שַׁעַר־עִירוֹ

"...even all that were in the gate of his city..."

According to our sages, this teaches that everyone closed their stores and came to pay their respects to Sarah. This is, incidentally, an obligation for the Jewish community. When one of the community's residents/members passes away, particularly an important member such as a rabbi or lay leader, the community should close their stores and attend the funeral.

23:16 – וַיִּשְׁקֹל אַבְרָהָם לְעֶפְרֹן

"...Abraham weighed to Efron ..."

Efron's name is missing a letter *waw* here, to indicate, according to *Masekhet Baba Matsia* [87], that "he spoke much but did not even do a little," for in the end, *Efron* took a very large sum for the plot.

23:17 – וַיָּקָם | שְׂדֵה עֶפְרוֹן

"The field of *Efron* was established..."

Literally, the word, *"wayaqam,"* means "it rose up." Which teaches that the field rose in importance because it came into Abraham's possession.

24:1 – וַיהוָה בֵּרַךְ אֶת־אַבְרָהָם בַּכֹּל

"...And HaShem blessed Abraham in all things."

The word *"bakol,"* which means "in all things," has *gematria* [numerical value] equal to the word for son, *"ben"* [both equal fifty-two]. Therefore, Rashi teaches that he had to attain a wife for his son. As mentioned earlier, in *Masekhet Baba Batra*, Ribbi Meir suggests this teaches that Abraham did not have a daughter. He says that even though a daughter is desirable, he would not be able to find a suitable mate for her, and this would cause him anguish. Ribbi Yehuda suggests that it teaches that he did have a daughter.

24:2 - אֶל־עַבְדּוֹ

"…to his servant…"

This was *Eli`ezer*. We learn that this was an incredible test for *Eli`ezer*, for he had a daughter of his own and had entertained thoughts of giving her to *YitsHaq* to wed. Ribbi Yaakov Peretz teaches that *Eli`ezer* became righteous simply because of his environment. When one lives amongst the righteous, he becomes righteous.

24:2 – תַּחַת יְרֵכִי

"…under my thigh…"

Rashi explains that the *Gemara Sh'vuot* [38] teaches that anyone who takes an oath must hold in his hand a sacred object, such as a Torah scroll. The *Brit Milah* [circumcision] was Abraham's first *mitswah* [commandment] therefore he chose it, as the object upon which to make the oath.

Alternatively, this is because the oath related to Abraham's progeny.

24:12 – וַיֹּאמַר ׀ יְהוָֹה אֱלֹהֵי אֲדֹנִי אַבְרָהָם הַקְרֵה־נָא לְפָנַי
"He said, HaShem, God of my master Abraham, send me now please…"

Eli`ezer invoked Abraham's merit because he was unsure if he was worthy of the task.

24:14 – וְהָיָה הַנַּעֲרָ אֲשֶׁר אֹמַר אֵלֶיהָ הַטִּי־נָא כַדֵּךְ . . . אֹתָהּ הֹכַחְתָּ לְעַבְדְּךָ לְיִצְחָק
"The maiden to whom I will say 'please incline your pitcher… she shall be the one appointed for your servant *YitsHaq*' …"

The test is very significant. As we discussed earlier, the *mazal* [astrological sign] of the nation of *Yisrael* is the *d'li* [pitcher – Aquarius]. This is due to the nation of *Yisrael* being the "servant of HaShem's Torah, His teaching, which is symbolized by water, and we by spreading His word is akin to giving the world to drink. The *kad* [pitcher] is simply an ancient word for *d'li* (There actually is a lengthy discussion in Talmud [*Baba Qama*] regarding the interchangeability of these terms in regard to torts). Therefore, *Eli`ezer's* "test" for the future matriarch, the future wife of *YitsHaq*, is to determine who will be the progenitor of this nation of "water carriers."

24:14 – כִּי־עָשִׂיתָ חֶסֶד עִם־אֲדֹנִי
"...for You have shown kindness..."

In all our endeavors, we are obligated to do all we can, and then have faith that HaShem will complete that which we are unable. This is His kindness [*Hesed*]. For instance, in the area of marriage, we are obligated to try and find a suitable mate, however, it is clearly impossible to meet the myriad of suitable mates that exist in the world, or even in ones locale, to find one's soul-mate. Yet, we are obligated to go out and meet as many as possible, at which point we rely on HaShem to complete the task and deliver our soul mate to us.

24:16 – בְּתוּלָה וְאִישׁ לֹא יְדָעָהּ
"...a virgin, neither had any man been intimate with her..."

The Midrash explains that she was a virgin physically and no man had made any improper advances towards her, nor had she acted immodestly otherwise. Rashi tells us that she was pure in every way.

24:17 – הַגְמִיאִינִי נָא מְעַט־מַיִם מִכַּדֵּךְ
"...Let me sip a little water ..."

Eli`ezer asked to sip and she answered, "Drink." This represents when in the future the nations of the world will come to *Yisrael* asking for a taste of Torah, and they will be given their fill to drink.

24:19 – עַד אִם־כִּלּוּ לִשְׁתֹּת
"...until they have finished drinking ..."

Camels drink a tremendous amount of water. This was indeed a true act of kindness, deserving of *Eli`ezer's* astonishment.

24:29 – וַיָּרָץ לָבָן
"...And *Lavan* ran ..."

This verse seems to be out of place, for immediately afterward it is written, that "he saw the ring and the bracelets ..." This might be so, to emphasize his greed, for according to our sages, *Lavan* looked at the ring and the bracelets and recognized the man's wealth which inspired him to run to *Eli`ezer*.

24:31 – וְאָנֹכִי פִּנִּיתִי הַבַּיִת
"I have cleared the house ..."

Bereshith Rabba teaches that this refers to idol worship, for Abraham's family knew of his teachings and recognized that the idols would make his servant uncomfortable.

24:42 – וָאָבֹא הַיּוֹם
"And I came this day ..."

Ribbi A*Ha* teaches that the ordinary conversation of the servants of the Patriarchs is more pleasing before HaShem than the Torah of their children. He demonstrates this, by noting that in this section *Eli`ezer* statements are repeated and therein many important principles of Law where only given through hints [*Bereshith Rabba*].

24:47 – וָאֶשְׁאַל אֹתָהּ וָאֹמַר בַּת־מִי אַתְּ . . . וָאָשִׂם הַנֶּזֶם עַל־אַפָּהּ
"I asked whose daughter...and I put the ring ..."

Eli`ezer reversed the order, for earlier we read that he first gave her the gifts and then asked her. He did this so that there wouldn't be any contention about him giving her gifts without first knowing that she was from the proper family.

24:49 – וְאֶפְנֶה עַל־יָמִין אוֹ עַל־שְׂמֹאל
"... to the right or to the left ..."

"To the right," refers to the daughters of *Yishmael,* and to the left refers to the daughters of *LoT.*

24:50 – וַיַּעַן לָבָן וּבְתוּאֵל

"Then *Lavan* and *B'tuel* answered ..."

Rashi explains that *Lavan* jumped up and answered before his father, which demonstrated that he was a wicked person.

24:55 – יָמִים

"...days ..."

This is interpreted as a year, which was the custom; to wait a full year between betrothal and consummation of the marriage.

24:55 – אוֹ עָשׂוֹר

"...or ten ..."

This refers to months, which supports the interpretation of "days" as meaning one year.

24:57 – אֶת־פִּיהָ

"... from her mouth ..."

Bereshith Rabba teaches that from this, we learn that a woman is given in marriage only with her consent.

24:62 – וְיִצְחָק בָּא מִבּוֹא בְּאֵר לַחַי רֹאִי

"*YitsHaq* came from *b'er laHai ro-i* ..."

Bereshith Rabba teaches that he went to bring *Hagar* to Abraham that he should marry her (see below).

24:63 – וַיֵּצֵא יִצְחָק לָשׂוּחַ בַּשָּׂדֶה לִפְנוֹת עָרֶב

"*YitsHaq* went out to meditate in the field in the evening..."

"*Lishu-aH*," meditate, we are taught denotes prayer. *Bereshith Rabba* teaches that this is the minHa or afternoon prayer and they teach that *YitsHaq* thus established the *minHa* prayer.

24:63 – וַיִּשָּׂא עֵינָיו וַיַּרְא

"...he lifted up his eyes and saw..."

This phrase, as mentioned in earlier instances, indicates a deeper perception. *YitsHaq* recognized *Rivqah* as his soul mate, and she [in the next verse] recognized him as well.

24:65 – וַתִּקַּח הַצָּעִיף וַתִּתְכָּס

"…she took the veil and covered herself …"

One possible reason for this is that she recognized that *YitsHaq* was praying and did not want to distract him. Or because as *YitsHaq* prayed, the *Shekhina* was before him, and upon seeing it, she veiled herself, just as *Moshe* veiled himself when he was in HaShem's presence.

24:67 – וַיְבִאֶהָ יִצְחָק הָאֹהֱלָה שָׂרָה אִמּוֹ

"…into the tent of his mother, Sarah…"

In other words she took the role of Sarah, his mother, becoming the matriarch. *Bereshith Rabba* explains that as long as Sarah lived there was a light burning from one *Shabbat* to the next, and a blessing in the dough, and a cloud hanging over her tent, but when she dies these things ceased. When *Rivqah* entered the tent, these things returned.

It seems to me this seems to be an allusion to the *Beth HaMiqdash*, its loss and then redemption and its rebuilding. The cloud is the incense offering, the *Shabbath* lights—the lights of the menorah, and the blessing in the dough—the *leHem hapanim* [the showbread]. The matriarch represents the *SheHinah*, it seems to me.

25:1 – קְטוּרָה

"…*Qeturah* …"

This, according to Rashi, is *Hagar*, and she is called *Qeturah* because her deeds were as pleasant as incense (*Qetoreth*)

25:5 – וַיִּתֵּן אַבְרָהָם אֶת־כָּל־אֲשֶׁר־לוֹ לְיִצְחָק

"Abraham gave all that he had to *YitsHaq*."

That is, everything of significance. Ribbi NeHemia teaches that this means that he gave him the blessing of the legacy.

25:6 – נָתַן אַבְרָהָם מַתָּנֹת
"Abraham gave gifts ..."

Masekhet Sanhedrin [91] teaches that Abraham gave them the names of impure forces to manipulate the world. That is, the names of spiritual forces that can be used even when one is not in a state of purity. It has been suggested by some contemporary scholars that these are the basis for what is known today as "Eastern medicine" and "Eastern martial arts," etc. They note, in support of this theory, that Abraham sent these sons eastward. Another interesting parallel is the eastern group called "Brahmas." The similarity to the name "Abraham" can not be missed.

25:7 – מְאַת שָׁנָה וְשִׁבְעִים שָׁנָה וְחָמֵשׁ שָׁנִים
"...one hundred years and seventy years and five years ..."

When he was one hundred, he was like a man of seventy and when he was seventy, he was like a man of five, in regards to sin.

25:8 – בְּשֵׂיבָה טוֹבָה זָקֵן וְשָׂבֵעַ
"...good old age ..."

Rashi teaches that Abraham was blessed to see his sons reconcile before his death.

25:9 – יִצְחָק וְיִשְׁמָעֵאל
"*YitsHaq* and *Yishm`a'el*, his sons buried him..."

Bereshith Rabba teaches that the fact that *YitsHaq* is listed before *Yishma`'el* demonstrates *Yishm`a'el* repented and permitted *YitsHaq* to precede him in the funeral.

25:16 – שְׁנֵים־עָשָׂר נְשִׂיאָם
"...twelve princes"

Twelve signifies a complete nation. This can be compared to the twelve tribes of *Yisrael* and the twelve children of *Nahor*.

PARSHATH TOLDOTH

Overview

The parsha begins with *YitsHaq*'s and his wife *Rivqah* marriage and life together. According to our tradition, *YitsHaq* was thirty-seven when *Rivqah* was born, and she was three when they married. He waited ten years before having relations with her, and then they tried for ten years to have children. This is similar to Abraham and Sarah who spent ten years in *Yisrael* trying to have children. *YitsHaq* entreated HaShem to bless his wife with children. This is another clear demonstration that the nation of *Yisrael* is a complete miracle. The life and actions of our ancestors, and those of their descendent are proof that ultimately everything only come through HaShem's blessings.

Rivqah becomes pregnant with twins, and is informed that two nations occupy her womb. When the twins are born, the first is called `Esaw*, because he is a "complete" man. The second child is called *Ya`aqov* because he emerges clinging onto the heel of `Esaw*.

After coming in from the field, `Esaw* sees *Ya`aqov* cooking red lentils, and being hungry, asks his brother for them. According to the tradition, this was his father's mourner's meal, following the death of Abraham. *Ya`aqov* convinces `Esaw* to sell him his birthright in exchange. Not only does `Esaw* agree to the sale, which he actually 'despises' it, not appreciating its importance.

There is another famine in the land, and *YitsHaq* is forbidden (by HaShem) from going to *Mitsrayim* [Egypt]. Instead, he dwells amongst the *P'lishtim* [Philistines], and has a similar incident with his wife, as did his father. *YitsHaq* prospers amongst the *P'lishtim*, and when he becomes very powerful he is asked to leave.

After which, there are several incidents involving the wells (often a symbol for Torah) of Abraham, where the *P'lishtim* fill them up with dirt (often a symbol for idol worship). There is a great deal of contention between *YitsHaq* and the *P'lishtim*. *YitsHaq* continually acquiesces and moves on to a new location, but finally stands his ground at the last well. Due to this,, *AbiMelekh* makes a treaty with *YitsHaq*, as he had done with Abraham.

YitsHaq grows close to his mother's age at the time of her death, and realizes that he should make preparations in case he dies. It is common knowledge that one lives to a similar age as one's parents. He commands *`Esaw* to hunt and prepare some venison for him, with the intention of blessing him. *Rivqah*, recognizing the grave error this would be, commands *Ya`aqov* to deceive his father and "steal" the blessing. He is successful, and when the deceit is revealed, *YitsHaq* seems to recognize that his wife was correct and that *Ya`aqov* truly does deserve the blessing, for he does not cancel it.

Rivqah divines that *`Esaw* is plotting against *Ya`aqov* and convinces *YitsHaq* to send him to her family in *Padenah Aram*, to acquire a wife. *`Esaw* recognizes that his Canaanite wives are displeasing to his parents and takes another wife from the daughters of *Yishm`a'el*.

In Detail: *A selection of some verses of interest:*

25:19 – וְאֵלֶּה תּוֹלְדֹת יִצְחָק בֶּן־אַבְרָהָם
"These are the *toldoth* [generations] of *YitsHaq* son of Abraham ..."

The word "*toldoth*" literally comes from the root meaning to be born of, and while it is commonly translated as "generations," it can be rendered in a variety of ways, such as "this is what results from," or "this is the history of," or "this is the continuation of," or "genealogy" or more simply "chronology of."

Rashi offers another understanding, suggesting *toldoth* refers to *Ya`aqov* [Jacob] and *`Esaw* [Esau], "which are discussed in this parsha."

However, while I think that this has bearing, it's possible that the simple meaning is that we've finished the story of Abraham, and now, we are to relate the story of *YitsHaq*. That is, each patriarch has a story unto himself. I believe there are several hints to this understanding within the next few verses, which God Willing, I will explain there.

25:19 – אַבְרָהָם הוֹלִיד אֶת־יִצְחָק
"...Abraham gave birth to *YitsHaq* ..."

Rashi points out that since the text wrote "*YitsHaq*, son of Abraham," [this same verse] it seems superfluous to say, "Abraham begot *YitsHaq*." Rashi reminds us of the Midrash (discussed last parsha) that the scorners of the generation were saying that from *AbiMelekh*, Sarah conceived and bore *YitsHaq*." Therefore, according to Rashi, based on the Midrash, HaShem formed the features of *YitsHaq*'s face to resemble Abraham's, causing everyone to confirm, "Abraham begot/gave birth to *YitsHaq*."

While this is probably the simple meaning, I think there may also be another interpretation. Considering *YitsHaq*'s age, and that the Torah begins to discuss his deeds at this point, I would suggest that the phrase can be understood metaphorically. That is, Abraham gave birth, or generated within *YitsHaq*, the fear, and love of HaShem that manifest itself in his deeds. It is clear that a man does not "give birth" to a son physically, but we can recognize one as coming from the same stock, when we witness his actions in the world. In English, the expression "chip off the old block" gives voice to this idea.

25:20 – וַיְהִי יִצְחָק בֶּן־אַרְבָּעִים שָׁנָה
"*YitsHaq* was forty years old ..."

Forty years symbolizes the passages of a generation within the *Tanakh*. This, in my opinion is a hint that we are "starting a new chapter" of the patriarch's. *YitsHaq* comes into his own, so to speak, and begins a new "*toldoth*."

25:21 – וַיֶּעְתַּר יִצְחָק לַיהוָה לְנֹכַח אִשְׁתּוֹ
"*YitsHaq* pleaded to HaShem "*nokhaH*" [opposite/facing] his wife..."

Rashi tells us that the word "*nokhaH*" here means opposite, in that he stood in his corner and prayed, while *Rivqah* stood in her corner and prayed.

I think there may be a metaphoric meaning here as well. Considering that the word for pleading, according to Rashi, denotes urging and profusion, "*nokhaH*" might mean facing, as in facing his wife's dilemma and empathizing with it. *YitsHaq*, we might assume, was familiar with his own mother's travails in this regard and this may have inspired his entreaty.

25:21 – וַיֶּעְתַּר לוֹ יְהוָה

"…HaShem allowed himself to be entreated for him …"

Being precise with the language, Rashi adds, "but not for her." Rashi quotes the *Gemara* in *Masekhet Yebamot* [64] pointing out that the prayers of a righteous person who is the son of a righteous person are unequaled. Further, it is known that when one prays for someone else, those prayers have a greater efficacy.

25:22 – וַיִּתְרֹצְצוּ הַבָּנִים בְּקִרְבָּה

"The children struggled within her …"

This verse demands, "Interpret me," for it does conceals the nature of their struggle, as Rashi points out. The rabbis offered several interpretations, such that when *Rivqah* passed by a house of idol worship *`Esaw* struggled to come forth, and when she passed by a House of Torah Study, *Ya`aqov* struggled to come forth. Others suggest that they were struggling over the inheritance of the worlds—this world and the World to Come.

25:22 – אִם־כֵּן לָמָּה זֶּה אָנֹכִי

"…If so, why am I thus? …"

Rivqah seemingly questions her desire to become pregnant. Midrash *Rabba* teaches that *Rivqah* went to the houses of several mothers to see if they too had suffered so.

Yet, this seems difficult to me, for our Torah is sparse with her words and this seems to be a common concern, almost petty. We have already learned from the first parsha, that the travails of pregnancy would be difficult as a result of our expulsion from Eden. Surely there is something more profound happening here.

Due to the fighting within her belly, *Rivqah* seems to have recognized the inevitable conflict of her two sons, and this is a reflection of her future lament ("Why should I be bereaved of the two of you?"[27:46]) It seems to me that it is this insight, or even spiritual inspiration (*ruaH haqodesh*), which led her to inquire of HaShem (see below).

25:22 – וַתֵּלֶךְ לִדְרֹשׁ אֶת־יְהוָה

"...and she went "*lidrosh*" [to inquire/to demand/to divine] (of) HaShem ..."

The simple meaning seems to be that she beseeched HaShem directly. However, *Bereshith Rabba* teaches that *Rivqah* went to the House of Study of *Shem*. *Shem* and *Ever* had a house of study, unequaled, according to our tradition, where they "studied the word of HaShem," yet, they did not merit that the Jewish Nation should come from them directly, but instead it was Abraham who merited this. We are told that there were many individuals that recognized the Oneness of HaShem in the world, but unlike Abraham they kept this idea to themselves. The best analogy is to compare this to someone seeking warmth. One way to warm up is to put a coat on, but in doing so, you only warm yourself up. The other method, the "Abraham" method (which is why he merited the Jewish People should come from his seed), is to light a fire. In this way, one not only warms himself, but the entire room can share in the warmth.

25:23 – שְׁנֵי גֹיִים בְּבִטְנֵךְ

"Two nations are in your womb ..."

The word for nations, "*goyim*," is written defectively, that is with an additional letter "*yod*," instead of the letter "*waw*." Literally, this can be rendered "*Gey'yim*," "proud ones." The Midrash tells us that each one took pride in his world. The Radal adds, that *Ya`aqov*'s "world" was that of the World to Come (that is the perfected world, the ideal, which is connected to the spirit), and `*Esaw*'s was this world (the gross material world as it is).

According to the Baal HaTurim, this is a hint at the ten [the *yod* is the numerical equivalent of 10] nations that came to destroy the Holy Temple.

25:23 – וּשְׁנֵי לְאֻמִּים

"...and two peoples ..."

The word, "'*umim*," says Rashi denotes "kingdoms." These are the Kingdoms of *Yehudah* [Judea] and Rome.

25:24 – וְהִנֵּה תוֹמִם בְּבִטְנָהּ

"...And behold, twins are in her womb."

Here, the word for twins is written without an "*aleph*," unlike the twins of *Tamar* [*Bereshit* 38]. The Midrash tells us that this is because both of *Tamar*'s twins were righteous, whereas here, one was righteous and one wicked.

25:25 – וַיֵּצֵא הָרִאשׁוֹן אַדְמוֹנִי

"The first came out ruddy ..."

The word, meaning reddish "*ad'moni*," is related to the word for blood, "*dam*," suggesting that he will shed blood, according to *Bereshit Rabba*. However, its simple meaning suggests 'healthy.'

When the prophet *Sh'muel* first saw *Dawidh* [King David], he was aghast for *Dawidh* was ruddy, reminding the prophet of what he had learned concerning *Esaw*. In particular, we know that *Dawidh* had a red beard, as do many of his descendents. *Sh'muel* thought that he would be murderous just like *Esaw*. Therefore, HaShem had to reassure him that this one (*Esaw*) kills in accordance with his own will, while this one (*Dawidh*) does so in accordance with the will of the Sanhedrin [the Jewish Supreme Court] (Midrash *Bereshith Rabba* 63:8). Therefore, HaShem tells *Sh'muel*, "Arise, and anoint him for this is the one." (*Shmuel* I 16:12)

25:25 – וַיִּקְרְאוּ שְׁמוֹ עֵשָׂו

"...and they called his name *Esaw* ..."

The name means, "complete little man," for he was "complete" at birth. Rashi says this relates to his hair, "for he was complete with hair as one of many years."

However, I think this can be taken metaphysically as well, in meaning that `*Esaw* did not grow, and remained infantile in his character. We see this demonstrated in the few descriptions of his behavior; he reacts in accordance with his needs and emotions at the moment where a mature individual would have taken a broader perspective.

25:26 – וַיִּקְרָא שְׁמוֹ יַעֲקֹב

"...and his name was called *Ya`aqov* ..."

Noting that the text does not say, "they" called him, as it did with `*Esaw*, Rashi offers an interpretation, that HaShem called him *Ya`aqov*, though another interpretation is that *YitsHaq* named him. Regardless, the name relates to his grabbing of his brother's heel, "`*aqeb*."

Another possibility might be that the "they" referring to the naming of `*Esaw*, is both *YitsHaq* and HaShem, but *Ya`aqov*'s name comes only from *YitsHaq*, for, as is latter revealed, HaShem will call him "*Yisrael*."

25:27 – וַיְהִי עֵשָׂו אִישׁ יֹדֵעַ צַיִד אִישׁ שָׂדֶה

" `*Esaw* was a cunning hunter..."

Midrash *TanHuma* tells us that he was a cunning hunter "to catch and deceive his father." It relates that `*Esaw* asked his father very intricate questions of law, to give the impression that he was a pious man. We see this type of description applied later to *QoraH*, the one who opposed *Moshe Rabbenu* [Moses] in the Desert.

This reflects a powerful idea in Judaism: it is not about wisdom (alone), but awe of HaShem. Our rabbis teach that one whose wisdom proceeds his awe, both will falter, but for the one whose awe and fear of Heaven preced `*Esaw* e his wisdom both will be enduring. The very important commandment to learn Torah (we are taught it is equal to all other commandments) only has significance if it is in the context of fulfilling, executing, Torah. We are to fulfill HaShem's Will (which is expressed in Torah), and the only way we can know what that Will is, is through our learning of Torah. This is why we learn - not to add another framed certificate on our wall.

A careful reading of the Torah will reveal that HaShem demands our heart, our soul, our selves, not our disconnected intellect.

25:27 – וְיַעֲקֹב אִישׁ תָּם

"...and *Ya`aqov* was a *ish tam* [simple/ naive/perfect man] ..."

As we discussed with *NoaH*, the word "*tam*" is often translated as simple, naive, or honest. I would suggest "uncomplicated as a translation. To be "tam" means that one lives his life in wholeness, wherein he acts in a way that reflects his concern for his fellow. Opposed to the modern understanding of naive, which is usually understood as one having less awareness, the Torah suggests the opposite. To be concerned about one's fellow requires a greater awareness that penetrates not only the immediate situation, but also the impact of one's actions on other individuals and the world at large.

Here, Rashi suggests that the word denotes that he was "simple," meaning that he was not an expert in all these (pursuits of `Esaw), and that he was not sharp-minded in deceiving.

However, I have difficulty with this, for we see that Ya`aqov does know how to deceive, both with his father and, later with his uncle, *Lavan*. Yet, we learn that Ya`aqov is the personification of "Truth." On the surface, this might seem difficult. I would suggest, that it is not a measure of one's righteousness to refrain from something that he is incapable of doing, rather, a righteous individual is one who continually struggles against his nature to do the proper and just thing, following HaShem's Will.

25:27 – יֹשֵׁב אֹהָלִים
"...dwelling in tents."

The similarity between the word for "tents" and the word for "God" is not coincidental here. We learn from this that Ya`aqov was continually seeking a relationship with HaShem. It should be noted that HaShem made His Presence dwell first in the *Mishqan* [Tent of Meeting], after the Revelation at Sinai.

It seems to me that the word "tents" is plural, because he was both involved in (improving) this world and the World to Come.

25:28 – וַיֶּאֱהַב יִצְחָק אֶת־עֵשָׂו כִּי
"*YitsHaq* loved `*Esaw* because ..."

His love was conditional, based on what `Esaw brought him (which according to the Midrash was "deceiving words"). It should be noted that the word, love, here is in the past tense, suggesting, as taught in *Pirke Avoth* [5:16], that love contingent upon something only lasts as long as the need is being satisfied. Just as physical deteriorates with time, so too, does the love that was based on that superficial object.

25:28 – וְרִבְקָה אֹהֶבֶת אֶת־יַעֲקֹב

"...and [but] *Rivqah* loves *Ya`aqov*..."

Here, the word for love is in present tense, for it is not contingent upon anything, and thus is eternal (again as per *Pirke Avoth*).

25:31 – אֶת־בְּכֹרָתֶךָ

"...birthright..."

The birthright, by definition, is an idea of the future, of continuity. This episode demonstrates the key difference between the brothers, for *Ya`aqov* is continually future oriented.

25:32 – וַיֹּאמֶר עֵשָׂו הִנֵּה אָנֹכִי הוֹלֵךְ לָמוּת וְלָמָּה־זֶּה לִי בְּכֹרָה

"*`Esaw* said, 'Here, I am going to die, why do I need a birthright?"

Rashi teaches that *Ya`aqov* explained to *`Esaw* that the birthright of the first born (entitlement to offer sacrifices to HaShem) carried with it many warnings and punishments if the service was not rendered properly, therefore, *`Esaw* recognized that he would not be able to stand up to this and would die.

The plain meaning, however, is that *`Esaw* saw no need for the blessing because he was "going to die." Yet, Rashi brought this interpretation because it is clear from the context, that *`Esaw* did not feel death was imminent.

Rather, it seems to me, that *`Esaw*'s statement reflects his philosophy, and that of many modern individuals. *`Esaw* was a man of the present, and recognizing that he was mortal, did not comprehend the need for something as intangible as a birthright, which is a concept, a gift dependent, not only one's immediate future but on that of his descendents as well. If one only has "this world," then something as intangible as a "birthright" is worthless. *`Esaw* represents the epecurian philosophy of "eat, drink and be merry, for tomorrow we die."

25:34 – וַיֹּאכַל וַיֵּשְׁתְּ וַיָּקָם וַיֵּלַךְ

"...and he ate, and he drank, and he rose and he went..."

Why does the Torah bother with such details? It seems to

demonstrate how attached `Esaw was to the physical world. There isn't even a hint of the concept of "delayed gratification."

26:2 – אַל־תֵּרֵד מִצְרָיְמָה

"...Do not go down to *Mitsrayim* [Egypt]..."

Unlike Abraham (and *Ya`aqov*) *YitsHaq* is consecrated to the land through the `Aqeidah* [the binding of *YitsHaq*], and therefore was unable to leave *Erets Yisrael.*

26:5 – וַיִּשְׁמֹר מִשְׁמַרְתִּי מִצְוֹתַי חֻקּוֹתַי וְתוֹרֹתָי

"...and kept my charge, my *mitswoth* [commandments], my statues, and my laws..."

According to *Bereshit Rabba* "my charge" refers to precautions against violating HaShem's law, "*mitswoth*" to those matters which even if they were not written, would be logical to follow (such as do not murder), "my statues" refer to those rules which there are no explanation, per se, but are "decrees of the king" (such as the laws of kashruth), and represent an acceptance of HaShem's sovereignty, and "my laws" include the Oral Law that was revealed to *Moshe* at Har Sinai.

26:15 – סִתְּמוּם פְּלִשְׁתִּים וַיְמַלְאוּם עָפָר

"...the *P'lishtim* [Philistines] stopped them up and filled them with earth."

Targum Onkelos renders it "The *P'lishtim* hid," and the *Gemara, Masekhet PesaHim* [42], suggests that it is related to the closing of the heart. Others suggest that the dirt was a symbol for idol worship, and the wells for Torah learning. Thus, the places that Abraham had established as places of worship or learning the Word of HaShem had been corrupted by the *P'lishtim.*

26:16 – לֵךְ מֵעִמָּנוּ כִּי־עָצַמְתָּ מִמֶּנּוּ מְאֹד

"...leave us for you are much mightier than we."

This is the story of the Jew living amongst the nations. We enter with very little, usually in a time of distress (such as the famine), and yet we prosper beyond expectations (verse 11: "a hundredfold in that very year"). Then the people there become fearful and send the Jew away after taking over his property (the wells, see the next few verses).

26:18 – וַיָּשָׁב יִצְחָק וַיַּחְפֹּר ׀ אֶת־בְּאֵרֹת הַמַּיִם אֲשֶׁר חָפְרוּ בִּימֵי אַבְרָהָם אָבִיו

"YitsHaq dug again, the wells of water which they had dug in the days of Abraham, his father..."

YitsHaq walks in the path of his father, careful to open up the same wells and call them by the same names before digging wells of his own. A well of water is often a hidden reference to Torah and learning. I think there is a significant message hinted in this, concerning how one should develop, learn, and grow. Only through respect of one's ancestors, and by carefully following their path can one come to found a "well of living water," of one's own, and further, that it takes several attempts before one can dig a well without contention [verses 19-22].

26:35 – וַתִּהְיֶיןָ מֹרַת רוּחַ לְיִצְחָק וּלְרִבְקָה

"And they were cause for bitter spirit for *Rivqah* and *YitsHaq*"

`*Esaw's* wives, says *Bereshit Rabba*, brought idol worship into the camp which caused grief to *YitsHaq* and *Rivqah*. Others contend that the idol worship made it difficult for them to perceive the *ruaH haQodesh* [Divine Inspiration].

I think that another, simpler, meaning, relating to the text before and after, might be that it caused disagreement between *YitsHaq*, who loved `*Esaw*, and *Rivqah*, who still had a clear vision of their mission, and saw these Canaanite women as a breach of that mission. We should remember that Abraham did not want such women in his camp and sent his servant to fetch a wife (*Rivqah*) abroad.

27:1 – וַתִּכְהֶיןָ עֵינָיו מֵרְאֹת

"...his eyes were dim ..."

There are several explanations for this in our tradition. Rashi suggests that this was due to the smoke from the idol worship of `*Esaw's* wives. *Pirke D'Rebbe Eliezer* teaches that at the time of the `*Akeida*, the Heavens opened up and the *malakhim* [angels] cried and their tears fell upon his eyes causing them to be damaged. Another interpretation was that this occurred so that *Ya'aqov* should take the blessing.

I think that we can interpret it metaphorically as well; that *YitsHaq* was blind to the failings of his son, `*Esaw*, like so many parents who do not see their children in a true light. We can compare this to *Rivqah*'s clear vision and understanding.

27:5 – בְּנוֹ

"...his son ..."

Esaw is referred to as *YitsHaq*'s son where as in the next verse, *Ya`aqov* is referred to as "her son."

27:8 – שְׁמַע בְּקֹלִי

"...listen to my voice ..."

Rabbi Samson Raphael Hirsch points out that clearly there was discussion between *Rivqah* and *YitsHaq* concerning their two sons and their characters. However, now it became clear to *Rivqah* that she had to demonstrate to her husband that he had erred in his judgment. This is why the ruse is so simple, for *Rivqah* wanted to demonstrated how, if the straightforward son can deceive him, how much more so was *YitsHaq* being deceived by the "cunning hunter."

It should be noted that *Rivqah* cared for both of her children, as noted in her lament at losing both of them (verse 45), however, she still had a clear vision of the mission and enterprise that she had married into.

I find it noteworthy that she tells *Ya`aqov* (several times) to "listen to my voice," for the word, "*shem`a*" carries with it the meaning of understanding as well. HaShem continually beseeches *B'nei Yisrael* [the Children of Israel] to hearken to His voice, for that will lead us towards Him.

In this entire episode, all five senses are engaged, yet it is only the sense of hearing, of comprehension, that carries with it the idea of Eternal Truths.

27:15 – אֶת־בִּגְדֵי עֵשָׂו בְּנָהּ הַגָּדֹל

"...her eldest son, `Esaw's, choicest clothes ..."

According to the Midrash, these were clothes that `Esaw stole from *Nimrod*, who had acquired them from *Adam*. These clothes had the smell of Paradise on them, and `Esaw regularly wore them before his father out of respect.

27:19 – אָנֹכִי֙ עֵשָׂ֣ו בְּכֹרֶ֔ךָ

"I am (myself), `*Esaw* is your first born...."

This translation follows Rashi's interpretation. *Ya`aqov*, according to the sages, did not lie outright to his father, but allowed his words to be misunderstood. The literal translation of the verse is, "I am `*Esaw*, your first born." The *Ta'amim* (the traditional cantillation trope of the verse) can support Rashi's interpretation.

27:22 – הַקֹּל֙ קֹ֣ול יַעֲקֹ֔ב

"...the voice of *Ya `aqov* ..."

Rashi explains that this is because of the manner of speech, for here *Ya`aqov* speaks in the language of supplication, which is not the nature of `*Esaw*. I had difficulty understanding why Rashi would not bring a simpler meaning, namely, that the voices were different. However, after consideration, it seems that the voice quality of the two should be similar, they were twins, and very often it is difficult to distinguish between brothers who are different ages, or a father and a son, through the voice alone.

27:22 – וַיֹּ֕אמֶר הַקֹּל֙ קֹ֣ול יַעֲקֹ֔ב וְהַיָּדַ֖יִם יְדֵ֥י עֵשָֽׂו

"...He said, 'the voice is the voice of *Ya `aqov*, and the hands are the hands of `*Esaw*' ..."

Many commentators have tried to understand why *YitsHaq* loved `*Esaw* (see above). Some say that he loved because he wanted to educate him and bring him towards a life of HaShem. However, I think that while it might be true that he tried to reach out to `*Esaw*, it seems to me that this was because he loved him and not the reason that he loved him. Rather, I think *YitsHaq* loved `*Esaw* because `*Esaw* was a man of action, because he was a "do-er". We all respect a man that does something, even if we are not pleased with what it is that they do. *YitsHaq* recognized that to bring to fruition HaShem's promise, his son would have to be a "man of action." Therefore, he tried take this "man of action" and bring him to a level were his actions were noble and directed towards the family mission.

I think *YitsHaq* suspected, or even knew, that the boy before him was *Ya`aqov*. After all, *YitsHaq* was not lacking in intelligence, and a man who loses one sense, usually compensates for that by the improvement of his other senses.

Rather, once he recognized what was happening, he realized that his approach was incorrect. For he realized that here was his son, one with the voice of *Ya`aqov* and the hands of *`Esaw*, the only one who could accomplish the mission.

The voice of *Ya`aqov* represents understanding. Out of all the senses, and all five are present in this episode, the sense of hearing requires time and patience. Not coincidentally, it is the one sense that communicates the Truth in this episode. Twice, *Rivqah* beseeches her son to "listen to my voice," for listen suggests understanding. The sages also bring this idea. It is evident when we say the *Sh'm`a*. "Hearken! Listen Israel, HaShem is our God, HaShem is One!" This is a statement of Torah, commanding comprehension.

"The hands of *`Esaw*" represent doing, action. *YitsHaq* realizes that *Ya`aqov* is a man of action when necessary. He can get the job done, but more so, he will do with understanding and with the ability to listen to the Voice of God; *Ya`aqov* will be able to do in the present, but with an eye towards the future.

We see further evidence of this at the end of the parsha, for there "*Ya`aqov* hears his mother and father," while *`Esaw* only "sees." *`Esaw* recognizes the truth only for a moment, *Ya`aqov* is able to comprehend the truth and carry it with him into the future.

It is interesting to note, that the *halakhah* follows this interpretation. We learn, for instance, that in the appointment or election of an official, a leader, we should pay more attention to his awe of Heaven than his technical skills: "If he is an expert in the field but hasn't *yirath sh'mayim* [fear of heaven], we do not appoint him, whereas if he has *yirath sh'mayim* but lacks the technical skills, we appoint him and teach him the skills."

It is a clear that our sages understood that it is much easier to teach one technical skills than connect him to the concept of the Eternal.

27:33 – וַיֶּחֱרַ֨ד יִצְחָ֣ק חֲרָדָה֮ גְּדֹלָה֮ עַד־מְאֹד֒ . . . וָאֲבָרֲכֵ֖הוּ גַּם־בָּר֥וּךְ יִהְיֶֽה

"...and *YitsHaq* trembled...also he shall be blessed."

Rabbi Samuel Raphael Hirsch explains that *YitsHaq* trembled at first, perplexed and angry, and then he realized the truth of the matter, that his wife had been correct (see above) and therefore, *YitsHaq* confirmed the blessing he had given *Ya`aqov*.

27:41 – וַיִּשְׂטֹם עֵשָׂו אֶת־יַעֲקֹב . . . וַיֹּאמֶר עֵשָׂו בְּלִבּוֹ יִקְרְבוּ יְמֵי אֵבֶל אָבִי

"...`Esaw hated Ya`aqov...and `Esaw said, 'Let the days of mourning for my father be at hand..."

`Esaw* holds *Ya`aqov responsible, and not his father. Moreover out of respect for his father he decides to withhold his vengeance during his father's lifetime so as to not cause him grief. As it was then, so it is today with the modern day " *`Esaw's*" of the world hating the nation of Israel, for the blessings that HaShem bestows upon us.

27:42 – וַיֻּגַּד לְרִבְקָה

"...*Rivqah* was told..."

Yet, we learned that *`Esaw* contemplated these things in his heart, how could *Rivqah* have "been told." Rashi explains that she learned through *ruaH haqodesh*, that is Divine inspiration.

27:45 – לָמָה אֶשְׁכַּל גַּם־שְׁנֵיכֶם יוֹם אֶחָד

"...why should I be bereaved of you both ..."

This can be understood two ways, as either referring to *Ya`aqov* and *YitsHaq*, for *`Esaw* planned to commit his murder after his father's death, therefore, *Rivqah* would be mourning her husband and her son. Or, which seems to be the plainer meaning, that she would mourn the loss of both sons, for surely *`Esaw's* crime would not go unanswered.

27:46 – לָמָה לִּי חַיִּים

"...why am I alive..."

Note the parallel to 25:22, which suggests that there, as well as here, implies the larger purpose of life and not simply a complaint on her [physical] life.

28:2 – לֵךְ פַּדֶּנָה אֲרָם

"...go to *Padenah Aram*..."

YitsHaq sends *Ya`aqov* himself, as opposed to a servant as his father had done.

28:5 – אֵם יַעֲקֹב וְעֵשָׂו

"...the mother of *Ya`aqov* and *`Esaw*..."

This demonstrates that *Ya`aqov* indeed supplanted *`Esaw* for he is listed first.

28:7 – וַיִּשְׁמַע יַעֲקֹב אֶל־אָבִיו וְאֶל־אִמּוֹ

"*Ya`aqov* listened to his father and his mother ..."

He heard, and he comprehended (See above - 27:22). Compare with *`Esaw* in the next verse.

28:8 – וַיַּרְא עֵשָׂו

"*`Esaw* saw..."

Only then did he see, at the moment when his father blessed his brother and sent him away. Yet, he still did not comprehend the significance and importance, for although he took steps to remedy the situation, they were only surface steps, addressing a symptom and not the underlying situation. It should be noted that he did not divorce his earlier wives.

28:8 – כִּי רָעוֹת בְּנוֹת כְּנָעַן בְּעֵינֵי יִצְחָק אָבִיו

"...were evil in the eyes of *YitsHaq*, his father ..."

He recognized that they were evil in his father's eyes, but not his own. Even so, *`Esaw* is credited with honor his father throughout the Tradition, despite his other failings.

PARSHATH WAYETSE

Overview

Our parsha begins with *Ya`aqov* in flight. He leaves his home and travels towards *Haran*. At the border of *Erets Yisrael*, he has an encounter with HaShem. He has a dream about a ladder that extends from the Earth towards Heaven with *malakhim* [angels] ascending and descending the ladder. Upon awakening, he recognizes the significance of his encounter, dedicates the place where he slept, calling it *Beit El*, the House of God, and vows a vow to HaShem.

Ya`aqov continues on his journey and arrives near *Haran*. He sees shepherds near a well and learns that they wait till all of the shepherds assemble before rolling the stone off of the well. This is because the boulder is so large and heavy it needs several men to accomplish the task. He sees *RaHel* and is consumed with passion. He rolls the stone off the well, single-handed. In a way, we see a reflection of his father's words, "The voice is the son of *Ya`aqov*, but the hands are (now) the hands of `*Esaw*." Filled with passion, he kisses *RaHel* and then weeps.

He meets his uncle *Lavan* (his mother's brother), *RaHel*'s father. After spending a month with *Lavan*, *Ya`aqov* agrees to work for seven years in exchange for *RaHel*'s hand in marriage. *Lavan* agrees but deceives him, secretly substituting the older sister *Le'ah* in place of *RaHel*. *Ya`aqov* agrees to work an additional seven years for *RaHel*.

Le'ah bears *Ya`aqov* four children and *RaHel* asks *Ya`aqov* to pray for her, as his father had done for his mother, but *Ya`aqov* protests, seeing her statement as a lack of faith. *RaHel* gives her maid to *Ya`aqov* and has two children through her. *Le'ah* likewise gives *Ya`aqov* her maid, who also gives him two children. Then *Le'ah* has two more sons, and a daughter. Finally, HaShem "remembers" or notes *RaHel* and she bears a son as well.

Ya`aqov* negotiates his wages with *Lavan*. Yet, *Lavan* tries again to deceive *Ya`aqov. However, HaShem is with *Ya`aqov* and he succeeds immeasurably. Recognizing a change in *Lavan*'s attitude towards him, and a feeling a need to return home, *Ya`aqov* gathers his family and secretly heads towards *Erets Yisrael*. *Lavan* chases after *Ya`aqov* (ostensibly to recover stolen idols), but HaShem warns him in a dream against doing anything (good or bad). He catches *Ya`aqov*, they argue and finally agree to a settlement. In the exchange, however, *Ya`aqov* is not careful with his words, and declares that whoever stole the idols should die. Not knowing that it was his beloved *RaHel* that had taken them, he seals her fate. They erect a stone mound as a witness to their agreement and have a feast.

We don't learn any *mitswoth* from this parsha. However, we do learn several customs, particularly in regard to weddings. It is our custom to celebrate a marriage for seven days. During this time, the bride and groom are treated like queen and king. Festive meals are prepared for them and special blessings are pronounced over a cup of wine at the *Birkat HaMazon* [Blessing of the Meal] said at the conclusion of the meal. Originally the meals were prepared and brought to the bride and grooms' new home each night. Today, more often the couple is brought to others' homes for the meals.

Another custom, performed at the wedding itself, is a special ceremony wherein the groom places the veil on the bride himself before she is led to the *Hupah* [wedding canopy]. This is to insure that the bride he is marrying is the one he had originally selected. While today, many people use transparent veils, there are still many communities that use a very thick veil. The *Yemenites* use a veil that is laden with gold. It is also appropriate that the veil is lifted under the *Hupa* for the witnesses to see the bride at the time of the ring ceremony and the signing of the *Ketubah* [marriage contract].

In Detail: *A selection of some verses of interest:*

28:10 – וַיֵּצֵא יַעֲקֹב

"*Ya `aqov* went out..."

Rashi points out that the text did not need to tell us any more than "*Ya `aqov* went to *Haran*." He offers that this is to teach that anytime a righteous man leaves a place, it makes an impression.

It seems to me, that we learn something further from this. The purpose of *Ya`aqov*'s journey was to leave. He was not traveling to *Haran* as much as he was leaving *Be'er Sheb`a*. While the purpose of his journey was to find a wife, this purpose was devised once *Rivqah* recognized that *Ya`aqov* wasn't safe in *Be'er Seb`a*. He needed a reason to leave, but *Ya`aqov* clearly was going away from a perceived danger, and not towards and definitive goal.

28:10 – וַיֵּלֶךְ חָרָנָה

"...and he went towards *Haran*."

The way in which this is phrased (in the Hebrew) is not the usual form of expression. Instead of a prefix "*lamed*," the suffix "*hey*" is used to denote direction. Rashi reports that the plain meaning is he "went to *Haran*." However, it seems to me that this is the form that is used when the destination is not precise and clear; therefore, it seems it would be better translated as him "going towards *Haran*," that is, going in that general direction.

This is substantiated by the Midrash which tells us that along the way, *Ya`aqov* stopped to learn in the House of Study of *Shem* and *Eber*.

28:11 – וַיִּפְגַּע

"He arrived ..."

The word, "*wayifga`*" seems to come from the root, "to meet," or "to confront." Though many commentators translate the word to mean, "he went up," which is related to the "place" in which he arrived (see below).

To my ear, the phrase conveys certain suddenness, such as occurs on a long journey, especially one of flight. Suddenly, *Ya`aqov* was there at "the place," (see below) and as the text later suggests ("God was in this place and I, I didn't know it," verse 16). It took him by surprise. The word might brings with it the idea that *Ya`aqov*, at that moment, recognized the fact that he was leaving his home and everything he had known, and might not be able to return.

Another interpretation brought by Rashi, is that the word relates to prayer, meaning "to request" as it is used in chapter seven of the Book of *Yermiyahu*. The *Gemara* teaches that it is from this we learn that *Ya`aqov* instituted the evening prayer.

28:11 – בְּמָקוֹם

"*b'maqom* [at the place]..."

Rashi points out that the Torah does not mention the name of the place but leaves it ambiguous. It seems to me that the text is demanding "explain me."

Rashi teaches that the place was *Har Moriah*, where Abraham had offered *YitsHaq* on the altar (the *Akeida*). He arrives at this understanding, because there [*parshath Wayera*, Chapter 22], *Har Moriah* is also referred to as the place, "He saw the place from afar."

The *Gemara* in *Masekhet Hulin* [91] also suggests this. Further it tells us that a miracle occurred and the earth shrank, making the distance less for *Ya`aqov*, so he could arrive there when he did.

In my opinion, one can also interpret the verse as, "He encountered God," which is also one of the understandings offered by the Midrash. The word "*maqom*" often refers to the Omnipresent in the *Tanakh* [see, for instance, *D'varim* 33:27]. God is the place of the world, our rabbis teach, and not, God Forbid, the opposite that He is contained/limited by the world. Its use tends to be towards the more hidden aspect of HaShem, the Mystery, the Infinite.

Further support of this can be found in the *gematria* [numerical equivalent] of the word "*maqom*," which equals one hundred eighty-six [*mem* - 40, *quf* - 100, *waw* - 6, and *mem* - 40]. This is the same value as God's Name when each letter is squared [*yud* -10 (squared - 100), *hey* - 5 (squared - 25), *waw* - 6 (squared 36), and *hey* -5 (squared - 25)]. It also equals six times "*El*" the word for God (the number six represents all physical directions). *Maqom* is also double the value for shield, "*magen*" as in the "shield/protection of Abraham" or the "shield of David."

Not conflicting with the sages understanding, that *Ya`aqov* happened onto *Har Moriah*, the place of the *Akeidah* and the future Temple(s), I would suggest that he felt some spiritual connection, and therefore decided to tarry in that spot. He encountered it unexpectedly, was unsure as to its nature, but nonetheless stayed. After his dream, *Ya`aqov* recognized what he had sensed the night before, that had encountered, not merely a place of God, but had an experience of the Infinite, Himself.

28:11 – כִּי־בָא הַשֶּׁמֶשׁ
"...for the sun had set..."

This implies, according to *Midrash Rabba*, that suddenly the sun set prematurely, so that *Ya`aqov* should be forced to spend the night there. The sages point out the peculiar construction of the sentence as pointing towards this meaning.

28:12 – וְהִנֵּה סֻלָּם
"...behold a ladder..."

The word for ladder, "*sulam*" has the same *gematria* [numerical equivalent - 130] as the word "*Sinai*" (as in *Har Sinai*). It represents a link or a bridge between Man and HaShem.

There is a teaching that this was the ladder of history, and the *malakhim* [angels] are the princes of nations representing their rise and fall, with HaShem standing above, and outside history, and by extension, *Ya`aqov*, representing the Jewish Nation, is also outside the ladder of history and not governed by the same forces as other nations.

Another interpretation of the ladder is that it symbolizes the stairway leading to the top of the altar in the *Beth HaMiqdash* [Temple].

In truth all of these "interpretations" are correct, for each symbol represents both itself and the interpretation. The metaphor of a ladder connecting this world to HaShem is significant, for it represents His continual interaction with this world, albeit, through a series of "concealment." We, and the world we live in is under His constant guidance, but at the same time, the distance of the "ladder" gives us the gift of free-will, at least from our perspective.

28:12 – עֹלִים וְיֹרְדִים
"...ascending and descending..."

The order seems strange, for we would have assumed that *malakhim* would first come down (from Heaven) and then ascend. This, says Rashi, is to teach us that the *malakhim* that accompanied *Ya`aqov* in *Erets Yisrael* do not leave the land, and therefore they ascended Heaven when he arrived at the border, and different *malakhim* descended in order to escort him outside the Land.

It seems to me that this might also represent the concept that our actions in this world (first) effect the upper worlds, resulting in a chain like reaction bringing their results back towards this world. This in the language of the *Qabalah* is the concept of "`aliyath m"n" the causing the ascension of "female waters" and the *"yiridah of m"d"* (the descending of the male water).   In simple language, this is the concept of offering up prayer, and the reception, afterward, of spiritual bounty.

28:13 – נִצָּב עָלָיו֙

"...stood on/beside him/it ..."

This phrase is very ambiguous, for it could be referring to HaShem standing beside (or on/above) *Ya`aqov*, or the ladder.

It seems to me that the phrase is left ambiguous on purpose to convey several meanings. First, it implies that, in regard to both this world and the heavens, HaShem is outside and above their machinations. He is their Creator; He is not confined by any of the actions of these worlds.

Further, if we understand that HaShem stood beside *Ya`aqov*, we learn that HaShem stands by each of us, supporting us in our ascension towards Him.

28:13 – וֵאלֹהֵי יִצְחָק

"...God of *YitsHaq*..."

Midrash TanHuma points out that we do not find anywhere else in the *Tanakh*, where HaShem's Name is linked with a righteous individual while he is still alive. The Midrash suggests that the exception is made here, because *YitsHaq*'s eyes were dim, and he was confined to his house, and the *Yester Hara`* [evil inclination] had already left him, so that he was similar to one dead.

It seems to me, that another reason might be that *YitsHaq* was offered on the altar of the *Akeida*, and therefore had already been "sanctified" to HaShem.

28:16 – אָכֵן֙ יֵשׁ יְהוָֹה בַּמָּקוֹם הַזֶּה וְאָנֹכִי לֹא יָדָעְתִּי

"...HaShem is in this place, and I, I did not know it."

Rashi teaches that this indicates that that *Ya`aqov* felt he should not have slept in so Holy of a place.

The verse is peculiar in that the word for "I," is not necessary, the first person singular being expressed by the verb form. Further the word used for "I," "*anokhi*" is the less common form. The word implies the totality of one's being, as when used by HaShem Himself at Sinai, "*Anokhi HaShem Elokekha*, [I am HaShem, your God]."

This seems to me, to suggests that *Ya`aqov* had not recognized the significance of the encounter with the totality of his being. Upon awakening he recognized the depth of the encounter, but because of his circumstances, failed to engage it with his "whole self." This is something that *Ya`aqov* will remedy when he returns to this spot on his journey home.

28:17- וַיִּירָא
"He was in awe ..."

The word "*yira*" is often translated as "fear," however this is imprecise. While the word contains an element of fear to it, it is a fear based on respect and understanding of the awesomeness of HaShem, and not a fear that one might have, so to speak, of danger.

28:17 – אֵין זֶה כִּי אִם־בֵּית אֱלֹהִים
"...this is none other than the House of God ..."

Each of the three patriarchs related to the same place, and to HaShem, differently. Abraham referred to this as a "mountain," *YitsHaq* as a "field," and here, *Ya`aqov* refers to it as "a house." This teaches that each of them had a different relationship with, and a different way of relating to HaShem.

It occurs to me that, after we returned to *Erets Yisrael* from *Mitsrayim* [Egypt], and conquered *Yerushalayim*, these three terms are all used for the site of the *Beth HaMiqdash*. *Dawidh HaMelekh* [King David] purchases the "field," on a "mountain" to build the "house" of HaShem.

28:17 – וְזֶה שַׁעַר הַשָּׁמָיִם
"...this is the gate of Heaven."

Because the majesty of Heaven was opened up before him, or alternatively, a place where prayers will ascend to Heaven. It is taught that all prayers enter the gates of Heaven from the place of the *Qodesh HaQ'dosh'im* [Holy of Holies] on the *Har Habayit* [The Temple Mount], in *Yerushalayim* [Jerusalem]. This is true even when the *Beth HaMiqdash* does not stand, may it soon be restored.

It is important for Jews, no matter where they are in the world to face and direct their prayers towards the Land of *Yisrael*. If one is in Israel, one must direct his prayers towards Jerusalem. If one is in Jerusalem, one directs her prayers towards the Temple Mount and the Holy of Holies. One should focus one's prayers as if they are ascending to Heaven from between the two *keruvim* that rest on the Ark of the Covenant.

28:21 – בְּשָׁלוֹם
"...*b'shalom*..."

Rashi teaches that this is to be interpreted as "*b'shalem*," "perfect, complete," that he should return uncorrupted by *Lavan*.

It seems to me that since *Shalom* is also one of the names of HaShem, the phrase can be understood as "with *Shalom*," that is "with God."

29:2 – וְהִנֵּה בְאֵר בַּשָּׂדֶה
"...and behold a well in the field ..."

There are many interpretations of this verse in the *Midrash*. Some of them are as follows:

The first is that the well represents the well that supplied the Children of *Yisrael* water in the desert, and the three flocks of sheep represent *Moshe*, *Aharon*, and *Miriam*. The great stone represents the great miracles that were there.

Another interpretation: The well symbolizes *Tsion* (*Yerushalayim*) and "the three flocks," the three festivals, and "from there, they watered the flocks," they partook of the Divine Presence.

Another interpretation: The well symbolizes Sinai; the three flocks are the three classes of Jews: *Kohenim* [Priests], *Levi'im*, and *Yisrael*. The great stone refers to the Divine Presence.

29:10 – לְבָן אֲחִי אִמּוֹ . . . לְבָן אֲחִי אִמּוֹ . . . לְבָן אֲחִי אִמּוֹ
"*Lavan* his mother's brother ... *Lavan* his mother's brother ... *Lavan* his mother's brother"

The Torah brings the expression, '*Lavan*, his mother's brother,' three times. Interestingly, the *gematria* (numerical equivalent) of the expression is 148, which is the exact number of verses in this parsha. It is also equivalent to the expression, חלקי״י meaning, "my portion," usually referring to one's inheritance, in either this world, or the World To Come. Further, it is equivalent to מחני״ם, camps. All of this hints at the fact that *Lavan*, his mother's brother, will (unwittingly) become the source of Ya'aqov's portion(s) and the establishment the 'camps' of *Ya'aqov*. We see HaShem using *Lavan* as the vehicle for bestowing His blessing on *Ya'aqov*.

29:10 – וַיִּגַּשׁ יַעֲקֹב וַיָּגֶל אֶת־הָאֶבֶן

"*Ya`aqov* approached and rolled the stone ..."

This seems incredible, for the many shepherds felt that they were unable to move the stone, yet *Ya`aqov* was able to do so himself. In my opinion, this is to reinforce that which we learned in last week's parsha concerning the words, "the hands of `*Esaw*"; that *Ya`aqov* had the ability to be a man of action when the situation called for it.

29:11 – וַיִּשַּׁק יַעֲקֹב לְרָחֵל

"*Ya`aqov* kissed *RaHel*..."

According to the Midrash, he recognized her as his kinswoman. The parallel to the story of Abraham's servant *Eli`ezer*, though, seems clear to me. There is an immediate recognition of the future matriarch and the "match" is made, even before the important information of lineage is established. Both *Eli`ezer* and *Ya`aqov* are guided by Divine assistance. It is interesting to note, that preceding both instances each man had an encounter with HaShem, especially if we follow Rashi's interpretation that *Ya`aqov* prayed at "the Place."

29:11 – וַיֵּבְךְּ

"...and he wept..."

The Midrash says that he wept, for he had come empty-handed. Opposed to *Eli`ezer* who had come with laden camels when he sought a wife for *YitsHaq*. According to the Midrash, his brother `*Esaw*` had sent his son *Elifaz* after *Ya`aqov* to kill him, but when he encountered him, he was unable to carry out the act. He asked *Ya`aqov* what he should do concerning the command of his father and he answered that he should take all of his possessions for a "poor man is considered as one dead."

The Midrash offers a second reason: that he cried because he foresaw, through Divine Inspiration, that she would not be buried with him.

Another reason offered, is that he saw the men whispering after he had kissed her, saying, "Does this man wish to introduce immorality among us?"

It seems interesting to me that most of the interpretations understand the weeping to be one of sadness. It seems to me that he could have been weeping at the joy of finding his soul mate.

It also seems appropriate to compare *Ya`aqov*'s weeping here, with the weeping of *`Esaw* when *Ya`aqov* returns to *Erets Yisrael* (next parsha) and *Yosef* crying, both in his encounter with his brothers and with his father. Even after being reunite with his beloved son, *Ya`aqov* doesn't weep, but his son does.

29:12 – כִּי אֲחִי אָבִיהָ הוּא וְכִי בֶן־רִבְקָה הוּא

"...that he was her father's kin, and that he was *Rivqah*'s son..."

The Midrash interprets the statement as, "If *Lavan* comes to deceive me then I too am his brother in deceit, but if not, then I am the son of his honest sister."

It seems to me, that another reason that *Ya'aqov* calls himself her 'aH,' a word which while usually translated as 'brother' can often mean the more general term 'kin,' to emphasize that it was not inappropriate that he kissed her, for his intention is to betroth her, just as *Eli'ezer*, Abraham's servant, did with *Rivqah*. However, *Ya'aqov* did not have any rings or bracelets – he had nothing - to give *RaHel* in order to betroth her, except a kiss. And, it seems to me that this might have been considered sufficient for betrothal before the giving of the Torah at Sinai, though further study is warranted.

29:17 – וְעֵינֵי לֵאָה רַכּוֹת

"And *Le'ah*'s eyes were weak/soft ..."

The *Gemara* in *Baba Batra* [123] teaches that *Le'ah* thought she would become *`Esaw*'s wife (for she was the oldest and so was he), and would therefore cry regularly.

However, I think that the word, "*rakot*" can also be interpreted as "soft," possibly meaning beautiful.

Or, alternatively, that the word means weak, which is a subtle reference to *YitsHaq*'s sight, for one might interpret the episode involving *Lavan*'s deception with *Le'ah* (see below) as atonement for *Ya`aqov*'s deception of his father.

29:25 – וַיְהִי בַבֹּקֶר וְהִנֵּה־הִוא לֵאָה

"It came to pass, that in the morning, behold it was *Le'ah* ..."

We are taught in *Masekhet Megillah* [13] that *Ya`aqov* anticipated *Lavan*'s deceit, and therefore he had given signs to *RaHel* so that he might recognize the trick. However, *RaHel* saw that *Lavan* was bringing *Le'ah* to him, and did not want her to be put to shame, so she taught her the signs.

Our traditions states that due to *RaHel*'s modesty, she merited that King *Sha'ul* should descend from her. On the surface, this might not seem "modest," but the opposite. I learned an incredible insight of *Lev Shalom* concerning this question.

He suggests that the signs that *Ya`aqov* taught *RaHel* were the laws of *Nida, Halah,* and the kindling of *Shabbat* Lights. When *RaHel* realized that *Le'ah* would be brought to the wedding tent instead of her, she taught these laws to *Le'ah*, but she never told her that they were "signs." When *Ya`aqov* asked *Le'ah* concerning the laws, she answered, not knowing that she was being tested. Moreover *RaHel* never revealed to her sister what she had done for her. That is the modesty that merited the reward our tradition speaks about.

The reasons that *Lavan* tricked *Ya`aqov* are manifold. On one level, when *Ya`aqov* usurped the birthright of `*Esaw*, he "inherited" *Leah*. Originally *Leah* was destined for `*Esaw* and *RaHel* for *Ya`aqov*. Yet, this was not *Lavan*'s motivation.

Rather, through the *Qabalah*, we learn that *Lavan* had spiritual insight concerning the future of the Nation of *Yisrael* and wanted to prevent its fulfillment. He reasoned that if *Ya`aqov* married *Leah* first, then *Yosef* would not be born, and thus the entire story of *Mitsrayim* and our redemption from there would not occur, arresting the creation of the People of *Yisrael* at Sinai. However, by trying to prevent history, he unwittingly facilitated it. This is how all *rash`a'im* [evil individuals] serve HaShem through their evil plots.

29:34 – עַתָּה הַפַּעַם יִלָּוֶה אִישִׁי אֵלַי

"…my husband will be joined to me…"

Masekhet B'rakhot explains that the matriarchs had prophesy and *Le'ah* knew that the twelve tribes would issue from *Ya`aqov*, therefore, after three sons, *Le'ah* had fulfilled her portion.

Another possibility a friend of mine mentioned, was that with three children the father would be forced to assist his wife, for she only has two arms, and would need him to carry the third child.

30:1 – הָבָה־לִּי בָנִים

"Give me children …"

Rashi teaches that *RaHel* pointed to *Ya`aqov*'s father, who had prayed for *Rivqah* to bear children, and demanded that he do the same.

30:3 – וְתֵלֵד עַל־בִּרְכָּי

"…that she may bear upon my knee …"

This seems to be a common practice in those days, that one's servant can act as a surrogate mother, and that the children would be counted as her mistress's.

30:14 – דוּדָאִים

"…*dudaim* [mandrakes] …"

This is a violet plant according to *Masekhet Sanhedrin*. Rashi identifies it as Jasmine. Others say it was Cypress grass. It was a plant, whose root resembled a little man and according to the (herbal) medicine at the time, it was a treatment for infertility.

30:17 – וַתַּהַר וַתֵּלֶד לְיַעֲקֹב בֵּן חֲמִישִׁי

"…and bore to *Ya`aqov* a fifth son…"

This may be a subtle way of emphasizing that it is not mandrakes or the like which give one children, rather it is only through the Will of God.

30:21 – וַתִּקְרָא אֶת־שְׁמָהּ דִּינָה
"...and called her *Dinah* ..."

According to *Masekhet B'rakhot*, originally the fetus was conceived as a boy, but *Le'ah*, knowing that *Ya`aqov* was supposed to have only twelve sons (corresponding to the twelve tribes), and realized (through *ru'aH haqodesh* [spiritual insight]) that the fetus was a boy. It would then happen that her sister, *RaHel*, would have less of a share than the handmaidens. They each had two son, and *Le'ah* already had six. Therefore she prayed, and the fetus was changed to a female.

There is a disagreement between the *Yerushalmi* and the *Bavli* talmuds, regarding the offering of a *tefilath shaw* [a "pointless" prayer], such as upon seeing a fire in the distance and praying that it isn't one's own home – the fire already exists in a specific place, it's not only ridiculous to pray for it not to be one's home, there's a hint of contempt of heaven in such a prayer. On this both Talmuds agreed.

The disagreement arises in regard to praying for a boy, after one knows that his wife is already pregnant. After all, the fetus already exists. According to the *Bavli* one can only prayer for a boy (or a girl) only until the fortieth day, whereas the *Yerushalmi*, citing the case of *Le'ah*, says one can pray all the way up until the birth of the child.

30:27 – נִחַשְׁתִּי
"...I have observed the signs..."

Rashi teaches that *Lavan* used divination. This is an example of idol worship, the attempt to manipulate "the forces," and God Himself for one's designs.

30:35 – וַיָּסַר בַּיּוֹם הַהוּא
"He removed that day ..."

This is referring to *Lavan* removing the particular flocks.

30:36 – הַנּוֹתָרֹת
"...the rest..."

Rashi teaches that these were the sick, weak, and otherwise poor of the flock. The symbolism should not be lost. HaShem took the seemingly poor of the flock, the Nation of *Yisrael*, slaves to the mighty People of *Mitsrayim*, and through our relationship and Covenant with Him, they became the Chosen People, the Light of the Nations.

30:38 – וַיֵּחַמְנָה
"...and they became heated..."

Bereshith Rabba says, in the name of Rabbi *Hosh`ya*, that a miracle happened and the female sheep did not require a male to become pregnant.

To further our analogy from above, we learned of the women in *Mitsrayim* that each pregnancy brought multiple births, causing the ranks of *bnei Yisrael* to swell.

30:43 - וּשְׁפָחוֹת וַעֲבָדִים
"servants..."

Ya`aqov was able to sell his flocks at a high price and buy all these things.

31:4 – וַיִּקְרָא לְרָחֵל וּלְלֵאָה
"He called *RaHel* and *Le'ah* ..."

Rashi teaches that *RaHel* is named first because it was because of her that *Ya`aqov* joined with *Lavan*.

31:5 – רֹאֶה אָנֹכִי אֶת־פְּנֵי אֲבִיכֶן כִּי־אֵינֶנּוּ אֵלַי
"...I see your father's face is not towards me ..."

The simple meaning is that *Ya`aqov* saw that *Lavan* was displeased with him. However, Rabbi Shlomo Twersky offers an interesting interpretation. He suggests that that *Ya`aqov* was starting to see *Lavan* in a new light, that he had been away from his father for so long, that he was starting to see *Lavan* as "not all that bad." He was getting used to the deceit. At the moment he realized that he must leave in order that he should leave complete *[shalem* - see above] and not become corrupted by *Lavan*'s influence. Our descent begins when we justify the others' failings; the justifications of our own sins are soon to follow. Instead, the path towards righteousness is through recognizing one's error and working towards improvement.

31:15 – הֲלוֹא נָכְרִיּוֹת נֶחְשַׁבְנוּ לוֹ

"Are we not counted as strangers ..."

Instead of giving a dowry, as is the custom, he sold his daughters as wages, according to Rashi.

31:19 – וַתִּגְנֹב רָחֵל אֶת־הַתְּרָפִים

"...and *RaHel* stole the *t'rafim* [images]..."

Midrash Rabba teaches that she stole them to prevent her father from idol worship. Yet, this is difficult for me, for idol worship is not dependent upon the physical idols but the way in which one approaches the world and its Creator. Nevertheless, the *halakha* does make allowances for removing and destroying destructive and corruptive material even without permission from their owners.

31:24 – מִטּוֹב עַד־רָע

"...either good or bad ..."

Masekhet Yebamot [103] points out that the good of the wicked is harmful to the righteous. As with the expression regarding a bee — "I don't want your honey and I don't want your sting." I think what this means, is that they might be deceived by such goodness, and believe the wicked have repented, and therefore become less cautious.

31:32 – עִם אֲשֶׁר תִּמְצָא אֶת־אֱלֹהֶיךָ לֹא יִחְיֶה

"With whomever you find your gods, he shall not live ..."

Bereshit Rabba teaches that it is because of this curse that *RaHel* died. This teaches that we should be very careful with our words.

However, it seems to me, that *Ya`aqov* may also be mocking *Lavan* and his beliefs. Who worships a "god" that can be stolen?

31:42 – וּפַחַד יִצְחָק

"...the Fear of *YitsHaq* ..."

Ya`aqov* was afraid to say the God of *YitsHaq* for he knew that HaShem does not confer His name upon the righteous while living. Even though HaShem had done it Himself (see above), *Ya`aqov did not want to tempt fate, as it were.

31:46 – לְאֶחָיו

"...to his brothers ..."

This refers to his sons.

31:47 – יְגַר שָׂהֲדוּתָא

"...*yagar sahaduta* ..."

This is the Aramaic translation of the Hebrew name, "*Galed,*" meaning "the heap of witness." That *Ya`aqov* and *Lavan* speak a different language emphasizes their different understandings of the world and different interpretations of the preceding events. According to the *Qabbalah*, the spiritual forces of Good only understand the Holy Language of Hebrew, but the forces of spiritual damage, the forces of the 'husk', only understand the Aramaic language. Incidentally, for this reason, the *Qaddish* prayer is recited in Aramaic, in order to subdue the destructive spiritual forces that want to feed off of and deplete the Holy forces of blessing and plenty.

30:50 – אִם־תְּעַנֶּה אֶת־בְּנֹתַי

"...if you afflict my daughters ..."

Masekhet Yebamot [77a] says that this refers to denying them their marital rights.

30:53 – אֱלֹהֵי אַבְרָהָם וֵאלֹהֵי נָחוֹר

"...The God of Abraham and the god of *Nahor* ..."

The distinction between the One God and the pagan god of *Nahor* seems to represent a "divorce" between the two families. This seems to be born out in the text as well, for we do not see *Ya`aqov*'s sons returning to *Haran* to get wives. This marks the end of the relationship between the two parts of the family.

PARSHATH WAY'SHLA*H*

Overview

*Ya`aqov* sends messengers to determine his brother's intentions toward him. He discovers that `*Esaw* is approaching with four hundred men. Therefore, *Ya`aqov* makes preparations. We learn that he prepared an appeasement (gifts), he prayed, and he readied himself for war.

Ya`aqov* sends a tremendous bounty to his brother and then divides his camp into two. Finding himself alone on the other side of the *Yarden* [Jordan] river, he encounters what the Torah calls "a man." *Ya`aqov wrestles with this man, whom our tradition tells us, was the guardian angel of `*Esaw*. The angel is unable to prevail as daybreak approaches, and therefore touches *Ya`aqov* in the hollow of his thigh, wounding him. *Ya`aqov*, however, is able to force the angel to give him a blessing. The angel also gives him a new name, *Yisrael*.

*Ya`aqov* and `*Esaw* meet and embrace. After introducing `*Esaw* to his family, they part ways, `*Esaw* returning to his home and *Ya`aqov* heads first to *Sukkot* and then arrives in *Sh'khem*. There, his daughter, *Dinah*, is captured and raped by *Sh'khem*, son of *Hamor*, who afterward requested to marry her. The brothers say that they can't allow such a thing. Ostensibly, their objection is *Dinah*'s marriage to an uncircumcised man, so after much negotiation, the entire city of *Sh'khem* agrees and circumcise themselves.

On the third day, when the pain from circumcision is at its worst, *Shi'm`on* and *Lewi* enter the city and slay all the men. They take all the possessions and the women of the city as booty. *Ya`aqov* protests their actions (though he is not specific as to what he objects to) and continues on to *Beth-El* where he sets up an altar.

RaHel dies on the way, in *Beth-leHem*, while giving birth to a twelfth son, *ben'yamin*. We also learn of *YitsHaq*'s death at the age of one hundred and eighty years old.

The Torah then delineates the generations of `*Esaw*, and all the kings and princes of *Edom*.

We learn only one *mitswah* in this parsha, the prohibition to eat the "*Gid HaNasheh*," or sciatic nerve. This is taught as a tradition, as a remembrance, concerning *Ya`aqov*'s wrestling with the angel. *Sefer HaHinukh* tells us that the *mitswah*, through its subtle hint, provides us with a reminder, that even though Jews will suffer great tribulations in Exile at the hands of the nations, who are the descendents of `*Esaw* — in the end, we will eventually prevail.

The sinew must be completely removed, with all of its fat, from the meat before one can eat the thigh meat of a domesticated kosher animal. One who violates this prohibition, and eats the sinew, is punished by a flogging of thirty-nine strokes.

In Detail: *A selection of some verses of interest*:

32:4 – וַיִּשְׁלַח יַעֲקֹב מַלְאָכִים

"*Ya `aqov* sent *mal'akhim*..."

The word *mal'akhim* can mean both "messengers" and "angels" (angels are in effect messengers of God). Rashi, based on *Midrash Rabba*, contends that these were actual "angels." The Midrash contends that if a *malakh* escorted *Eli`ezer*, who was only a servant of the household, how much more should *Ya`aqov* be escorted by them, considering he is the inheritor of the blessing and responsibility as HaShem's chosen.

Abarbanel, however, suggests that these "angels" are human merchants who had just "coincidentally" met `*Esaw*. He too would agree that they were sent by HaShem, but in this case, the messenger was unaware of his patron.

32:5 – עִם־לָבָן גַּרְתִּי

"...with *Lavan* I dwelled ..."

Rashi teaches that *Ya`aqov* was stressing that he remained a resident and was not made a prince or an important person. He went to great pains to inform `*Esaw* that he hadn't any reason to hate him, that the blessing of their father (that he would be master over his brothers) had not been fulfilled.

Interestingly, the *gematria* [mathematical equivalent] of the word "I dwelled [*garti*]" is six hundred and thirteen. This hints that *Ya`aqov* lived with *Lavan* for many years, but did not forsake the six hundred and thirteen *mitswoth* nor learn evil from *Lavan*. *Ya`aqov* is informing his brother that despite the distance and the time, he did not lose his identity.

Another possibility for emphasizing that he dwelt with *Lavan* might be a hidden warning to *`Esaw*. As if to say, I lived with the master thief, and not only survived, but became successful, it might behoove you to treat me with caution.

32:6 – וַיְהִי־לִי֙ שׁ֣וֹר וַחֲמ֔וֹר
"I have oxen and asses ..."

Again, *Ya`aqov* is stressing that the blessing his father bestowed upon him is not being fulfilled, so *`Esaw* need not worry. The blessing promised, "dew of Heaven and of the fat places of the earth." Livestock is from neither.

32:7 – בָּ֣אנוּ אֶל־אָחִ֖יךָ֙ אֶל־עֵשָׂ֔ו
"We came to your brother, to *`Esaw* ..."

Rashi suggests that the messengers (angels) said to *Ya`aqov* that even though he may still call him and relate to him as "brother," *`Esaw* continues to act wickedly against him.

I think there might be other ways of understanding this verse. It's possible that the *mal'akhim* are reminding *Ya`aqov* that *`Esaw* is (still) his brother, and just as *Ya`aqov* remained unaffected by the passage of time, *`Esaw* is still the same man of *Ya`aqov*'s youth.

This might be what prompts the Holy *Zohar* to teach us that *Ya`aqov* wasn't immediately worried about *`Esaw*, for he knew the respect that his brother had for his father, and assumed that *`Esaw* wouldn't kill him while his father was still alive. This is why, the *Zohar* teaches, that *Ya`aqov* chose now to appease him now, when there was a possibility of changing his attitude.

Another possibility is that the language recalls the tragic episode of the first brothers, *Kayin* and *Hevel*, with all of its implications.

32:8 – וַיִּירָא יַעֲקֹב מְאֹד וַיֵּצֶר לוֹ

"*Ya`aqov* was terribly afraid and distressed ..."

We must examine why the Torah uses two words here when one would suffice. According to *Midrash TanHuma* and *Bereshit Rabba*, *Ya`aqov* was both afraid of being killed and distressed that he might have to kill others.

On the surface, the statement from the Midrash and Rashi, that *Ya`aqov* was concerned about killing, "others," seems to be a general concern for the safety of innocent bystanders, yet like most of Torah, very little insight is gained through a superficial reading.

In the *Gemara*, a group of rabbis, amongst them Ribbi Meir, is referred to at "the others," instead of by name, due to their opposition to the *Nasi* [president of the *Sanhedrin*]. Ribbi Meir is the son of a convert from Rome, that is *Edom*. The text seems to be suggestion that *Ya`aqov*, through prophetic insight, was afraid, not of killing the present-day person of his brother, but rather the future Torah that would be brought forth from the lips of Ribbi Meir.

32:8-10 – וַיַּחַץ אֶת־הָעָם . . . לִשְׁנֵי מַחֲנוֹת: . . . וַיֹּאמֶר יַעֲקֹב אֱלֹהֵי אָבִי אַבְרָהָם וֵאלֹהֵי אָבִי יִצְחָק

"...he divided the people...into two camps ... And *Ya`aqov* said, God of my fathers ..."

Rashi teaches that *Ya`aqov* prepared himself for three things, for a gift, for prayer and for war. This should be compared with the advise *Ya`aqov* gives *Yehudah* before his encounter with *Yosef* (see *parshath Miqets, Bereshith* 43:11).

32:11 – קָטֹנְתִּי

"[literally] I am (made) small ..."

Masekhet Shabbat [32] understands the word to mean, "I am (or, have become) unworthy," meaning that *Ya`aqov* feared that all of the kindnesses which HaShem had shown him had "used up his credit," so to speak, in Heaven and that he thus might not prevail against *`Esaw.*

The Ramban, following this understanding, interprets the verse to mean, "I am less because of all the mercies and truths You have done for me, your servant."

This is a powerful lesson, that if *Ya`aqov* the forebearer of the Jewish People felt thus, how much more should we feel "small" before all of the wonderful gifts and *Hesed* [acts of kindness] HaShem has performed for us, *Ya`aqov*'s children.

32:11 – בְּמַקְלִי
"...with my staff ..."

The Midrash says that this verse teaches that *Ya`aqov* used his staff to split the *Yarden* and pass over. This is of course a foreshadowing of the entrance into the Land of Israel by his descendents under the leadership of *Y'hoshu`a*. It seems to me there is another way of understanding the expression as well.

On the simple level, *Ya`aqov* is simply acknowledging to HaShem that when he first passed over the *Yarden* on his way to *Lavan*, he had nothing but his staff and now HaShem has provided him with two full camps.

On the more esoteric level, *Ya`aqov* may be acknowledging that the gold, cattle, servants and other possessions are not his, but ultimately belong to HaShem. All that *Ya`aqov* has, that is all he can rely upon, is his staff, his support, namely, HaShem.

32:15 – עִזִּים מָאתַיִם וּתְיָשִׁים עֶשְׂרִים רְחֵלִים מָאתַיִם וְאֵילִים עֶשְׂרִים
"Two hundred she goats and twenty he-goats ..."

We learn in *Bereshit Rabba* that *Ya`aqov* sent enough males sufficient for the needs of the females, with all of the animals. It further interprets from this the required marital duties of the husband, depending upon his occupation. That is that one's obligation is contingent upon the outside demands placed upon an individual.

32:21 – אֲכַפְּרָה פָנָיו
"...*akhap'rah fanaw*..."

Literally, "I will make/cause atonement of his face," Rashi understands this to mean, "I will undo his wrath." Ibn Ezra understands it to mean "I will cover his anger," while the Ramban interprets it to mean that *Ya`aqov* intends to offer a "gift of redemption."

Yet it might be understood thus. Relating to the continuation of the verse, which states, "I will see his face, perhaps he will accept me," I think we might be able to understand the beginning of the verse as stating, "I will overturn or deny his face." The root word also carries the meaning of "denial." That is, I will cause his face to change from that of anger and denial of me to that of acceptance.

32:23 – וְאֶת־אַחַד עָשָׂר יְלָדָיו

"...and his eleven children ..."

Rashi points out that we know he has twelve children including *Dinah*. *Bereshit Rabba* addresses this, and teaches that *Ya`aqov* had locked *Dinah* in a chest lest *`Esaw* see her and wish to marry her. For this, we are taught, *Ya`aqov* is punished, for he withheld his daughter from his brother, and perhaps she would have caused him to repent and return to the path of HaShem. Instead, she fell into the hands of *Sh'khem*.

32:25 – וַיִּוָּתֵר יַעֲקֹב לְבַדּוֹ

"*Ya`aqov* was left alone..."

Masekhet Hulin [91] teaches that he had forgotten small jars and returned to retrieve them.

I think it is significant that, like his leaving *Erets Yisrael* on his journey towards *Lavan* where he was "left alone," here too he is left alone, despite all of his possessions. There, *Ya`aqov* was not truly alone, he only felt so, but due to his dream recognized that "HaShem was in that place." Here too, *Ya`aqov* seems to be "left alone," yet has an encounter with "a man." This time though, instead of simply passively observing the *malakhim* ascending and descending, *Ya`aqov* becomes a part of the experience, wrestling with it until the morning. He does not reflect on it as a past event, but relates to it in the present.

32:25 – וַיֵּאָבֵק אִישׁ עִמּוֹ

"...and there was a man with him ..."

Bereshit Rabba explains that this was the guardian angel of *`Esaw*. Their words have support from his description as a "man," and *`Esaw* being named because he was "completely formed," that is "a little man," at birth. Also his angel is called "a man."

32:27 – כִּי אִם־בֵּרַכְתָּנִי
"You should bless me ..."

Rashi states, "Confirm for me the blessing which my father blessed me and for which `Esaw is contesting." It seems to me that *Ya`aqov* has been fighting for this blessing all his life, and it has been a tremendous struggle for him.

32:28 – מַה־שְּׁמֶךָ
"What is your name?"

It should be noted that this is the same question his father asked *Ya'aqov* when he presented himself (surreptitiously) to receive the blessing.

32:29 – לֹא יַעֲקֹב
"...not *Ya `aqov* ..."

It will no longer be said that the blessing came to you through insinuation and deceit [the name *Ya`aqov* is similar to the word for deceit or crooked], but through straightforward methods [*Yisrael* is similar to *yashar*, straight]. Rashi's understanding of this verse reflects this idea.

It seems to me that Rashi is addressing a difficulty in the text. Unlike Abraham who after his name change from *Abram* is never referred to again as such, the name *Yisrael* is not an exclusive name for *Ya`aqov*. It seems that the Torah only bestows this name on the patriarch when he acts in accordance with his role as the progenitor of the Nation of *Yisrael*.

32:29 – כִּי אִם־יִשְׂרָאֵל
"...but *Yisrael* ..."

The word *Yisrael* can be understood as "one who wrestles with God." When Jews merit it, we are crowned with the title "Children of *Yisrael*" for we must continually wrestle with our understanding of HaShem's Will in order that we might fulfill it.

33:1 – וַיִּשָּׂא יַעֲקֹב עֵינָיו
***Ya`aqov* lifted up his eyes...**

He understood the intent of his brother. We have discussed the idea behind this expression previously. Further support of this is that he saw with him four hundred men. Four hundred is represented by the letter "*taw*," which, according to the *Gemara* [*Masekhet Shabbat* 104a], represents "truth." However, according to "*Otioth of Ribbi Aqiba*," the letter "*taw*" represents indulgence of earthly pleasure. This also has significance for `*Esaw* who saw himself as a man of "this world," uninterested in matters of spirit, that is, the "other world." Thus, when *Ya`aqov* "lifted his eyes," he recognized the true nature of his brother.

33:1 – אַרְבַּע מֵאוֹת אִישׁ
"...four hundred men ..."

Another understanding of the four hundred men might be that they represent the "*taw*" [the numerical value of this letter is four hundred], placed on the forehead by the *malakh Gabriel* as related in the vision of *Yehezkel*. It was written in ink for the righteous, and in blood for the wicked, symbolizing "you shall live," and "you shall die," respectively [*Masekhet Shabbat* 39]. Here, *Ya`aqov* "lifted" his eyes to read the "*taw*" on his brother's forehead to divine if he was approaching in righteousness or wickedness.

Four hundred is also the *gematria* for the word "*saq*" which is the sackcloth of mourning. This sackcloth is what Jews wear when mourning the destruction of the *Beth HaMiqdash* [the Holy Temple] that was destroyed by the descendents of `*Esaw*. Further, the *Beth HaMiqdash* was destroyed because *Yisrael* (the nation) was acting more like `*Esaw* and indulging in worldly pleasures at the expense of spiritual achievements.

33:4 – וַיָּרָץ עֵשָׂו לִקְרָאתוֹ וַיְחַבְּקֵהוּ
" `*Esaw* ran to him and embraced him..."

`*Esaw* is a man who is always overcome by the moment. He allows his passions to rule him. Rashi explains that here he was so moved when he saw his brother bow out of respect for him.

33:4 – וַיִּשָּׁקֵהוּ

"...and kiss him..."

In the Torah there are dots over all of the letters. In *Bereshit Rabba* there are many interpretations of this. Some interpret this to mean that he did not kiss him wholeheartedly. However, Ribi Shimon Bar Yokhai (others say *ben Eli`ezer*) said that despite the fact that *`Esaw* hates *Ya`aqov*, he was so overcome with passion for the moment that he did kiss him wholeheartedly. Another interpretation is that the dots symbolize that *`Esaw* went to bite *Ya`aqov*, but his neck was turned to marble and *`Esaw*'s teeth were blunted and loosened.

33:11 – קַח־נָא אֶת־בִּרְכָתִי

"Take, please, my blessing..."

Ya`aqov* gives *`Esaw his blessing. How ironic, considering the history of the two, where first *Ya`aqov* buys *`Esaw*'s birthright, and then deceives his father for the blessing that was intended for *`Esaw*. Further, he forces a blessing from *`Esaw*'s guardian angel. *Ya`aqov* finally recognizes that he has enough, and is able to give freely his blessing to his brother.

33:11 – יֶשׁ־לִי־כָל

"...I have enough ..."

Yet, *`Esaw* said "I have a lot." We learn that the wise is happy with whatever he has, for whatever he has, is "enough." Yet, the one who only lives in this world may have a tremendous amount, and even though it might seem like more than he needs now, he will not be satisfied and soon it will not meet his expectations.

33:14 – עַד אֲשֶׁר־אָבֹא אֶל־אֲדֹנִי שֵׂעִירָה

"...until I come to my lord in *Se`ir* ..."

Bereshit Rabba points out that *Ya`aqov* never went to *Se`ir*, and therefore asks "When will he go?" It answers that he will go there in the Days of the *MashiaH*, as it is written "Rescuers will go up to *Har Tsion* to judge *Har `Esaw*."

32:18 – וַיָּבֹא יַעֲקֹב שָׁלֵם
***"Ya`aqov* came *shalem...*"**

Literally, the word, *shalem* means "whole." *Masekhet Shabbat* [33] teaches that he was whole in body, for his lameness was healed, whole in his wealth, for he lacked nothing, and whole in his knowledge, for he did not forget his learning while living with *Lavan*.

I think it may also include whole in his relationship with HaShem and whole in his security, for he encountered his brother; he faced his worst fears, and prevailed. Any doubts that he might have had were completely dispelled. He was also whole in his relationship with HaShem. One should compare this with the previous parsha, (*Bereshith* 28:21).

33:18 – עִיר שְׁכֶם
"...to *Sh'khem* ..."

This is the first place that his grandfather Abraham came to when he arrived from *Paddam Aram* as well.

34:1 – בַּת־לֵאָה
"...the daughter of *Le'ah...*"

Bereshith Rabba asks if she wasn't also the daughter of *Ya`aqov*? It answers that she was called the daughter of *Le'ah* because like her, *Le'ah* was one who would "go out."

This is difficult for me, for the idea of "like daughter, like mother," doesn't fit exactly in this instance. The verse referring to *Le'ah*'s "going out," referred to her "going out" to meet her husband, as Rashi points out. This to me is an entirely different idea than going out "to look with the daughters of the land."

Instead, I would suggest that like *Le'ah* who was originally intended for the *bakhor* [firstborn], *Dinah* was also originally intended as a wife for *`Esaw*, but due to the actions of *Ya`aqov* (see above, he hid *Dinah* in a chest), both of the women were married to someone else. This may be what the Midrash is hinting at, suggesting that the "going out" was from their predestined framework, from their intended husband.

34:5 – וַיַּחֲרֵשׁ יַעֲקֹב

"And *Ya`aqov* was silent ..."

This represents the opposite of his father's limitations. *YitsHaq* was unable to see the situation clearly, but he was able to act. Here, *Ya`aqov* hears and understands but is unable to respond.

34:5 – עַד־בֹּאָם

"...with guile..."

Rashi interprets this as, "with wisdom," and suggests that there wasn't any guile, really, for as the text continues they had "defiled *Dinah*..."

34:25 – שְׁנֵי־בְנֵי־יַעֲקֹב

"...two of *Ya`aqov*'s sons..."

Rashi quotes the Midrash, stating that they were his sons, yet they did not behave as such, for they did not take council from him regarding this matter.

34:25 – בֶּטַח

"...in security/unaware/unresisted ..."

Rashi states simply that this was because they were in pain. He then adds that there is a midrashic understanding that they had faith in *Ya`aqov*'s merits.

34:31 – וַיֹּאמְרוּ הַכְזוֹנָה יַעֲשֶׂה אֶת־אֲחוֹתֵנוּ

"...as with a harlot..."

In other words, should she be treated as a woman without protection and recourse?

It seems to me, that there are two forms of marriage according to the *Tanakh* (Bible), and the expression '*zonah*' which is normally translated through it's usage today, as a harlot. However, it seems to me that it would be better understood as a type of concubine, that is a wife without a *ketubah* or marriage contract. In other words, wife of secondary status, but still a wife. This is suggested by the words root, which is related to food and sustenance. Thus, we see in *Shoftim* (Judges) 11:1 "And *YiftaH* the *Gil'adi* was a mighty man, the son of a wife-*zonah*. For *Gil'ad* bore *YiftaH*. We therefore see that the Sages of

Blessed Memory, enacted a prohibition [*Baba Kama* 89a], forbidding a man from marrying, or even being with his wife for even an hour without a *ketubah* (marriage contract). Further, the Talmud [*Yebamoth* 89a] adds, "What is the reason for that the Rabbis instituted that all wives must have a *ketubah*? So that it divorcing a woman should not be taken lightly. Therefore, the Sages of Blessed Memory established [*Ketuboth* 10b] the minimal amount for a brides dowry.

35:1 – קוּם עֲלֵה בֵית־אֵל
"...Arise, ascend to *Beth-El* ..."

Midrash TanHuma teaches that HaShem suggests by this, that it is because of their delaying in *Sh'khem* that he was punished through his daughter.

35:2 – אֶת־אֱלֹהֵי הַנֵּכָר
"...strange gods..."

Rashi points out that they acquired these from the spoils of *Sh'khem*. Yet, it seems to me considering that *Ya`aqov* acquired slaves and servants previously, he may have been addressing them, for they may have still retained the trappings of their former culture.

35:4 – וְאֶת־הַנְּזָמִים אֲשֶׁר בְּאָזְנֵיהֶם
"...the earrings in their ears ..."

It seems to me that this foreshadows the future incident of the Golden Calf. It's important to note, that earrings often represented servitude, as with the Hebrew Servant who wishes to remain in perpetual service to master (see *parshath Mishpatim*).

35:8 – תַּחַת הָאַלּוֹן
"...under the oak ..."

It can also be interpreted as "under the other one." *Bereshit Rabba* tells us that at the same time, *Ya`aqov* is informed of the death of his mother.

35:9 – וַיְבָרֶךְ אֹתוֹ
"...and blessed him ..."

Rashi brings *Midrash Rabba* which adds, "the blessing for mourners." I don't understand why the simple meaning isn't enough, that HaShem blessed him. It might be because he already received a blessing?

35:11 – אֲנִי אֵל שַׁדַּי
"I am *El Shadai*..."

Interestingly, when HaShem changed Abram's name to Abraham, He also called himself *El Shadai*, meaning God that which is sufficient.

35:13 – וַיַּעַל מֵעָלָיו אֱלֹהִים
"...God went up ..."

HaShem is enthroned on the patriarchs.

35:13 – בַּמָּקוֹם
"...in the place ..."

This refers to *Har Habayit*, the Temple Mount.

35:22 - וַיֵּלֶךְ רְאוּבֵן וַיִּשְׁכַּב אֶת־בִּלְהָה פִּילֶגֶשׁ אָבִיו
"...that *R'uben* lay with her..."

According to *Masekhet Shabbat* [55], *R'uben* took his father's bed, which had been in *RaHel*'s tent till her death, and placed it in his mother's tent. *Ya`aqov* had moved it to *Bilhah*'s tent. *R'uben* saw this as an insult to his mother, and so that she should not be shamed at having the maid-servant become a rival wife to her, he took the bed and put it in his mother's tent. However, because he disarranged the beds, he is attributed as having "lay with her."

35:29 - וַיִּקְבְּרוּ אֹתוֹ עֵשָׂו וְיַעֲקֹב בָּנָיו
"...and his sons *'Esaw* and *Ya'aqov* buried him."

We are familiar with the Midrash, that points out here, unlike with *Yishm'ael* and *YitsHaq*, *'Esaw* precedes *Ya'aqov* in the verse, indicating he never accepted his *Ya'aqov*'s role eminence. However, according to the more straightforward, simple meaning, there, *Yishm'ael* was the son of a concubine, but here, both brothers are the sons of the same wife, and *'Esaw* was actually born first. Further, it seems to me, that after all that *Ya'aqov* has been through, he no longer has a need for to impose his position on his brother. He has clearly received the blessing. Further, even though *'Esaw* vowed to kill his brother when their father passed away, there doesn't seems to be any tension in this chapter of their story. All of the conflict and competition seems to be a thing of the past for the brothers, if not their descendents.

PARSHATH WAYESHEV

Overview

$Ya`aqov$ settles in the land of his father, the land of Canaan. After which, the story of *Yosef*, his son through *RaHel*, unfolds. *Ya`aqov* shows favoritism to *Yosef* which causes jealousy amongst his brothers. *Yosef* has several dreams, which seem to depict him lording over his brothers. This increases the animosity that they feel towards him, and they plot to kill him.

Yosef, at his father's request, travels to where his brothers are pasturing the flocks. On the way, he meets the *malakh* [angel] *Gabriel* who directs him to where the brothers are. At first, they decide to kill him, but *Re'uven* convinces them to throw him in a pit instead, hoping that he can rescue him later. While they have a meal, a caravan of *Bnei Yishmael* [Ishmaelite] merchants "happens" by. *Yehudah* suggests that they sell *Yosef* to the merchants instead of killing him. The brothers agree. Eventually, *Yosef* gets sold to *Potifar*, one of the ministers to *Par`oh*, the king of *Mitsrayim* [Egypt]. The brothers slaughter a goat and sprinkle its blood on *Yosef*'s coat, before showing it to their father. *Ya`aqov* is grief stricken and cannot be comforted over the loss of his son.

There is a brief interlude in the story of *Yosef*, while the Torah focuses on the story of *Yehudah*. He leaves his brother after the sale of *Yosef*, marries a Canaanite woman, and has three sons. He marries off his eldest, *`Er* to a woman named *Tamar*. *`Er* is "evil in the sight of God" and dies. Therefore, *Yehudah* gives *Tamar* his next son *`Onan*, following the custom of a *Levirate* marriage. *`Onan*, not wanting his seed to bear his brother's name, sins before God (wasting his seed on the ground) and dies as well. *Yehudah*, not knowing the reason his two older sons died, fears for his youngest son, so he sends *Tamar* to her father's house. He tells her that when his son his older, he will marry her.

Yehudah's wife then dies. And later, he goes to oversee his sheep shearers and on the way encounters *Tamar* who is playing the role of a harlot to entrap him. *Yehudah* does not recognize her, and has relations with her. He leaves her with a pledge in lieu of payment.

It then becomes known that *Tamar* has becomes pregnant, and *Yehudah* is ready to have her executed (for an obvious adulterous affair - as a *Yibum* [one waiting for a levirate marriage] she is not allowed relations with anyone other than those suitable for such a marriage).

Tamar discreetly produces his pledge as that which belongs to the father of the child. She is careful not to directly name *Yehudah* as the father, but lets him accept responsibility. Which in fact, *Yehudah* does. He recognizes the pledge, and accepts that by withholding his son from *Yibum* [Levirate] marriage with *Tamar*, she is more righteous than he. As, technically at the time, *Yehudah* was suitable to take her as a levirate marriage. (Originally it encompassed any kinsman of the deceased husband. Today it applies only to his brother). Subsequently, *Tamar* bears twins to *Yehudah*.

Then the story of *Yosef* continues. *Yosef* prospers in his master's house, but soon, *Potifar*'s wife makes advances towards him. Spurned, she frames *Yosef* and tells her husband that he seduced her. *Potifar* throws *Yosef* in jail. There he encounters two men, the chief butler and baker of *Par`oh*. They each have a dream and *Yosef* interprets them. His interpretation comes to pass, and the butler is restored to his position, but, despite his promise, he seems to forget *Yosef*.

In Detail: *A selection of some verses of interest:*

37:1 – וַיֵּשֶׁב יַעֲקֹב בְּאֶרֶץ מְגוּרֵי אָבִיו

"And *Ya`aqov* settled in the land of his father's travels..."

Rashi points out that the Torah wrote a great deal concerning where `*Esaw* dwelled, and his descendents, as well as their areas of conquest and settlement. However, for the patriarch *Ya`aqov*, the Torah reserves only one verse.

Rashi offers several poetic allegories. First, he suggest it is like finding a rare pearl amongst many pebbles. Second, he compares it to a spark in a pile of flax. Despite the tremendous amount of "straw," that is the descendents of `*Esaw*, the one spark of *Ya`aqov* will be able to ignite the fire of Torah and consume the stubble of `*Esaw*, as it is written, "And the House of *Ya`aqov* shall be a fire and the House of

Yosef a flame, and the House of *`Esaw* for stubble." [*`Ovadia* 1:18]

However, it seems to me that there may also be another reason. On the basic level, it seems logical that the text should list the expanse of *`Esaw*'s dwellings in total and be done with it, so that it can focus on the main story at hand, which is the continuation of the inheritance of Abraham. In other words, the Torah pauses to inform us of a secondary player in our saga, and then continues with main story at hand.

On a different level, I think the Torah has a deeper message. Despite *Ya`aqov* efforts to convince *`Esaw* that the "blessing hadn't become manifest (see last week's parsha)," the Torah tells us that the reverse is true, "*Ya`aqov* settled in the land of his father's sojourning." This tells us two very important things:

First, we learn that it is *Ya`aqov* and not *`Esaw*, despite his vast holdings, that dwells in the land of their father. *Ya`aqov* inherited the land, not *`Esaw*.

Further, we learn that *Ya`aqov* settled; after all of his wanderings, he was able to settle. This also seems to be a further entrenchment of the seed of Abraham in what will become known as *Erets Yisrael* [The Land of Israel]. Wherein *YitsHaq* only sojourned in the land, *Ya`aqov* is able to "settle."

37:2 – אֵלֶּה ׀ תֹּלְדוֹת יַעֲקֹב יוֹסֵף
"These are the *toldoth* [generations] of *Ya`aqov*, *Yosef*..."

Again, we encounter the word "*toldoth*." As I pointed out in earlier studies, this word carries multiple meanings. Simply, it means "generations," but clearly that exact meaning doesn't apply here, for then we would expect a list of all of *Ya`aqov* sons, instead of the beginning of *Yosef*'s story. Rather, it seems to mean that this is "the result of," or "what comes from." In other words, *Yosef*'s story is intrinsically linked to *Ya`aqov*'s story. *Ya`aqov*'s story continues with the *Yosef*'s narratives.

Alternatively, *Bereshit Rabba* offers other possibilities. It suggests that the entire being of *Ya`aqov* worked for *Lavan* only for *RaHel* and that *Yosef*'s appearance was similar to *Ya`aqov*'s, and that whatever happened to *Ya`aqov* happened to *Yosef*. Another explanation is that *Ya`aqov* sought to dwell in peace, but then the troubles of *Yosef* came upon him. This later explanation is a springboard for the idea that the righteous do not merit rest in this world, but only in the World-to Come. This world, is the world of the "preparation of the field," so to speak, and only after our death can we hope to gain the true rest of the harvest.

37:2 – וְהוּא נַעַר אֶת־בְּנֵי בִלְהָה וְאֶת־בְּנֵי זִלְפָּה נְשֵׁי אָבִיו
"...he was a lad [na`ar] with the sons of *Bilhah* ..."

This is a curious expression. Rashi tells us it is because the sons of *Leah* scorned them, while he befriended them.

We should note that *Bilhah* is the maid of *RaHel*, which might suggest that *Yosef* had closer relations with her sons. It should be noted too, that in all the listings, *Bilhah* is listed before *Zilpah*.

It seems to me also that the word, "*na`ar*" echoes the story of *Dinah* and might imply the idea of going out and "looking" for trouble, as it did with her story. The simple meaning though, it would seem, is that he would be a lad with them, in the sense that a boy plays with other youths.

37:2 – וַיָּבֵא יוֹסֵף אֶת־דִּבָּתָם רָעָה
"...*Yosef* brought a *dibatam ra`ah* [an evil report of them]..."

Rashi teaches that he told his father that the brothers ate a piece of flesh cut off from a living animal. This is confirmed by *Ba`Al HaTurim*, who teaches that the *gematria* [numerical equivalent] of *dibatam ra`ah* is equal to the phrase "They ate a limb from a living animal." He also accused them of degrading the sons of the handmaidens by calling them "slaves" and were suspect regarding forbidden unions. Of course none of this was actually true, though the Midrash describes events in a way that to a non-discerning eye, it may have looked like they did commit such offenses.

Therefore these three evils befell *Yosef*. The brothers slaughtered a goat when selling him, he was sold as a slave, and his master's wife chased after him in *Mitsrayim* [Egypt].

We further learn the word "*dibah*" is from the same expression, "making talkative the lips of those that are asleep." [*Tehillim* 7:10] This suggests an interesting moral lesson. Evil results from a lack of awareness. The word for evil in Hebrew is רַע [r`a], while the word for being awake or aware is a reversal of these two letters – עֵר [`er]. The more we work on our 'awareness' of others, as well as HaShem's Will then the further we move away from perpetuating evil. This is especially true with our speech to and about others.

37:3 – בֶּן־זְקֻנִים

"...the son of his old age..."

Rashi offers us the simple meaning that he was born to him in his old age.

However, this seems curious to me, for his brother *Binyamin* was born after him, when *Ya`aqov* was much older. One possible explanation for this difficulty is that because his beloved *RaHel* died giving birth to *Binyamin*, he reminded him of the loss of his wife. Whereas *Yosef* reminded him of *RaHel* when she was alive. He reminded him of his youthful love, so to speak.

Another possibility is that *Yosef* reminded *Ya`aqov* of himself when he was that age, therefore "of his old age" refers to the nostalgic effect of watching a son who is similar to oneself. He relived his youth through *Yosef*.

Another solution is found in *Targum Onkelos*, which understands the this phrase to mean "he was a wise son to him."

37:3 – כְּתֹנֶת פַּסִּים

"...*k'tonet passim*..."

This is traditionally translated, in accordance with the Radak, as a coat of many colors, understanding *passim* as "striped." However, Rashi tells us that *passim* denotes a cloak of fine wool. Ibn Ezra interprets it as an embroidered coat. Shadal interprets it as a full-length coat, whereas Hizkuni says that it is a coat specifically designed to convey favoritism.

Another interpretation uses the letters of the word as the initial letters of *Potifar*, *SoHarim* [merchants], *Yishmaelim* [Ishmaelite], and *Midyanim* [Midianites]. Because of this coat, and what it represented, he was sold to these four.

37:4 – וַיִּשְׂנְאוּ אֹתוֹ וְלֹא יָכְלוּ דַּבְּרוֹ לְשָׁלֹם

"...they hated him, and they could not speak peaceably to him..."

Rashi teaches that from within their condemnation, we learn their praise, for they did not speak one way with their mouths and another with their hearts.

37:8 – וְעַל־דְּבָרָיו

"...and for his words..."

That is, the evil reports that he would tell his father. *Or HaHayyim* however suggests that this means that *Yosef* asked his brothers to interpret the dreams for him.

37:9 – וַיַּחֲלֹם עוֹד חֲלוֹם אַחֵר

"He dreamed again, a different dream..."

The two dreams represent the two types of success and blessing. The first one, the binding of sheaves, was concerning earthly, material blessing. The second, involving the heavenly bodies, represents spiritual, heavenly blessing. It seems to me that this is significant, as it was *Ya`aqov*, his father who took both of these blessings from *`Esaw*.

37:10 – וַיְסַפֵּר אֶל־אָבִיו וְאֶל־אֶחָיו וַיִּגְעַר־בּוֹ אָבִיו

"He related it to his father and to his brothers..."

First he told it to his brothers alone, and then repeated it in the presence of his father. It seems to me that the brothers may have forced him to repeat it before their father, hoping, as did in fact happen, that *Ya`aqov* would reprimand him for it.

37:10 - וַיִּגְעַר־בּוֹ אָבִיו

"...his father reprimanded him..."

Rashi suggests that he was reprimanded not for the dreams, but for disclosing them and bringing enmity on himself. It should be noted that *Ya`aqov* also had dreams of divine significance, but he did not disclose them, but rather guarded the matter, waiting for them to become manifest. We are admonished not to flout our blessings, as even just deserved rewards can invite enmity and jealousy.

37:10 - הֲבוֹא נָבוֹא אֲנִי וְאִמְּךָ וְאַחֶיךָ לְהִשְׁתַּחֲוֹת לְךָ אָרְצָה

"...Shall we come, your mother and I ...to bow down before you?"

Ya`aqov pointed out that the dream had an element of absurdity to it, for *Yosef*'s mother, *RaHel*, was already dead, and could not conceivably bow down before *Yosef*. Rashi points out however that this was referring to *Bilhah* who raised him as a mother. The Ramban however suggests that *Bilhah* too passed away before the family descended into *Mitsrayim* and that the moon refers to the children of the brothers. Just as this is absurd, *Ya`aqov* tells him, so is the rest of the dream. Rashi suggests that *Ya`aqov* did this, in front of the brothers, in order that he might "remove the matter from their hearts," — that they would not envy him.

This last point is an important one, for both *Ya`aqov* and the brothers were aware that dreams are powerful and often time communicate certain truths. Our sages teach that dreams are one sixtieth (that is, a taste)[7] of prophecy. Yet dreams, unlike prophecy are dependent on interpretation and can be misconstrued. In addition, dreams can be simple nonsense, and even those that contain truth, will always have a certain degree of nonsense or absurdity attached to it [*Masekhet Brakhot* 55a].

Dreams are very significant, but they can come from the side of the *klipah*, through a *shed* (demon) whispering in one's ear or they can come from the side of *qedushah* [holiness]. In the later case, the dream usually comes at the end of one's sleep cycle (it doesn't cause one to awaken because of the dream) and one remembers it upon awakening. There are other indications, and it is important that one discuss "significant" dreams with a rabbi or Torah scholar who understands such things. Usually a dreamer knows if a dream is "significant" even if he doesn't understands its implications, in which case, he should seek out a scholar's advice.

37:11 – וְאָבִיו שָׁמַר אֶת־הַדָּבָר

"...and his father guarded/kept the matter."

Similar to the incident with *Dinah*, *Ya`aqov* does not act in a decisive way, but waits, regarding the matter. Rashi teaches that he was waiting

---

7 One-sixtieth is the legal measure of taste in regard to prohibitions regarding food, such as an admixtures of milk and meat. Less than this amount is considered null.

for it to come to pass. A wise man knows when to take action and when to wait for the appropriate moment.

Yet, it seems to me, that this is a hint pointing to the earlier suggestion that *Ya`aqov* reprimanded *Yosef*, not for the dream itself, but for revealing it (Rashi on the previous verse).

37:12 – בְּשְׁכֶם
"...in *Shkhem*."

It seems to me that mentioning of the place is significant. For it was in this same place were we read (34:1-31) about the rape of *Dinah*. There too, *Ya`aqov* did not act, he was silent. In response, the brothers of *Dinah* took matters into their own hands and acted, inappropriately according to the simple understanding of *Ya`aqov*'s reaction to their deed. Here, the brothers also take matters into their own hands after their father "kept the matter (to himself)." It seems to me that there might be a connection between these incidents and the actions of *Ya`aqov* and his sons. This might be another reason for the use of the word "*na`ar*" previously, in regards to the evil reports (see above, verse 2).

37:14 – מֵעֵמֶק חֶבְרוֹן
"...from the valley of *Hebron*..."

This is very curious for, in fact, *Hebron* is situated on a mountain. Rashi suggests that this refers to the depth of counsel of the righteous Abraham who was interred in *Hebron*, and the covenant of the pieces which prophesized *Yisrael*'s decent into *Mitsrayim*, for it is this journey of *Yosef* which will set into motion all that was foretold.

Of course, the simple meaning is that the term *Hebron*, includes more than the actual city, but relates to the area and the villages within, which include many hills and valleys.

37:15 – וַיִּמְצָאֵהוּ אִישׁ
"A man found him..."

Rashi tells us that this was the *malakh* [angel] *Gabriel*. *Gabriel* is the *malakh* of justice, and is referred to as 'man' throughout the *Tanakh*. It seems to me significant that the man finds *Yosef*, just as *Ya`aqov*'s first spiritual encounter "found" him.

37:17 – נָסְעוּ מִזֶּה

"...they have traveled from this [here] ..."

The text literally says, "this." *Yosef* says he is seeking his brothers, and the man tells him that they have removed themselves from the concept of brotherhood with *Yosef* [Rashi]. It seems to me that it is significant that the *gematria* [numerical equivalent] of "this" is twelve. The brothers, it should be noted, numbered twelve, suggesting that they have moved away the idea of being a united nation.

37:17 – נֵלְכָה דֹּתָיְנָה

"...let us go to *Dotan*..."

Simply, this is a place name. On a different level, "*Dotan*" is similar to the word "*datoth*," meaning "law," or "legal tools." This might be suggesting that the brothers went to seek a legal means to kill *Yosef* [Rashi] or that they will go and take the law into their own hands in their disposition of *Yosef*.

37:18 – וַיִּרְאוּ אֹתוֹ מֵרָחֹק

"They saw him from a distance..."

The brothers did not see *Yosef* as a brother, as one of them, but someone distant and like a stranger to them.

37:18 – וּבְטֶרֶם יִקְרַב אֲלֵיהֶם

"...before he came near..."

Before *Yosef* could make a gesture of consolation, or before they recognized him as family, they purposely maintained their distance (they did not allow for sympathetic feelings to interfere) from him so that they would be able to carry out their plot.

37:23 – וַיַּפְשִׁיטוּ אֶת־יוֹסֵף אֶת־כֻּתָּנְתּוֹ אֶת־כְּתֹנֶת הַפַּסִּים אֲשֶׁר עָלָיו

"...they stripped *Yosef* of his coat, the coat of many colors..."

Rashi, in explaining the awkward construction which mentions the coat twice, teaches that this refers to two things, the first to his robe and the second to the coat that his father gave him. It seems to me, however, that the Torah could simply be emphasizing the symbolic importance the coat had for the brothers, in that it demonstrated their father's favoritism.

37:24 – וְהַבּוֹר רֵק אֵין בּוֹ מָיִם
"…and the pit was empty, there wasn't any water in it."

It seems logical that if the pit were empty, that would mean that it would not have any water in it. This begs the question as to why the Torah would mention such a fact.

The *Gemara* [*Shabbat* 22] teaches that this implies that while there wasn't any water in the hole, there were snakes and scorpions. The significance it seems is that nothing is completely "empty." Nature abhors a vacuum. When devoid of life-giving qualities, dangerous elements eventually enter the space. Thus, in life, when some empties his life of Torah and God (water is often a symbol for both), eventually he will be invaded by "snakes and scorpions,." that is, evil and debilitating ideas and actions. It is as impossible for a vacuum to exist (for long) in the spiritual realm as it is in the physical world

37:25 – וַיֵּשְׁבוּ לֶאֱכָל־לֶחֶם
"They sat down to eat bread…"

Midrash Rabba point out that through this crime, *Yosef* will end up supplying, not only the brothers, but also the whole world with bread.

37:26 – וַיֹּאמֶר יְהוּדָה אֶל־אֶחָיו מַה־בֶּצַע
"*Yehudah* said to his brothers, 'What profit is it…'"

Midrash Rabba notes that although *Yehudah* is mercenary in his actions here, he saw no alternative to saving *Yosef.*

37:28 – וַיַּעַבְרוּ אֲנָשִׁים מִדְיָנִים
"Men of *Midyan* passed by…"

Rashi points out that this was yet another caravan, for *Yosef* was sold many times. The brothers sold *Yosef* to the sons of *Yishmael* who sold him to the men of *Midyan*.

37:29 – וַיָּשָׁב רְאוּבֵן
"*Re'uven* returned…"

The obvious question is, where was *Re'uven*? Rashi offers two explanations. The first is that it was his day to go and minister to their father. Rashi, borrowing from the Midrash, also uses the word return as meaning, performing "*tshuvah*." Literally this means return but here its spiritual sense, that is repentance, is implied. Rashi suggests that *Re'uven* was wearing sackcloth and fasting in an effort to repent from disarranging the couch of his father after *RaHel's* death.

However, it seems to me, that another reading is possible. *Re'uven* could have been physically present during the entire episode, yet, when he looked into the pit, and saw it full of scorpions and snakes, he repented of the brothers' actions.

Yet, after he repented, he became distressed and then returned to the conspiracy of the brothers, as it says, "He returned to the brothers," for as he says, *Yosef* was already gone, he was lost, thus he had no choice, "And as for me, how shall I come?" He would be unable to come before his father and reveal the truth, therefore, "They took *Yosef's* coat ..."

37:31 – וַיִּשְׁחֲטוּ שְׂעִיר עִזִּים
"They slaughtered a goat..."

Just as *Ya`aqov* tricked his father with the slaughtering of a goat, so was he tricked by his sons.

37:32 – הַכֶּר־נָא הַכְּתֹנֶת בִּנְךָ הִוא אִם־לֹא
"Do you know/recognize whether it is your son's coat or not"

The Midrash teaches that it is *Yehudah* who says these words, and it will come back to him. *Tamar* will ask him "Do you know, now, whose are these (referring to the pledge that he had left with her)?"

37:35 – וַיֵּבְךְּ אֹתוֹ אָבִיו
"...and his father wept for him ..."

Midrash *Rabba* teaches that this refers to *YitsHaq* weeping for *Ya`aqov*, because of the grief that his son, *Ya`aqov*, felt. However, the Midrash informs us that *YitsHaq*, through prophecy, knew the truth. He said, though, that if HaShem had not revealed the truth to *Ya`aqov*, how could he do so. Therefore, while in *Ya`aqov's* presence he wept, but upon leaving he did not observe the mourning rites.

37:36 – סְרִיס פַּרְעֹה שַׂר הַטַּבָּחִים

"...an officer of *Par`oh, sar hatabaHim*."

There are many different interpretations of this title. *TabaH* literally means butcher. Ibn Ezra suggests that he was the chief executioner. Rashi teaches that he was in charge of those who slaughtered the king's cattle.

38:1 – וַיְהִי בָּעֵת הַהִוא

"It came to pass..."

Rashi teaches that this section is introduced here, in the middle of the story of *Yosef* to teach that after seeing the grief they brought to *Ya`aqov*, the brothers turned on *Yehudah* and said, "Why did you say to sell him, if you had said to return him, we would have listened to you."

However, I think that this interlude is placed here so that we can witness the spiritual path of *Yehudah*, which descends and then rises far above the other brothers. *Yehudah*'s loss of his own sons may help him to understand the pain of his father's loss. This, and the truth revealed through *Tamar*'s actions, engenders in him a maturity and understanding that allows and compels him to be a leader amongst his brothers, and take the initiative when they go to *Mitsrayim*.

38:1 – וַיֵּרֶד יְהוּדָה

"...*Yehudah* went down ..."

To my mind, this can only suggest spiritually. *Yehudah*, after suggesting the sale of *Yosef* and delivering the coat to his father, begins a spiritual descent. His descent begins with a self-imposed exile; he removes himself from his family. From there, he diverts himself, changing directions, associating with *Hirah*, a man of *Adulam* and then marries a Canaanite woman.

38:12 – וַיַּעַל . . . תִּמְנָתָה

"...he went up...to *Timnah*..."

However (as Rashi points out), in the story of *Shim'shon* [Samson], we learn that *Shim'shon* descended to *Timnah*. Rashi suggests that it was situated on a mountain slope and thus depending on one's direction one either ascended or descended.

Yet is seems to me that this too, can be explained in terms of a metaphysical ascent or descent (Rashi actually may be hinting at this too). There, as the Midrash points out, *Shim'shon* was descending. He went to marry a heathen woman. However, here, *Yehudah*'s ascent into *Timnah* will be the beginning of his return. Here he meets *Tamar*. After she "forces" him to do the right thing, *Yehudah* is able to take the initiative and step forward. His journey to *Timnah* is the beginning of *Yehudah*'s return. From here, he will begin to take responsibility for his actions. This "path of ascent" will continue until he stands before *Yosef* in *Mitsrayim*, a leader responsible for his charge and prudent in his actions.

38:14 – בְּפֶתַח עֵינַיִם
"...she sat in *petaH `Eynayim*..."

Literally this means at the "opening of the eyes." To my mind, this means clearly that this is where *Tamar* will open *Yehudah*'s eyes to his responsibility.

Rashi interprets it as, "at the crossroad on the way to *Timnah*. That is where one opens one's eyes to see which direction to take."

The Midrash says that she "lifted up her eyes to the gate (*petaH*) to which all eyes (*`eynayim*) are directed, that is to HaShem and the Gate of Prayer.

In fact all these interpretations are simultaneously true. It is from this point, where *Yehudah* will lift up his eyes, to decide which direction he needs to take his life, and he will decide to direct it towards the path of Heaven.

38:18 – חֹתָמְךָ וּפְתִילֶךָ וּמַטֶּךָ
"...your signet, your cord and your staff..."

Rashi, based on Targum Onkelos, interprets this as the ring with which you sign/seal and your cloak, with which you cover yourself.

Bereshit Rabba understands it as the signet, which alludes to royalty (the kingship will come from *Yehudah*), the cord, which alludes to the Sanhedrin (in connection with the thread of blue in the *tsi-tstith*) and your staff, which alludes to the *Melekh HaMashiaH* (the staff of the strength of HaShem).

It seems to me that she takes his "symbols of leadership," so that she can offer him the true mantle of leadership, that is, responsibility.

38:23 – פֶּן נִהְיֶה לָבוּז
"...lest we be put to shame."

Rashi explains, lest the matter becomes known and it will be a disgrace.

38:25 – לְאִישׁ אֲשֶׁר־אֵלֶּה לּוֹ אָנֹכִי הָרָה
"...I am with child through the man whose things are."

Rashi teaches that she did not want to shame him in public; therefore she shifted the onus of the truth to him. Our rabbis learn from here, that it is better to have oneself thrown into a fiery furnace than to shame one's fellow in public.

38:26 – וַיַּכֵּר יְהוּדָה
"*Yehudah* acknowledged ..."

In the Hebrew text there isn't an object written for the verb. I would suggest that this implies that *Yehudah* recognized more than the objects themselves. He recognized the truth, not just of this situation, but also of his role with *Yosef,* and his responsibility towards his father, and towards HaShem.

38:26 – מִמֶּנִּי
"from/than me ..."

The word, "*mimeni*" can be understood as "than me," as in "she is more righteous than me," of "from me," in that *Yehudah* is acknowledging that the child is from him.

Rashi offers another explanation, based on the Midrash suggesting that it was a Heavenly Voice that declared "from me," that is, that all these things came to pass "By Me and from Me." It seems to me that, amongst other things, *Yehudah* might also be recognizing this; that all things are by and from the Hand of Heaven.

38:26 – לֹא־נְתַתִּיהָ לְשֵׁלָה בְנִי

"...I did not give her to *Shelah*..."

In the end, *Yehudah* redeemed *Tamar* (through *Yibum*), and *Tamar* caused *Yehudah*'s redemption, and from their union will come the Redeemer.

39:6 – כִּי אִם־הַלֶּחֶם

"...except the bread..."

Rashi suggests that this is a euphemism to his wife, but the Torah uses "clean" language.

39:6 – וַיְהִי יוֹסֵף יְפֵה־תֹאַר וִיפֵה מַרְאֶה

"...*Yosef* was of beautiful form ..."

He began to eat and drink well, and curl his hair, teaches Rashi. HaShem said, "You're father is in mourning and you are curling your hair!" With that He incited the "bear" against him, as it states, "So it was after these things..."

39:8 – וַיְמָאֵן |

"He refused ..."

The *ta'amim* [musical notation or cantillation trope that are traditionally used when reciting verses from the Torah] suggest that even though he refused, it was a struggle for him, for he was sorely tempted.

39:9 – וְחָטָאתִי לֵאלֹהִים

"...and sin against God ..."

All of the descendents of *NoaH* (that is, all of humanity) are forbidden to engage in illicit relationships.

39:11 – וַיָּבֹא הַבַּיְתָה לַעֲשׂוֹת מְלַאכְתּוֹ

"...when he went into the house to do his work ..."

Masekhet Sota [37] teaches that there is a disagreement between Rav and Shmuel regarding what the work was. One says it was actual work, while the other says that he had tired and was intending to succumb to her, however, as he approached her, he saw an image of his father and resisted.

40:8 – הֲלוֹא לֵאלֹהִים֙ פִּתְרֹנִ֔ים

"Do not interpretations belong to God?"

In other words, they are not a random event but a sublime truth that can be discerned.

40:13 – יִשָּׂ֣א פַרְעֹה֙ אֶת־רֹאשֶׁ֔ךָ

"...lift up your head ..."

Rashi tells us that this denotes counting. This same expression is used for counting the Children of Israel in the desert. Here, it suggests that when *Par`oh* counts his servants the butler will be numbered among them.

40:20 – יֹ֣ום הֻלֶּ֣דֶת אֶת־פַּרְעֹ֔ה

"...the birthday of *Par`oh* ..."

This is the only mention of a birthday celebration in Torah. Despite this, the *Ben Ish Hai* recommends that all Jews celebrate their birthdays by dressing in festive clothing and having a festive thanksgiving meal, acknowledging the gift of life that HaShem has bestowed. It is my family's tradition to do this on our birthday and on the anniversary of our *brith milah* – when we entered into the covenant of HaShem.

40:23 – וְלֹֽא־זָכַ֧ר שַֽׂר־הַמַּשְׁקִ֛ים אֶת־יֹוסֵ֖ף וַיִּשְׁכָּחֵֽהוּ

"The chief butler did not remember *Yosef*, but forgot him."

We learn from Rashi that because *Yosef* put his trust in a man, and did not trust in HaShem he was confined for an additional two years. As it is written in *Tehillim* [40:5], "Happy is the man who has made HaShem his trust, and has not turned to the arrogant." 'Arrogant' is interpreted there to mean 'the *Mitsri* [Egyptians]'.

It seems to me that this is a foreshadowing of the future when *Par`oh* forgets of *Yosef*, and all that he accomplished for Egypt. There seems to be an implicit warning that political and other worldly relationships are temporal and arbitrary. The only One Who does not forget, but remembers His people, is HaShem.

PARSHATH MIQETS

Overview

The story of *Yosef* continues. *Par`oh* has several disturbing dreams that his advisers cannot interpret. After two years, the butler remembers what *Yosef* did for him, and at the appropriate moment tells *Par`oh*. *Par`oh* has *Yosef* raised up from the pit of prison to see if he can interpret his dreams. Not only is *Yosef* able to interpret the dream, crediting HaShem with the wisdom of the interpretations, he also offers *Par`oh* concrete advise as to how to employ countermeasures against the dire predictions of the dreams. *Par`oh* is impressed with *Yosef*, and raises him up to be his viceroy, placing all of *Mitsrayim* [Egypt] in his control.

Yosef designs and executes a plan wherein he is able to preserve much of the excess produce during the years of plenty as a hedge against the years of famine. *Yosef*'s plan is successful and soon, the entire world turns to *Mitsrayim* to purchase food.

Ya`aqov begins to feel the effects of the famine in Canaan and decides to send his sons to purchase grain. *Yosef* recognizes them, but they do not recognize him. *Yosef* accuses the brothers as being spies, and demands that the brothers return to their father and return with their younger brother as proof that they are not spies. He holds *Shim`on* captive lest the brothers not return. However, when *Ya`aqov* hears this, and *Reu'ven* suggests that they return with *Binyamin*, *Ya`aqov* forbids them to do so.

Some time later, when the famine continues, and the family is short of grain again, *Ya`aqov* sends them to *Mitsrayim* again. *Yehudah* reminds his father that they may not return there without *Binyamin*. *Yehudah* offers himself, as a guarantor for *Binyamin*'s welfare, and *Ya`aqov* acquiesces.

At first they are treated as royal guest, however, *Yosef* plants a goblet in the bag of *Binyamin*, and sends his servants after them, to accuse them of theft. Upon discovering the goblet in *Binyamin*'s sack, *Yosef* declares that he should be made a bondsman, but the rest of the brothers may return to their father, "in peace." The parsha ends here, in a cliffhanger type ending, as we wait to see how the brothers will resolve this.

In Detail: *A selection of some verses of interest:*

41:1 – וַיְהִי מִקֵּץ שְׁנָתַיִם יָמִים
"It was at the end of two years..."

Yosef's liberation is delayed by two full years. Rashi suggests at the end of the last parsha that this was due to *Yosef* putting his trust in someone other than HaShem. He had asked the chief butler to remember him when he was restored to his position, and Rashi suggests that this was a sign of *Yosef* putting his trust in someone other than God.

However this is difficult for me. While everything is attributable to HaShem, it is our obligation to make an effort in this world and operate to the best of our abilities, keeping in mind that it is not our scheming that brings results, but the Will of God. Therefore, it's not that *Yosef* was necessarily at fault for telling the butler to remember him. Rashi may be hinting at the way *Yosef* asks the butler, which, can almost be seen as a lament against, and a refusal to accept his situation as "fair." It's not inappropriate to act in this world to improve our situation, but at the same time we act, we need to accept our current situation with the happiness and confidence that everything is for the good. This is the most difficult aspect of serving our Creator: moving forward, acting - doing the best we can to fulfill His Will as we understand it - and at the same time accepting, and being happy with, our current situation as that in which HaShem has determined is, at that moment, the best of all possible situations we can be in. Fulfilling serving HaShem in joy, as we are enjoined, is, to an extent, living a paradox.

In *Yosef*'s case, it was HaShem who caused the butler to forget until the most appropriate time, for had the butler remember and tried to do something two years earlier, the results might not have been the same. When *Par`oh* needed someone, that was the time to remember the "dream interpreter" in jail. The time was not right until that moment. We see another example of this with the different reactions

Reu'ven and *Yehudah* receive from *Ya`aqov* about returning to *Mitsrayim* with *Binyamin*.

Yosef obviously "needed" to spend another two years in jail. We do not know what occurred during those two years, but they definitely matured and strengthened him to the point where he would be able to meet *Par`oh*, interpret his dreams and suggest a course of action based on the interpretation.

We see a continual maturing of *Yosef*'s abilities. Initially, he had dreams but did not seem to be able to interpret them, nor did he explicitly ascribe them to God. Then we see him able to interpret the dreams of others, and further, he developed a sensitivity to the Source of those dreams. Finally, when he meets *Par`oh* he not only is able to interpret the dreams but is able to suggest an appropriate course of action based on the information in the dreams.

41:1 – וְהִנֵּה עֹמֵד עַל־הַיְאֹר

"...he was standing on *hay'or* [river]..."

This is the River Nile, says Rashi, for no other river goes by this name. The Nile is called thus because, says Rashi, the entire country is formed into man-made "*y'oraim*," [rivers], that is canals, and periodically the Nile rises into them and fills them, irrigating the country.

It is significant that *Par`oh* is standing on the River Nile in his dream (though he later, in relating the dream tactfully says that he is standing on its banks. See below.). The Nile was worshiped by the people of *Mitsrayim*, it was considered one of their gods.

Par`oh's standing on the Nile emphasizes the pagan view of life, which is that one can control and manipulate the gods. Pagan worship views the individual as the center of the universe. The Jewish view of the universe is diametrically opposed to this. HaShem is the center and the individual must bend his will to God's, even if it is contrary to the individual's own conscience.

It seems to me that this difference is illustrated subtly by comparing the dream of *Par`oh* and *Ya`aqov*'s dream of the ladder extending to Heaven. There the text reads, "And behold, HaShem stood upon him/it [28:13]." According to this understanding the "him/it" refers to *Ya`aqov*.

41:2 – יְפוֹת מַרְאֶה

"...beautiful in appearance..."

While the simple meaning is that the animals were of the finest quality, well fed and healthy, Rashi offers another possibility. He states that their being "beautiful in appearance" is a sign of the days of plenty, because it is during such times that creatures appear pleasing to each other "for the eye of one creature is not envious of his fellow."

It seems to me that there might be another way of understanding this as well. The text stresses that the animals "appeared" beautiful, yet, as we know appearances can be deceiving. All of us are experienced with the apparent beauty of a windfall only to find later that its promise was hollow. In truth, the Torah is hinting that material success can only appear beautiful, for eventually all physical beauty fades.

41:4 – וַתֹּאכַלְנָה

"They ate up..."

Rashi teaches that this is a sign that all the joy of plenty will be forgotten in the days of famine. It seems to me that the language suggests a certain urgency, as if the years of famine overtook the years of surplus without warning, as if there were an almost instantaneous transformation from one year to the next.

41:4 – וַיִּיקַץ פַּרְעֹה

"...so *Par`oh* awoke."

He awoke to the idea that there was a problem. Here, *Par`oh* simply awakens, whereas in verse seven it states, "he awoke and behold it was a dream." We see a progression of *Par`oh*'s awareness.

Why would God send *Par`oh* dreams warning him of the famine? It seems that this is in order that *Par`oh* would need *Yosef*, liberate him from prison, appoint him over *Mitsrayim* [Egypt], so that first the brothers and then the entire family of *Ya`aqov* would journey to *Mitsrayim* in fulfillment of the prophesy that HaShem told Abraham. It was necessary for *Yisrael* to go down to *Mitsrayim*. We often look at the world too simplistically, assuming that the cause and effect are only immediately realized, whereas HaShem's plan is more complex, usually leaving us to understand only after the chain of events manifests itself. Then (if at all) we look back and see how it "had to be that way."

41:7 – וְהִנֵּה חֲלֹום
"…and behold it was a dream."

And therefore it was in need of interpretation. It is possible that here, where it says that he awoke and behold, it was a dream, means that he remembered this dream. However, at the time that he awoke, in verse four, he did not remember that dream until the second one. It seems to me that the both dreams took place in the same night.

To the Western ear, the phrase, "it was a dream," will most probably be heard as, "it was only a dream," suggesting a certain dismissive nature to it as if it doesn't require much concern.

However, this is the opposite of the text's intentions. "It was a dream," demands a response by *Par`oh*. He cannot ignore it. The West's vulgar materialism does not leave any room for the unseen. This blindness prevents the Western man for recognizing HaShem's role in History and in each of our lives, and has orphaned him in a cold and sterile world.

41:8 – וַתִּפָּעֶם רוּחֹו
"…his soul was troubled…"

Bereshit Rabba tells us that there were two agitations, one being the forgetting of the dream and the second, the concealment of its interpretation.

41:8 – חַרְטֻמֵּי
"…*Harutumei*…"

Generally, this word is translated as magicians. It seems to be a Hebraicized Egyptian word. Rashi understands the word to mean literally, "those who are aroused (the root of which is "*Har*") through the bones (the Aramaic root of which is "*tam*") of the dead.

It seems to me that the word might come from a combination of the words, "*Harut*," meaning "to engrave" and the word, "*tamei*," meaning "defiled." One could understand this as the method of their pagan practice. "Engraving" is a meditative method described in *Sefer HaYitsirah*, and here, the pagan's used methods that were connected to the side of *tumah* (impure).

Or one can understand the term metaphorically, describing the magicians as those whose impurity is etched or engraved on them, meaning that the effects of their defiled practice became indelible. When one approaches the Infinite in an effort to manipulate the forces of the universe for one's own end, one contorts one's own soul beyond repair.

This explains the phenomena of paganism being revitalized in the modern era. The modern era has become more and more egocentric, and the spiritual expression of such narcissism is paganism. It is the "spiritual" side of the moral decay of the Western world.

41:8 – וְאֵין־פּוֹתֵר אוֹתָם לְפַרְעֹה
"...but no one could interpret them..."

According to Rashi, that is no one could interpret the dream to *Par`oh*'s satisfaction. *Bereshit Rabba* teaches that the magicians understood the dream to mean that *Par`oh* would have seven daughters, and he would have to bury all seven daughters. This did not ring true to *Par`oh*.

From this we learn that the dreamer understands his dream intuitively, subconsciously, and is able to identify a correct interpretation. This was hinted at with the Butler and Baker in last week's parsha. *Par`oh* recognizes the wisdom of *Yosef*'s words, for as soon as he offers an interpretation, *Par`oh* recognizes it as true.

41:14 – מִן־הַבּוֹר
"...out of the "*bor*" [pit]..."

There seems to be an allusion here to verse 37:28 wherein the merchants drew *Yosef* "out of the pit." *Yosef* is cast into "the pit" and raised out of it several times, apparently by men, but *Yosef* recognizes that it is HaShem Who is the Source of his success. There may also be a connection to his father *Ya`aqov*, who went down into the pit (*she'ol*) out of despair.

41:16 – בִּלְעָדָי אֱלֹהִים יַעֲנֶה אֶת־שְׁלוֹם פַּרְעֹה
"...It is not in me, rather God will answer..."

That is to say, that all of my abilities are a gift of God. I, without

God, am nothing but an empty vessel that God will use to answer *Par`oh*. This is not false-modesty, but rather a declaration of Truth. *Yosef*'s simple statement is a *Qidush HaShem* [Sanctification of God's Name]. From this we learn that one should not be embarrassed or shy of Truth. Even in a room full of pagans, in front of the king of the country, one who holds his life in the balance, *Yosef* declared this simple Truth. He did not hold his tongue for fear of the response.

41:17 – הִנְנִי עֹמֵד עַל־שְׂפַת הַיְאֹר
"...I was standing on the bank of the Nile..."

Earlier, the dream was explained that *Par`oh* stood on the Nile in actuality. However, according to Rashi, *Par`oh* changed this slightly, because he did not want others to hear that he was standing on what the Children of *Mitsrayim* regarded as a god.

I have difficulty understanding why this would have been a problem for the people of *Mitsrayim*. After all, *Par`oh* was also considered a god, or at least an avatar. Rather, it may have been *Yosef*'s pious declaration, which gave *Par`oh* pause. When he encountered the Truth of *Yosef*'s declaration, he became embarrassed at his naivete in thinking that he could stand on any god.

41:25 – חֲלוֹם פַּרְעֹה אֶחָד הוּא
"...the dream of *Par `oh* is one..."

That is the dream has one source, namely God. The duality of the dreams represents the multiplicity of life but the singularity of the Source. It also represents that the reality of which the dreams speak is already prepared by God and is at hand.

41:34 – וְחִמֵּשׁ אֶת־אֶרֶץ
"...and *Himesh* the land..."

Rashi interprets this word in accordance with Targum Onkelos meaning let them hasten.

I think that it may be possible that this word is related to "*Hamushim*," meaning armed. Here it might mean "to ready," or "to alert," as in "prepare and alert the land..."

Other commentators suggests that it comes from the word for five, "*Hamesh*," suggesting that the *Par`oh* take a fifth of everything from the land to store in preparation for the coming lean years.

41:35 – וְיִקְבְּצוּ אֶת־כָּל־אֹכֶל

"And let him gather food..."

Part of the solution to the dream is that the fat cows are still within the lean ones. That is, that with proper planning one can carry the years of plenty through the years of lean.

41:38 – אֲשֶׁר רוּחַ אֱלֹהִים בּוֹ

"...in whom rest the Spirit of God..."

Or HaHayyim points out that this was a unique phenomenon for *Par`oh*, that they would be unable to find such a man, either amongst them or outside of their circles. The Rashbam suggests that *Par`oh* means by this, "one who can interpret dreams and is wise in the ways of the world."

It is my experience, that even those who are very distance from Torah and God still recognize, intuitively, His messengers.

41:39 – אַחֲרֵי הוֹדִיעַ אֱלֹהִים אוֹתְךָ אֶת־כָּל־זֹאת אֵין־נָבוֹן וְחָכָם כָּמוֹךָ

"After God has caused you to know all this there isn't one as modest and wise as you."

Or HaHayyim points out that *Par`oh* recognizes that not only is *Yosef* wise and modest, but he also has the Spirit of God within him, and therefore there isn't a more suitable candidate. In other words, real wisdom is from God.

The Rambam teaches [*Hilkhot Melakhim* 1:7], that when one is confronted with a choice for a leader (or by extension any role of responsibility) and there is one candidate who is an expert in his field but lacks Fear of Heaven, and another who possess Fear of Heaven but lacks expertise or ability, one is obligated to appoint (or elect) the one who possesses Fear of Heaven, for expertise can be taught but recognition of HaShem cannot.

One who fears Heaven will base his decisions on what is good and best, on what is in keeping with the universal absolute truths of the universe. One who does not have fear of heaven will ultimately make decisions based primarily on what is good and best for his position and prestige. Woe to the nation that chooses leaders who do not fear

God.

41:40 – אַתָּה תִּהְיֶה עַל־בֵּיתִי

"You shall be over my house..."

Yosef is first a steward in someone's home, then he is the steward of the prison, and now he is the steward of the land of *Mitsrayim*.

Yosef demonstrates an clear recognition of God's Hand in everything and the true role of man in the world.

It seems to me that there may be a hint here that, like *Yosef*, we are not really in possession of anything, it is all God's. Instead we are simply stewards, the custodians of the King's possessions.

Further, this is the role of a true Jewish leader, in particular the king, whom HaShem gives to sit over His people Israel. His role is to "manage" and "sustain" and sustain the people in the name of the King of Kings, and therefore is ultimately subordinate to Him, just as *Yosef*, despite his role, his still subordinate to *Par`oh*.

This is the role of the *MashiaH ben Yosef*, the steward who prepares the way for the final redemption. It is my opinion, with the help of Heaven, that in our generation there have been several *Tsadiqim* who have represented this aspect of *MashiaH ben Yosef*. There needs to be several because the People Yisrael are so scattered, that there needs to be a 'steward' for each of the various congregations. It is striking that *Hakhamim* (Rabbis) as disparate as *Hakham* Yosef Hayyim [the *Ben Ish Hai*], Ribbi NaHman of Breslov, the Gaon of Vilna, The *Hida*, the *Ba`al HaTanya*, and others all had similar messages about the keys to the the redemption. May we merit its actualization soon.

41:40 – יִשַּׁק כָּל־עַמִּי

"...all my people will be *yisaq* [ruled]..."

Targum Onkelos renders this as "all my people will be sustained." There is a correlation between being sustained and being ruled, for the true role of a good ruler is the providing of sustenance and guidance for his people.

41:43 – אַבְרֵךְ
"...avrekh..."

This can mean, "bow the knee," in other words, when he appeared people would announce him so that people would be able to bow before him out of respect. The Targum Onkelos renders it as "father" or "counselor" [*av*] of the king [*rakh* in Aramaic].

The Midrash interprets it differently. Ribbi Yehuda suggests, "He was a father/elder [*av*] in wisdom, though tender [*rakh*] in age." Ribbi Yosi *ben Durmas'qit* disagrees strongly saying that the word means only, "knees," that everyone entered and went out by his permission (bending the knee, so to speak).

Today, the term is used for a married full-time student of Torah who has not yet reached the level of *"Talmid Hakham* [student of wisdom]."

41:44 – אֶת־יָדֹו וְאֶת־רַגְלֹו
"...his hand or foot..."

Targum Onkelos translates this as meaning that no man shall raise his hand to wear a sword, or his foot to ride a horse. It seems to me that both the hand and foot are symbols of man's independence and therefore is suggesting that everyone was under *Yosef*'s complete control. As a sustainer of the nation, their lives depended upon him. This is analogous to our relationship to God, wherein we see ourselves as independent, yet every action we take, and every direction we travel depends, in reality, upon the Grace of HaShem.

One can compare this to the anointing of the *kohanim* [priests] of *Yisrael.* They are anointed by placing a drop of blood and oil on the their thumb and large toe, along with their ear lobe (for the ability to listen).

41:45 – צָפְנַת פַּעְנֵחַ
"...Tsaphenath pa`ne'aH..."

Rashi suggests that the name means, "he that explains hidden things." However, as Rashi and Ramban point out, *pa`n'aH* is not found in any form anywhere else in the *Tanakh.* Ibn Ezra suggests that it might be an Egyptian word.

41:45 – פּוֹטִי פֶרַע
"...Poti fera'..."

Rashi, based on *Masekhet Sota* [13a], tells us that this is *Potifar* (whom *Yosef* originally served) but he was called *"fera"* which means to un-man because he later emasculated himself, because he desired *Yosef* for sodomy. Ramban adds that he was embarrassed by this and therefore entered into the service of pagan worship as a priest. Others understand his emasculation to have taken place long before he met *Yosef*. His daughter *Osnat* therefore would have been adopted. The Midrash teaches that she was the daughter of *Dinah* and *Shkhem*, who was abandoned after the entire episode.

41:45 – כֹּהֵן אֹן
"...priest of *On*..."

This is the Egyptian sun god.

41:48-49 – וַיִּקְבֹּץ אֶת־כָּל־אֹכֶל | ... כִּי־אֵין מִסְפָּר
"He gathered up all the food...for it was without number."

It seems to me that this might be a metaphor for the *MashiaH*, who will gather the Jews from every city, and bring us into *Yisrael*.

41:50 – בְּטֶרֶם תָּבוֹא שְׁנַת הָרָעָב
"...before the year of the famine came..."

Masekhet Ta`anit [11a] tells us that it is from this verse that we learn that a man is forbidden to have relations during years of famine.

41:55 – וַתִּרְעַב כָּל־אֶרֶץ מִצְרַיִם
"All of the land of *Mitsrayim* was famished..."

At first it seems curious that the rest of *Mitsrayim* did not prepare itself for the famine that was to come. I would have assume that news of *Par`oh*'s dream and its interpretation would have been widespread, motivating everyone to take similar actions. Rashi answers this difficulty teaching that all the grain that the people stored rotted. Only *Yosef*'s remained intact.

41:56 – וַיִּשְׁבֹּר

"...he *(Yosef) wayishbor* [sold]..."

The word "*wayishbor*" is an interesting word. Rashi says it denotes both selling and purchasing. Its root means to break up (and sell).

However, my teacher taught me an interesting nuance to the word. For the root, "*seber*," with the letter שׂ "*sin*" as opposed to the letter שׁ "*shin*" as the initial letter, means, "hope." [It should be noted that the difference between the two letters involves the moving of a simple dot from the right to the left of the letter.] In the text of the Torah, the letters of the text are unmarked, so it is impossible to distinguish between the letters "*shin*" and "*sin*."]

Moreover, the tribe of *Yosef*'s son, *Efraim*, will be distinguished as being unable to differentiate phonetically between the *shin* and the *sin* [*Shoftim* 12:6]. *Yosef* provides hope in the face of disaster, hints the text. So to, in the end of days, the *MashiaH ben Yosef* (the predecessor to *MashiaH ben Dawidh*) will provide hope to the world at its darkest hour.

Further, in the next verse, "And all the earth came towards *Mitsrayim* 'lishbor E-l *Yosef* ...'" This phrase is traditionally translated as "came to *Yosef* to buy (corn)." However, to do that requires one to understand the words in a different order than that rendered. If we ignore the markings [which aren't in the Torah but are part of the Masoretic tradition], the text could read, "And all the earth came towards *Mitsrayim* [which means Egypt but literally means the place of narrowness/distress] to hope in the God [the word E-l, depending on how it is rendered can be the preposition "to" or a name for God] of *Yosef* because the hunger was strong in all the earth." This too, says my teacher, is a hint of the end of days, when all the word will be hungry for knowledge, they will turn and hope in the God of *Yosef*."

42:3 – וַיֵּרְדוּ אֲחֵי־יוֹסֵף עֲשָׂרָה

"*Yosef*'s ten brothers went down ..."

It is strange that the brother's are called "*Yosef*'s brothers," and not "*Ya`aqov*'s sons." Rashi tells us that we learn from this that they repented of selling him and were determined to ransom their brother *Yosef* at any price, for they knew that he had been sold into *Mitsrayim*. In other words they now saw themselves as his brothers, and were determined to redeem him and correct their sin.

However, it seems to me that their repentance is not complete, for we see they only waited for a convenient opportunity to embark on the mission. Since they were already going to *Mitsrayim*, they would try and redeem him, however, all the years hence, they did not interrupt their lives to seek their brother. Only when *Yehudah* stands opposite *Yosef* and offers himself in place of *Binyamin* is the repentance truly achieved.

42:7 – וַיִּתְנַכֵּר אֲלֵיהֶם

"...made himself strange to them ..."

Rashi says that this was done by speaking roughly to them, for this was foreign to the sons of *Ya`aqov*.

42:8 – וַיַּכֵּר יוֹסֵף אֶת־אֶחָיו וְהֵם לֹא הִכִּרֻהוּ

"*Yosef* recognized his brothers, but they did not recognize him ..."

Rashi brings *Masekhet Ketubot* [27b] which says that this is due to the fact that *Yosef* was without a beard when they left him, and his brothers had full beards.

Yet, it seems to me that *Yosef* only thinks that he recognizes his brothers, that is, that they are the same men who sold him into servitude. He will discover that this is not true, that they (especially *Yehudah*) have repented of the crime, and are not the same brothers of his youth.

There is also an echo here, of *Yaaqov*'s recognizing the coat of splendor and *Yehudah* recognizing the pledge he left with *Tamar*.

42:9 – וַיִּזְכֹּר יוֹסֵף אֵת הַחֲלֹמוֹת

"*Yosef* remembered the dreams ..."

It seems to me, that here we see proof that everything *Yosef* did, he did for the sake of Heaven. He remembered "the dreams", but not "the pit", nor that the brothers sold him to *Mitsrayim* (Egypt). In other words, his actions now are not done out of a sense of vengence or revenge for the way his brother's treated him, but rather to bring to fulfillment the vision of the dreams. It is important to note, that according to the Torah, prophecy is not simple a vision of future events, but includes signs and portends that demand action on our part to bring those visions to fruition. Thus, we saw throughout the story of our father, Abraham, as well as with *YitsHaq* and *Ya'aqov*, who all acted in order to fulfill the Promise which HaShem promised them.

42:9 – מְרַגְּלִים אַתֶּם

"...you are spies ..."

The brothers had accused *Yosef* of being a spy; for he had been a talebearer, bring evil reports to his father.

42:9 – אֶת־עֶרְוַת הָאָרֶץ

"...the nakedness of the land ..."

That is the exposed parts, the areas of weakness that they might be able to invade. Another interpretation is that this peculiar choice of word exposes that the essence of *Mitsrayim* was its licentiousness.

42:13 – שְׁנֵים עָשָׂר עֲבָדֶיךָ אַחִים | אֲנַחְנוּ . . . וְהָאֶחָד אֵינֶנּוּ

"...twelve brothers ...and one who is not."

Bereshith Rabba explains that they were accused of being spies because they each entered through a different gate. They explain that they did so because of the "brother who was not." They said that they had spread throughout the city in search of him.

42:14 – אֲשֶׁר דִּבַּרְתִּי אֲלֵכֶם

"...That is what I said..."

Soforno understands that *Yosef* claims here that "the one who is not" went back to make a report. That is, *Yosef* uses the vagueness of the brothers' statement against them.

Though it seems to me that he might be hinting at the "game." He says it is because of "that one," the "one that is not" that I am accusing you of being spies. In other words, I am accusing you of being spies because you sold that one – me – to *Mitsrayim*.

42:21 – אֲבָל

"...*aval* ..."

Targum Onkelos renders the word, "in truth." They presented

themselves as honest men, but they know their guilt. *Yosef* is trying to determine, if in fact they have become upright, which paradoxically means, they would have to acknowledge their guilt.

42:23 – וְהֵם֙ לֹ֣א יָ֣דְע֔וּ כִּ֥י שֹׁמֵ֖עַ יוֹסֵ֑ף כִּ֥י הַמֵּלִ֖יץ בֵּינֹתָֽם
"They didn't know that *Yosef* understood them, for there was an interpreter between them ..."

Yosef used an interpreter when the brothers spoke with him, so that he could further conceal his identity, and so that the brothers would not know that he understood their language when they spoke amongst themselves. Rashi tells us that the interpreter was *Yosef*'s son *Menashe*h.

42:24 – אֶת־שִׁמְעֽוֹן
"...Shim`on ..."

Bereshit Rabba tells us that *Shim`on* was the one chosen for it was he who threw *Yosef* into the pit, and it was he who said, "Behold, the dreamer comes."

However, it seems to me that there is also a subtle connection to his name, which comes from the word "to hear." In naming him, *Leah* announced that because God had seen that she was hated, He had given her a son [29:33]. Through *Shim`on*'s captivity, *Yosef*'s father, *Ya`aqov* will come to hear that *Yosef* was hated. Further, through the unity that the brothers show during the ordeal, and their repentance, *Yosef* will come to "hear" and understand that he is no longer hated by them.

42:24 – וַיֶּאֱסֹ֥ר אֹת֖וֹ לְעֵינֵיהֶֽם
"...before their eyes ..."

According to *Bereshith Rabba*, *Yosef* only had *Shim`on* bound before their eyes, but afterward, he released him and gave him food and drink.

42:36 – שִׁכַּלְתֶּ֑ם
"...shikaltem ..."

That is, rendered me childless, bereaved.

42:36 – יוֹסֵף אֵינֶנּוּ וְשִׁמְעוֹן אֵינֶנּוּ
"...*Yosef* is not, and *Shim*`on ..."

Ya`aqov* repeats their phrase for *Yosef*, and uses the same expression for *Shim*`on*. Does this suggest that *Ya*`aqov* understands the nature of *Yosef* being "not?" Further, *Ya*`aqov* seems to be accusing the sons of being responsible for *Yosef*, just as they are for *Shim*`on*.

42:38 – לֹא־יֵרֵד בְּנִי עִמָּכֶם
"He said, 'My son shall not go down with you ..."

Bereshith Rabba teaches that *Ya*`aqov* did not accept the words of *Reu'ven*, for his words seemed foolish, for one's grandchildren are like one's own children. How could he suggest that *Ya*`aqov* kill them? Further, it seems to me, the statement is so extreme that it echoes a false zealousness. Either it was insincerely delivered, or *Reu'ven* demonstrated an insensitivity to his own children, that would make him insensitive to his father's loss. *Yehudah*, on the other hand, will identify with his father's bereavement, for he too has lost children. Therefore, *Ya*`aqov* accepts *Yehudah*'s word. This demonstrates that a leader must know how to identify with others in order to communicate effectively and sincerely.

43:2 – וַיְהִי כַּאֲשֶׁר כִּלּוּ לֶאֱכֹל אֶת־הַשֶּׁבֶר
"...when they had eaten the grain ..."

The Midrash points out that *Yehudah* wisely waited until the situation became critical again, so that his father would have to worry about the lives of all his children, including *Binyamin*. A true leader knows not only how to act but when to act.

43:6 – וַיֹּאמֶר יִשְׂרָאֵל
"*Yisrael* said ..."

I have tried to understand when and why the Torah uses the name "*Ya*`aqov*" and when "*Yisrael*." There seems to be a general sense that when *Ya*`aqov* acts, particular in a way that leads towards the destiny of the Jewish people, he is called *Yisrael*. Therefore, it seems that here the emergence from the tragedy of *Yosef*'s disappearance begins, even if *Ya*`aqov* himself is unaware of it, for he recognizes that he must now act, and he does, bearing the name, "*Yisrael*."

43:9 – אָנֹכִי אֶעֶרְבֶנּוּ מִיָּדִי

"I will be his guarantor..."

Yehudah says, essential the same thing as *Re'uben*, but because his words are not wild and scary (for what man would slaughter his own grandchildren), they bring *Ya`aqov* comfort. *Ya`aqov* recognizes the responsibility of the pledge.

Also, *Yehudah* has demonstrated his faithfulness to redeeming his pledge with *Tamar*. He has proven himself a faithful guarantor.

43:9 – וְחָטָאתִי לְךָ כָּל־הַיָּמִים

"...I shall have sinned against you all the days."

Rashi teaches that the phrase "*kol hayamim*" includes also the World to Come.

43:11 – קְחוּ מִזִּמְרַת הָאָרֶץ

"...take of the choice fruits ..."

It is interesting to note that all of these gifts, where the listed wares of the *Midiyan* merchants whom *Yosef* was sold to. Also, it seems to me that *Ya`aqov* is making similar preparations for his children's encounter with their brother as he made with his brother *`Esaw*. He prepares a gift, evokes prayer to HaShem, and subtly tells them, if all else fails, to be prepared for war (in the next verse where he tells them to "take" their brother).

43:14 – וְשִׁלַּח לָכֶם אֶת־אֲחִיכֶם אַחֵר

"...that he may release to you your other brother ..."

Bereshit Rabba suggests that *Ya`aqov* was touched by Divine Inspiration, for the word "other" seems to be superfluous. Therefore, it suggests that "brother" designates "*Shim`on*" and "other" designates "*Yosef*."

43:23 – אֱלֹהֵיכֶם וֵאלֹהֵי אֲבִיכֶם

"...your God and the God of your fathers..."

Rashi understands this as "Either through your merits or through the merits of your fathers, God has rewarded you."

43:33 – וַיִּתְמְהוּ הָאֲנָשִׁים אִישׁ אֶל־רֵעֵהוּ

"…and the men marveled one with the other."

According to *Bereshit Rabba Yosef* did this using a cup, suggesting that he was able to divine their birthright.

44:9 – אֲשֶׁר יִמָּצֵא אִתּוֹ מֵעֲבָדֶיךָ וָמֵת

"With whomever it be found …"

This is reminiscent of the oath that *Ya`aqov* made to *Lavan* concerning that which *RaHel* had taken. *Yosef* immediately mitigates it.

44:10 – גַּם־עַתָּה כְדִבְרֵיכֶם כֶּן־הוּא

"…and now, therefore it shall be according to your words …"

That is, despite that according to your words, everyone should be held accountable for the act of one of the brothers, only the one with whom the goblet is found will be made a bondsman.

44:14 – וַיָּבֹא יְהוּדָה וְאֶחָיו

"*Yehudah* and his brothers came …"

Yehudah is listed at the head, for he had taken the lead and had promised to be a guarantor for *Binyamin*.

44:17 – וְאַתֶּם עֲלוּ לְשָׁלוֹם אֶל־אֲבִיכֶם

"…but you, go up in peace to your father …"

This is filled with irony, for how could they return to their father, "in peace," without the beloved son. *Yosef* has placed the test before his brothers to see if they truly have done *tshuvah* [repentance]. In a sense, it seems to me that *Yosef* is asking them how they were able to "go up in peace" to their father after they had sold him into bondage.

HANUKAH STUDY

The laws of the *Hanukah* lights are found in the chapter '*B'mah Madliqim*' (*Gemara* Tractate Shabbath). The conclusion of the Gemara is that all oils (fuels) and all wicks are fit for lighting the *Hanukah* lights. At the same time, it also establishes that the appropriate measure of fuel must be sufficient for the lights to remain lit for a half an hour. Also, the time of lighting the lights is from the setting of the sun until "*kila regel min ha shuq*", an expression whose literal meaning suggest that time when everyone (every foot) has left the marketplace. Further, the sages establish that the *mitswah* of the *Hanukah* lights is minimally one light per household. Only after detailing all if the laws of *Hanukah* does the *Gemara* bring the story of the miracle of the flask of oil that took place when the *Hashmona'im* (Hasmoneans) liberated the *Beth HaMiqdah* (the Holy Temple) from the Pagan Greek forces. This well known story relates that when the *Hashmona'im* liberated the Beth HaMiqdash (Temple) from the Greeks, they found only one flask of unpolluted oil. The flask contained oil that was only sufficient to light the Menorah for one day, but miraculously lasted eight, enough time to allow them to replenish the supply from nearby Tekoa.

On the surface, the laws of *Hanukah* are perplexing, and require thorough examination. For example, it is incumbent upon us to understand why we are allowed to light the lights with oils and wicks that don't present a clear bright flame. Further, why are we obligated to light at a time when the sky is only beginning to darken? And why it is important to light in, or adjacent to the public domain?

It would seem reasonable and logical that for the purpose of publicizing the miracle (Shabbat, folio 23b), that we should need to be scrupulous concerning the quality of the oils, insuring that they feed the wicks consistently and cleanly, and that the wicks would provide clear bright light. Further, one would expect that the time that the lights need to remain lit would be long, in order to provide maximum recognition and exposure to the public at large. We also need to ask why the time of lighting is from sundown, for even though the lights will be seen during twilight, they would certainly be more recognizable, if they were lit after nightfall, when the lights will be more distinct against the night sky.

Moreover, we need to understand why the *mitswah* is specifically incumbent on each household, and not each person in Israel. Is there any other *mitswah*, other than *Hanukah* that has such a designation? In addition, we need to understand why the *Hanukah* light needs to be placed at the entrance to one's home, so that it is recognizable as to which household the light belongs. We need to explore why the light needs to be on the left side of the entrance, facing the *mezuzah* on the right side of the entrance, as well as all the other very specific details of this *mitswah*.

No study would be complete if we didn't explore the subtleties and source for the difference of opinion between the House of Shammai and the House of Hillel concerning the most splendorous and majestic way of embellishing the *mitswah*. According to the House of Shammai, the greatest way to adorn the *mitswah* would be to light eight lights on the first night, and diminish a light each successive night, so that on the last night of the festival, one would light only one *Hanukah* light. On the other hand, we are all familiar with the House of Hillel's adornment, where we begin the festival by lighting one light, and add a light each successive night, until we finally light eight lights on the last night. Both of these opinions, however, beg the question, why wouldn't it be considered an even greater adornment if we were to light eight lights all eight nights?

In my humble opinion, it seems to me, that the key to understanding all the various details of the laws of *Hanukah* lights will come to light if we delve into the basis for this disagreement between the House of Hillel and the House of Shammai. As is well know, in every disagreement between these two schools of Talmudic thought, both opinons are considered "the very words of the Living God" (Babylonian Talmud, Tractate Eruvin, folio 13b).

The sages, in their discussion of the adornment of the *mitswah* (Shabbath, folio 21b), provide a clue. They teach us that the the source for the House of Shamai's adornment is Temple offerings of the Sukkoth Festival, while the House of Hillel relies on the axiom that one increases in holiness, and not decrease.

And yet, both reasons flow from the same source and root: the Holiday of Sukkoth. As we know, the *Kohen Gadol* (the High Priest) Yo*H*anan the son of

Hanukah Study

Matatiyahu established and arranged the Festival of *Hanukah* and the lighting of the lights based on the fact that the Nation of Israel was unable to celebrate the holiday of Sukkoth at its appointed time because of the war with the Greeks (as brought by the Arukh HaShul*H*an, Section Ora*H* Hayyim, Section 671, paragraph 2, according to Maccabees II, 10:6-7). In fact, we learn that the first celebration of the Festival of *Hanukah* was celebrated with the four species of Sukkoth. For subsequent generations, Yo*H*anan established the lights to remember the miracle.

It's also clear that there is a direct link to the inner esoteric meaning of *Hannukah* with the inner esoteric meaning of the Festival of Sukkoth, and in particular the special holiday on the eighth day upon Sukkoth's conclusion, Shemini *Hag* ha'Atseret, which serves as a model for the last day of *Hanukah* known as *Zoth* (this is) *Hanukah*. (Incidentally, we are also given insight as to why today, we need to 'enwrap' this important joyous festival, Shemini *Hag* ha'Atseret, in the rabbinical cloak of Sim*Hath* Torah. See my study on the holiday of Sukkoth for an in-depth exploration of this deep concept).

The Holy Zohar (parsha Tetsaweh, folio 187a) sheds some much needed light on the connection. It teaches that an essential component of the offerings of Sukkoth is to prevent the destructive external forces from draining and suckling the tremendous light -- blessing and abundance -- that Israel receives during Shemini *Hag* ha'Atseret.

It states:

"And further, all of them are called Sukkoth in their fullness [that is when it is written in its long form, סוכות, with the letter *waw*]. And when they are written in their shortened form סכות [without the letter *waw*], this indicates the lower world, that requires these seven holy days to nourish the great appointed ones on the other nations (that is the source of spiritual nourishment for the seventy nations), and prevents them from diminishing the happiness she (Israel) enjoys from and with her 'husband' (The Holy One), In order to confuse and redirect these forces from the main source of spiritual nourishment, their offerings (those in the name of the other nation) is significantly greater from other times of the year, so that they will focus on them, and not become involved afterwords with happiness and joy of Israel., which is Shemini *Hag* ha'Atseret."

"Come and see, while these other appointed ones (of the seventy nations) enjoy and consume the nourishment that Israel prepares for them, they prepare and repair the throne for the Holy One below, and raise it up above through the species, and their joy and praise and their encircling of the mizbea*H* (altar), then she goes up and receives blessing and happiness from her husband."

"Meanwhile the remaining Forces who are Anointed on the Nations consume and devour and feed. And she (the Holy Presence) embraces the souls in pleasure above, as is said. Because she descends and embraces all of the blessings and all the holiness and all the pleasures. And for those seven days, Israel draws her near through their actions which they perform -- they draw her (the Holy Presence) close. Therefore she descends and embraces her children and rejoices with them for one day. And that day is the eighth day (Shemini *Hag* ha'Atseret), because all of the other seven days are included within it. Therefore it is the eighth, and all eight days are as one. Therefore it is called 'Atseret, that is gathered and joined, for they are all gathered together into this one day. And, it is called 'Eighth', for there is no eighth except inclusive with the seven."

Thus, it seems to me in my humble opinion, that this is also the underlying purpose of the Joy of the Drawing of the Water, when the sages and righteous would sing and dance every night of the Sukkoth holiday while the floor of the Courtyard was washed with water drawn from the spring. These festivities, it seems to me, were also designed to distract and confuse the external forces so that they would focus on the seven days of Sukkoth, and not draw their attention the Eight day, so as not to drain the abundance and blessing designated for Israel.

To our great distress, the *Beth HaMiqdash* was destroyed, and therefore we are unable to offer an abundance of offerings in order to confuse, distract and deter those external destructive forces. Thus, there is a continual danger that they will drain the blessing of abundance that is designated for Israel.

This may be the key to understand the underlying principle of the Festival of *Hanukah*, and why the Kohen Gadol Yo*H*anan established for each household to light the *Hanukah* lights in order to publicize the miracle.

One needs to understand that in lighting the *Hanukah* lights, we are in effect redeeming and conveying the Light that fell into the Husk, which is called the 'Public Domain', and draw that Light toward every home in Israel, which is designated as 'Private Domain', and represents the realm of Redemption. Since, we unfortunately are currently bereft of the *Beth HaMiqdash*, we are left, each of us, with just the four *amoth* (cubits) of our Private Domain, each to his own, of redemption.

We can now see how the underlying reason of Beth Hillel and Beth Shammai are essentially the same. Both of them represent the concept of redeeming the sparks of Holy Light that fell into the Husk of External Destructive

Forces, and to deflect the Appointed Ones of the Nations of the World from suckling and depleting the bounty that is designated for Israel.

According to the teachings of the Holy Ari, z"l, as well as our teacher, the Rash"ash, may their merit guard, the essential purpose of lighting the *Hanukah* lights is not to bring light **to** the public domain, but rather to bring light **from** the public domain towards the home. We see this explicitly in the practice of lighting the first light furthest from the entrance, and each day lighting the new light closer and closer to the home's entrance. This would be in accordance with both Beth Hillel and Beth Shamai.

We know, that in the language of our Sages, the Marketplace, as well as the Public Domain are expressions designating the Husk, and the three lower worlds of '*BiYA*', the world of Exile. On the other hand, the home is designated as Private Domain, representing the supernal world of *Atsiluth*, which represent Redemption. The entrance to the home represents the three lower *sefiroth* (sub-domains) of *netsaH*, *hod* and *yesod* which receive the bounty from above.

Through our sins, and the destruction of the *Beth HaMiqdash* (Temple), this 'doorway', which is in the shape of the Hebrew letter *Het*, fwll into the Husk. The left jamb which represents the *sefirah* of *hod* fell to a depth of eleven 'egg' measures, which, not coincidentally is the measure for the amount of oil used in the *Hanukah* light. When we light the *Hanukah* lights, we elevate the Light, the two drops, represented by the letters of *yod* and *hey*, from the holy name of טטפפי"ה, that fell into the Public Domain, and redeem them to the Private Domain, to their place in holiness.

The Time of Lighting

We learn from the esoteric texts, that it is impossible to elevate this Light that fell into the Husk during the daytime. This is because daytime is under the rule of holiness, and one can't descend into the Husk at a time time of full Light to bring up these two small Lights that fell. Likewise, during the nighttime, we do not have the power and strength to free these Lights from the hold of the destructive external forces.

Therefore, the only time that it is possible to elevate these Lights that fell is at the time of dusk, from sundown until a half an hour into the twilight. At that time both the bounty of holiness diminishes, allowing us to descend, while at the same time the external forces have only begun to take hold, and they haven't reach the fullness of their strength. At that time it is possible to elevate those two drops of Light, and return them to the left leg, the left jamb of the doorway, returning them to the world of *Atsiluth*. Each night we redeem a small amount of the Light that fell, until the eighth day of *Hanukah*, *Zoth* Hanukah. This models the *Hashmona'im* who upon redeeming the *Beth HaMiqdash*, divided that one jar of oil into eight measures, lighting an eighth each of the eight nights (Beth Yosef).

According to the *Pri Ets Hayyim* (*Sha'ar* Hanukah, chapter four), "Know that we light them (the lights) with the setting of the sun, because this is the quality of night, and it thus descends to the worlds of *BiYA* to "provide its 'prey' to her house and law to her youth," (*Kohelet*) We then draw that Light upward. One should note that the language of 'with the setting of the sun', is the same language that the Rambam uses to designate the time of lighting.

It seems to me, that the intention of the Maran, Beth Yosef, in his Shul*H*an Arukh when he wrote "the end of sunset" was to be specific to the time when the ball of the sun dips below the horizon, and not like those who hold that the time of lighting is at the beginning of the setting of the sun, that is, when the sun begins to descend in the sky towards the horizon.

Tiqun-Reparation of the Sefirah of Hod,
The Left Jamb of the Home's Entrance,
Which Represents the Partsuf of Nuqbah

Even though, as is known, the *Sefira* of *NetsaH* (the right jamb of the 'doorway') also became blemished, it was restored and redeemed through the efforts of Mordekhai and Esther. As a result of the miracle of Purim, *NetsaH* was elevated to its rightful place. It returned to function with increased intensity that led to the rebuilding of the (second) *Beth HaMiqdash*. However, while the *Sefira* of *Hod* began to be repaired a step at a time, each stage was beset by faltering. The first stage in its reparation began with our patriarch Ya'aqov, in his return to the Land of Israel from his sojourn with *Lavan*. The Torah hints to this when it describes Ya'aqov returning for the small jars, which represent the Lights of *Hod* that fell into the Husk. But, as we know, the "man", the spiritual protector of Esaw, prevented this elevation of Light. Again, this is hinted at in the verse, "And the 'man' wrestled with him, and injured Yaaqov's hip joint". The hip joint of the left thigh, represents the *Sefira* of *Hod*.

Afterwords, at the time of the erecting of the *Mishqan* (Tabernacle), the tribal leaders rectified the *Sefira* of *Hod* through their offerings. Yet, even though they were successful in elevating the Lights of *Hod* to their proper place, their success was not complete, because the Holy One delayed the erection of the *Mishqan* to the month of Nisan, even though its construction was completed on the 25th of the month of Kislev (the date of *Hanukah*). The reason for the delay was because if the dedication of the Holy *Mishqan* was in the month of Kislev (that is, during the winter months), then if Israel would sin in the future, then the Holy One would have to pour out His Wrath on His People Israel. Instead of the stones and wood of the building. Therefore to mitigate this, the dedication of the *Mishqan* was delayed until the spring/summer month of Nissan. According to the esoteric understanding, the summer months represent the quality of impermanence. Thus, if Israel fell into sin, as they ultimately did, the Holy One would pour out His Wrath on the stones and wood of the building. This, as we know, resulted in the eventual destruction of the *Beth HaMiqdash* (the Temple), but the nation itself survived.

The *sefirah* of *Hod* was further rectified through the efforts of *Elqanah* and *Hanah*, but this too was delayed, because the *Miqdash* was not yet built. Though their son, *Shmu'el*, who was on par with Moshe and Aharon, wanted to restore the *sefirah* of *Hod*, it did not come to pass through his hand, because the *Miqdash* wasn't built in his lifetime to replace the *Mishqan*.

The continuation of the reparation was supposed to be in the next generations, those of *Dawid* and *Shlomo*, but was instead delayed until the time of the *Hashmona'im*. They, in their war with the Greeks and the Hellenists, were were able to affect a major rectification, and eight out of ten levels of the *Sefirah* were restored, but the last two remaining levels, that of *yesod* and *malkhuth* (of the *Sefirah* of *Hod*) were not redeemed. because the *Hashmona'im*, who were a priestly family, took the kingship unto themselves, and did not restore the temporal leadership to the tribes of *Yosef* and *Yehudah*, which represent those levels respectively. Since they refused to restore the Davidic Dynasty, it fell to latter generations to elevate those two levels, which are hinted at through the letters *yod* and *hey*, two drops from the holy name of טפטפי"ה of *Hod*, and return them to their proper place.

This is the reason, according the Sages of Blessed Memory, as to why there isn't a scroll for the festival *Hanukah* (that is, *Hanukah* doesn't have a sanctioned canonical writing, and is not included in the Hebrew Bible), but only one for Purim. In the language of the *Gemara* (*Yoma* folio 29a): Why is Esther compared to the dawn? Just as the dawn represents the conclusion of the night, so too Esther represents the culmination of all the miracles. What about *Hanukah*? asks the *Gemara*, which was several years later. It answers that Purim was the last miracle of which permission was granted to commit to (sanctioned and sanctified -- canonical) writing.

Hanukah Study

As we discussed, the miracle of Purim completed the rectification of the *Sefira* of *NetsaH* (the right jamb of the entrance way). Therefore the Sages of Blessed Memory dedicated an entire Tractate to the Festival of Purim, the Tractate of *Megillah*. But, the Festival of *Hanukah* does not have its own Tractate, because its rectification is not yet complete (and not for the reason that some have suggested. Namely, that Ribbi Yehudah HaNasi took issue with the *Hashmona'm* for not restoring the Davidic Dynasty, of which he is descended from).

Essentially, what we are doing when we light the *Hanukah* lights is to return the Light from the Public Domain and restore it to the Private Domain, not to light up the streets of the public domain. Therefore, the very lighting of the lights fulfills the *mitswah*, even if the oils and wicks don't create a brilliant flame, and if only for a brief time. Even with fuels and wicks that are not fit for Shabbath lights, we fulfill the *mitswah* of Hanukah.

For Shabbath, the main reason for Shabbath lights is not the act of kindling, but that the home be well lit, which symbolize the peace of the home, and represents the unification of the of the *partsuf* of *zu"n* in the world of *Atsilut*. However, the essential purpose of the *mitswah* of lighting the Hanukah lights, is the act of lighting itself, and not necessarily the resulting light.

When *Hanukah* falls on Shabbath, one needs to elevate the 'foot' from the 'marketplace' (that left leg or jamb of the entrance-way) before the additional time of accepting Shabbath, because at the moment of the additional time of Shabbath, all the worlds rise several levels, and the holiness that is submerged in the Husk also rises.

Therefore one who normally accepts Shabbath from the time of *plag haMinHah* (approximately an hour and a quarter before sunset) in accordance with Ribbi Yehudah, one must light the *Hanukah* lights, a half an hour beforehand, to represent the elevation of the *Sefira* of *Hod*, as discussed above. Then, at the beginning of Shabbath, all of the worlds rise up with the *Hod*, that also continues to rise up. Through this, it is given additional strength to elevate even more so. Thus, according to the *Rash"ash*, of blessed memory (page 40 of his book *Nahar Shalom*), one need not be particular in adding enough oil in order for the lights to remain lit a half an hour after sunset, because the essential aspect of the *mitswah* isn't the light, but the lighting. However, in any case it is meritorious to insure that there is sufficient oil, initially, that the lights remain lit until a half an hour after sunset.

At the conclusion of Shabbat, the obligation to light the Hanukah lights begins from the recitation of the verse, *"Wayhi no'am,"* whose purpose is to return the worlds to their original place (carrying with them the sanctity of Shabbath). At this moment, the obligation to light begins, because the *sefira* of *Hod* returns to the Husk below, and through lighting the Hanukah lights we elevate it again. Therefore, lighting doesn't depend on sunset at the conclusion of Shabbath, but rather the prayer service of *'Arvit*. In this too, one need not be especially particular about the amount of time the light remain lit, because, as we know, the holiness of Shabbath continues until midnight.

Each of the eight days of *Hanukah*, our service is to elevate and return the various and specific aspects of the *sefira* of *Hod*. This is represented in the blessing through the different vowelization of HaShem's Name which we visualize at the time of recitation. The letters *yod* and *waw* of HaShem's name are vowelized with the vowelization that represent the specific *sefira* of *Hod*, while the two letters of *hay* are vowelized with the vowelization for the *sefira* of *Hod* itself. Some *siddur'im* (prayer books) which represent *kawanoth* meditations reflect this, and this is explained at length in various books of the *Qabbalah*. It is an easy reflection for one to focus on during the lighting, and goes as follows: First night – יְהֹוָה, second night – יְהֹוָה, third night – יְהֹוָה fourth night – יְהֹוָה, fifth night – יְהֹוָה, six night – יוֹהֹוָה, seventh night – יוֹהֹוֹוהֹוֹ, and the eighth night – יְהֹוָֹה.

On *Zoth* Hanukah, that is the last night of *Hanukah*, we also have an additional service, to enlighten the Light of the two remaining main *Sefiroth*, those of *Yesod* and *Malkhut*, which the *Hashmona'im* failed to redeem. We do this so that they will eventually have the strength to be elevated and redeemed. Therefore many righteous individuals throughout the generations are accustomed to dress in festive whites at the time of the lighting the *Hanukah* lights, and remain awake the entire last night, learning in order to awaken these two rectifications represented by the qualities of *notser* and *naqeh*, and the *sefiroth* of *yesod* and *malkhut*.

The Place of the *H*anukah Light

The chapter *B'mah Madliqim* (in Tractate Shabbath, 21b) states: "The rabbis teach that the *mitswah* of the Hanukah light is to place it (them) at the entrance to one's home, from the outside, but if one resides above ground level, on an higher story, one should place it in the window that opens to the public domain. We've already examined the the concept of bringing light from the public domain towards the home, which represents the redemption of the Lights of *Hod* from the Husk to the realm of holiness.

Hanukah Study

The *Sha'ar HaKawanoth*, in the section concerning *Hanukah*, teaches that one should follow the instructions for lighting the lights, as instructed in the Beth Yosef's commentary on the Turim, and its compendium, the Shul*H*an Arukh. However, the version of text in the Shul*H*an Arukh that is brought in the *Sha'ar HaKawanoth* is slightly different from the version in our current published copies of Shul*H*an Arukh.

This is the language of the *Sha'ar HaKawanoth*: "Therefor on the first night, one should light the first light from the right, which is the furthest from the entrance from the other seven lights. On the second night, one lights the second light, which is closer to the entrance from the first, and afterwords, turn to his right and light the first light. One should continue in this manner for the remaining nights until we find that on the last night one lights the light on the left side, the light which is the closest to and adjacent to the entrance, beginning with it and turning to the right side, the closest one from previously, and then this proceeds until the first light of all of them, is on the far right, is lit last on the last night."

This version, of the Ari, *z"l*, in the *Sha'ar HaKawanoth* has the additional expressions: "the most distant from the entrance," and "the one that is closest to the entrance from the first light". Also, it explains that on the last night, one lights the light that is "closest and adjacent to the entrance." This version has caused many difficulties for later authorities, such as the Gaon, Hakham Yosef Hayyim, of blessed memory (the Ben Ish Hai), that according to his own words is forced to interpret the Ar"i, *z"l*'s description of lighting the lights from within the home. But this is difficult, because we know explicitly that the essential performance of the *mitswah*, initially, requires the lights to be lit outside the home, adjacent to the public domain.

However, in my humble opinion, it seems that the true solution to the apparent difficulty, is that the intention of the Ar"i, *z"l* (and the Master Shul*H*an Arukh as well), requires us to set up the lights perpendicular to the entrance to the home, and not parallel. In discussing this solution with my teacher, he agreed that my interpretation seems to answer the difficulty, except that due to our living in the exile, he, himself, was accustomed to lighting from withing the home, as described in the Ben Ish Hai. Further, he testified that even when he lived in Jerusalem, everyone was accustomed to light within the home, due to the hatred of the non Jewish population. Thus, even though he agreed that theoretically, my explanation fit well with the description, and solved the apparent difficulty, he cautioned that we don't have an actual tradition to rely on.

However, later, I saw that Rabbi Yehudah Getz, *z"l*, and his students, do light the *Hanukah* lights in this manner. It thus seems to me that it is the one method that encompasses both the words of the Ar"i *z"l* and the Shul*H*an Arukh. Further, it clearly represents the esoteric meaning perfectly of conveying the Light of *Hod* from the public domain, the Husk, to the entrance of the home. Therefore, here is how I suggest it should be performed:

One should set the lights up on the left side of the entrance, a hands-breadth adjacent to it. One should set up the lights perpendicular to the entrance. When one lights the lights, one should stand on the left side of the entrance, facing the *mezuzah* with the lights between him and the entrance and the *mezuzah*. Thus, the lights will be in a line from the public domain towards the entrance of the home.

On the first night, one lights the light furthest from the entrance, and on the second night one lights the light closer to the entrance first, and then turns to his right to light the light that he had previously lit the night before. This process continues until the eighth night when one lights the light closest to the entrance, the newest light, and then turns to his right to light the other earlier lights. See the following illustration:

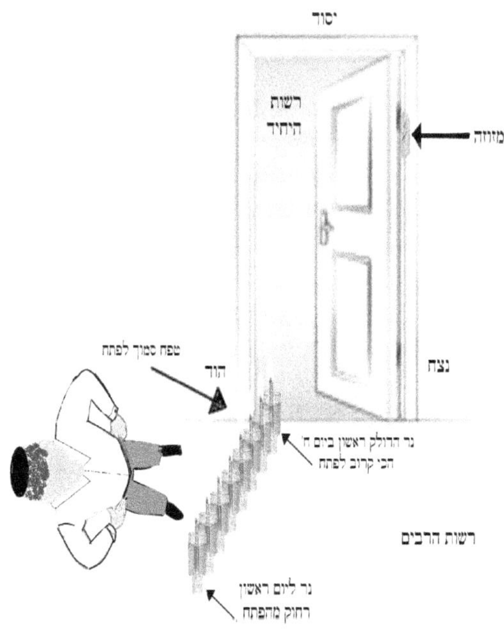

And all of this is correct when one's home (or his private courtyard) opens to the public domain, because, as we discussed, the point is to symbolize the bringing of the Lights of *Hod* to the home. And this is the language of both the *Gemara* and the Shul*H*an Arukh: "The Hanukah light should be set at the entrance to one's home adjacent to the public domain, from the outside. If one's home is adjacent to the public realm, set it at the home's entrance, if one has a courtyard before one's home, set it at the entrance to the courtyard."

However if one doesn't have a private home or courtyard adjacent to the public domain, then this method is not relevant, Therefore, the *halakhah* continues: "If one lives on above ground level (on the second (or more) floor, and thus one doesn't have an entrance to the public domain, place the lights in a window adjacent to the public domain. And in a time of danger, when one can't safely fulfill the *mitswah* this way, place the lights on one's table (within the home) and this is sufficient."

So, today, when most people don't have a private home, but live in an apartment building, one can't place the lights in the public domain, that is outside the building, because then it would be impossible to recognize each light for each home. Therefore, one should place outside the entrance to one's apartment, using the public space of the building as the public domain, and draw the Light towards the home. This is especially true if there are other residents who would pass by the apartment.

Yet, if it is impossible to place the lights at the entrance to the apartment, then one should place them in the window that faces the public sphere. And if this is still not possible, one can place the lights inside, next to the entrance to the home, as described by the Ben Ish Hai (Year One, Laws of Hanukah, #4).

And, as the language of the Gemara says, this will be sufficient, because the root and principle of the *mitswah* of the Hanukah Light is as we have learned. There is Light that is designated for Israel, and it is our role and responsibility to redeem them from the external forces, and prevent those forces from draining the bounty and blessing. The *Gemara* relates (Shabbath 21b): "If a camel carrying flax passes through the public domain, and the shopkeeper sets his *H*anukah light outside his shop, and the flax ignites and sets everything aflame, the shopkeeper is exempt (from damages)." This emphasizes the importance of elevating these sparks that shoot out from beneath the hammer.

There is a very esoteric understanding of this passage in the *Gemara*, because the *gematria* (numerical equivalent) of the word for the shopkeeper (חנוני) is equal to the name Yo*H*anan, who of course was the High Priest. This is also the *gematria* for the expression "הודו ליהוה כי טוב *Hodu L'Shem Ki Tov*" that is, "Give thanks to HaShem for He is good," Further, the camel represents the sefira of *Hod*, (see the Holy Zohar, parshat *Way'Hi*, folio 214a), and flax is the material used for the uniform of the priest, for which the Hebrew expression is the *gematria* 89 (Hanukah), while spark equals the numerical equivalent of the word for shield, and both of them are the holy sparks that shoot out from beneath the hammer, the Hebrew word for which represents the four hundred men of *'Esaw*, that is the Husk, and the gematria of Hanukah (89) is equal to the holy name of the lights that fell into the Husk,

It is sufficient, because through the performance of the *mitswah* of the Hanukah lights we fulfill the verse (Ovadia 1:18): "And the House of Ya'aqov will be a fire, and the House of Yosef a flame, and the House of 'Esaw will be as straw set aflame and consumed; and there will be no remnants of the House of 'Esaw, because HaShem has spoken." Gd Willing, the Holy One will return the Light of the Holy Presence to His Home, the Beth HaMiqdah. May it be rebuilt, soon and in our day. Amen.

PARSHATH WAYIGASH

Overview

Our parsha begins at the climax of last week's parsha. *Yosef* (still unknown to the brothers) has just declared that *Binyamin* must stay as an indentured servant, but the other brothers can return to their father in peace.

At this point, *Yehudah* steps forward. He is clearly agitated with the games, and he confronts this viceroy of *Par`oh*. He tells him that *Binyamin* is in his charge and offers himself in place of *Binyamin*, while at the same time complaining of their treatment and the obvious manipulation at his hand. *Yosef* is unable to restrain himself and reveals himself to the brothers.

Yosef reveals himself, but tells them not to worry. It is clear that it was HaShem's plan that *Yosef* should be sent to *Mitsrayim* so that the family might survive the famine. He has the means to provide for their sustenance. With *Par`oh*'s approval, *Yosef* sends the brothers back to *Ya`aqov* in order that the entire family might come to *Mitsrayim* during the famine.

The brothers return to their father, who is overwhelmed at the news. He, at first doesn't believe it but is convinced through a message *Yosef* sends, reminding *Ya`aqov* of the last subject that they had been studying together before his disappearance.

The family descends into *Mitsrayim* [Egypt], stopping in *Beersheba* where *Ya`aqov* offers an offering to HaShem. He receives permission to continue to *Mitsrayim*, and a promise that HaShem will return him to the land.

Ya`aqov* is reunited with *Yosef*, and is introduced to *Par`oh. The family settles in the land of *Goshen*, which is prime land for their flocks.

The famine continues to devastate the world. The people of *Mitsrayim* come to *Yosef* to buy food. However, the first year they use up all their money, so they must trade their cattle and horses, and such for food in the next year. In the year following, having nothing left, they sell their land and themselves as bondsmen to *Yosef* (for *Par`oh*) in exchange for food. *Yosef* decrees that one fifth of all their labors are to be paid to *Par`oh* as a tax in subsequent years. Only the lands of the pagan priests are not touched, as *Par`oh* regularly apportioned them food, so they had no need to sell themselves.

In Detail: *A selection of some verses of interest:*

44:18 – וַיִּגַּשׁ אֵלָיו יְהוּדָה

***"Wayigash elaw Yehudah…[Yehudah* drew near to him]"**

According to *Bereshith Rabbah* [93:6], the word, "*wayigash*" has been used in three different contexts throughout the *Tanakh*. It has meant "to console [*Yohoshua* 14:6]," "to do battle [II *Shmuel* 10:13]," and "to pray [I *M'lekhim* 18:36]."

It is striking that these three concepts reflect both *Ya`aqov*'s approach to *`Esaw* [32:4-26] and his advise to *Yehudah* when he (*Ya`aqov*) gave permission to take *Binyamin* to *Mitsrayim* [43:11-13 - see my explanation in the previous parsha concerning the expression "take your brother…"]. There seems to be a valuable message here about the preparation one should take before approaching one's adversary. One should never limit one's approach, but be able to attack a situation from several angles, each one both complete in its own right and complimenting the other options. A good leader is never stymied when one avenue is closed, because he has already prepared several different approaches.

Further, there seems to be another subtlety hidden within these verses. Most commentators, and it is apparent from the text itself, comment about the similarity between *Yosef*'s story and *Ya`aqov*'s. Both men had conflict with their (older) brother(s), both are forced to journey outside *Erets Yisrael*, both are successful in their adopted home, and so on.

Yet, it seems to me, there is another parallel hidden within the verses, that between *Ya`aqov*'s journey, and his son *Yehudah*'s. It is not as readily apparent as that of *Yosef* and his father, but, in some sense, I believe it may be deeper and truer.

Parshath Wayigash

Like *Ya`aqov*, *Yehudah* instigates a deception of his father that is
ostensibly over who is (or should be) the favored child. The
deception, interestingly, is carried out, in both instances through the
vehicle of a goat (*Ya`aqov* uses the goat's hair to deceive his father;
Yehudah (leading the brothers) slaughters a goat and uses the blood to
deceive his father). The goat, it should be noted, carries with it
tremendous symbolism, including that of atonement. Because of this
deception, both men enter into self-imposed exile from the family,
and it is in that exile that their actions come back to haunt them. They
are made painfully aware, through the agency of outsiders, of the
effect of their own actions. At some point, both men return from
their exile (now with a family), and are forced to confront, not only
their past deeds, but also the brother who was the focus of those
actions, and both prepare for any eventual outcome of that
confrontation.

It is at that confrontation, or immediately preceding it, that both
Yehudah and his father meet themselves. One explanation of *Ya`aqov*'s
wrestling with the angel was that he was wrestling with himself, or
that in wrestling with him he also encountered and realized his true
self.

One understanding of "*Wayigash elaw Yehudah*," is that in the act of
confronting *Yosef*, *Yehudah* met himself, that is, he mad a complete and
total repentance for his previous actions. This interpretation of
Yehudah's action has support. *Itture Torah* translates "*wayigash Yehudah*"
as "*Yehudah* drew near" and it answers the question of to whom, with
"to himself." [Vol. I, p. 389]. *Yehudah* drew near to himself and met
himself. He realized who he was, and what he had done.

Another hint is revealed in the *gematria* [the numerical equivalent of
the words] of "*wayigash aylaw*" which is equal to three hundred and
ninety-three. This value can be written with the letters *yod, peh, gimmel,*
and *shin*, spelling the word, "*Yifgash*," "he meets." This would render
the verse simply, "He meets (or will meet) *Yehudah*." *Yehudah*, through
repentance comes to meet himself, and in doing so allows *Yosef* to
reveal his true identity in return.

According to Saadiya Gaon, one does not fully do *tshuvah*
(repentance/return) until one finds oneself in the same position that
caused the sin in the first place, and is able to act differently. *Yehudah*,
displaying no jealousy or envy for an obviously favored younger
brother, *Binyamin*, redeems him, and does not allow him to be taken

away from his father. *Yehudah* has accomplished true *tshuvah*. Even though he had been poised on the point of *tshuvah* since his promise to his father, it was not until this moment that it became truly effective. Thus, he was able to genuinely "go up," his status rising in the eyes of HaShem.

Yehudah usurped the leadership from his older brother *Reu'ven*. *Ya`aqov* receives the inheritance instead of `*Esaw*. Both of them tried to gain the leadership, originally, through their own cunning, which led to their further estrangement from their goal. Yet, both realized that leadership and gained the blessing, when they were able to rise to the challenge confronting them and act with full knowledge of who they were, and what needed to be done.

Yosef and *Yehudah* will both wear the crown of *Yisrael*. *Yosef*'s crown will be the first and the most apparent. Yet, *Yehudah*'s crown, may be more subtle, but it is a subtleness that runs much deeper and has more permanence.

I heard a teaching in the name of Rabbi Shlomo Carlebach. In the End of Days, there will be two Anointed Kings in *Yisrael*, first the *MashiaH ben Yosef*, who is destined to make us aware that there is a problem; that there is something wrong with the way we are living. While this is an essential part of healing, and redemption, it is not an end in itself. It is the *MashiaH ben* David (who comes from *Yehudah*), who will then come to teach us how to fix that which is broken.

44:18 – וַיִּגַּשׁ אֵלָיו יְהוּדָה

"*Wayigash elaw Yehudah...*[*Yehudah* drew near to him]"

The *Ba`Al HaTurim* points out that the *gematria* [numerical equivalent] of this phrase is equal to the *gematria* of the phrase "*zehu l'haleHem `im Yosef*," "This one is to battle with *Yosef*."

In recent times, many people have seen the establishment of the State of Israel as the "*MashiaH ben Yosef*," [Messiah son of *Yosef*]. This idea is difficult for religious Jews to accept, as the modern State of Israel is a far cry from the promised restoration of a Torah oriented Kingdom, a return to fully living under HaShem's rule, which includes the rebuilding of the *Beth HaMiqdash* [The Holy Temple], and the restoration of the Sanhedrin as the court of the land.

It might be possible to resolve this dichotomy, if we understand that

Redemption comes in stages. According to the Vilna Gaon, he represents the first, physical, stage of redemption, whereas the *MashiaH ben Dawidh* [Messiah son of David] represents the later spiritual and final stage of redemption. In fact, I've heard from Rabbi Yoel Shwartz that the *gematria* of *Tsionuth* [Zionism] is the same as *MashiaH ben Yosef* (556).

This would make the revelation by the *Ba`Al HaTurim*, all the more significant. It suggests a battle for the souls of the nation between the bankrupt values of Secular Zionism (which at its core is a rejection of HaShem and His Torah) and the Torah values of the religious community of Israel.

We could compare this with the first redemption, where the nation of Yisrael is physically redeemed from *Mitsrayim* [Egypt], before making the journey to Sinai and receiving the Torah, allowing for their spiritual redemption.

44:18 – וְאַל־יִחַר אַפְּךָ בְּעַבְדֶּךָ
"...and not let your anger burn..."

Rashi teaches us that from this, we learn that *Yehudah* spoke harshly to *Yosef.*

44:18 – כִּי כָמוֹךָ כְּפַרְעֹה
"...for you are like *Par`oh* ..."

The simple meaning, as Rashi teaches, is that *Yosef* had the power of *Par`oh*, and this is of course discernible from the earlier text itself.

Bereshit Rabba, however, understands this to mean one of several other possibilities. The first, that just as *Par`oh* was smitten with leprosy, because he held Sarah captive for one night, so will *Yosef* become smitten if he holds *Binyamin*.

Another interpretation is that *Yehudah* is hinting that, if *Yosef* provokes him, not only will he kill him, but also he intends to destroy *Par`oh* as well.

44:20 – וְאָחִיו מֵת
"...and his brother is dead ..."

Rashi explains that due to the fear of *Yosef*'s request, a false statement issued from his mouth. This should be contrasted when they told *Yosef* earlier, that their brother "was not."

44:22 – וָמֵת
"...and die..."

The language is somewhat ambiguous here, and the subject of the verse could be either *Ya`aqov* or *Binyamin*. That is, if he (*Binyamin*) leaves his father, then it will cause his father "to die." This doesn't necessary have to be a literal death, but one similar, or even greater that the "death" that *Ya`aqov* suffered at the loss of his son *Yosef.*

Or, as Rashi suggests, the brothers worried that *Binyamin* might die while traveling, because this is how his mother died. Rashi seems to assume that since this idea is brought out later, that here, *Yehudah* must be referring to *Binyamin*.

44:28 – אַךְ טָרֹף טֹרָף
"...he was devoured by beasts..."

Yosef seems to be waiting for this very statement. Through *Yehudah*'s telling of the events, *Yosef* learns that his father believes him to be dead, and that this has caused him much grief. It should be noted that *Yosef* did not know that the brothers told their father that he had been killed. Rather, it is possible that *Yosef* believed that his father had abandoned him, or that he was a part of the betrayal. This might explain why *Yosef* persisted in this ruse, not to test to brothers but to "rescue" his younger brother *Binyamin* (his only full brother) from the rest of the family and protect him.

44:32 – כִּי עַבְדְּךָ עָרַב אֶת־הַנַּעַר מֵעִם אָבִי
"For your servant became a guarantor for the youth to my father ..."

Thus, the story comes full circle, just as *Yehudah* was the one who suggested the sale of *Yosef,* here, he informs *Yosef* that he has sold himself as a guarantee for *Binyamin*. This is repentance at its purest form. When *Yosef* hears this he realizes that he does not need to be the protector of *Binyamin*.

44:34 – כִּי־אֵיךְ אֶעֱלֶה אֶל־אָבִי

"For how can I return to my father ..."

Yosef suggested that they return to their father "in peace." *Yehudah* informs him that this is not possible. They are not the same brothers who were able to return "in peace" to their father after their sale of *Yosef* into slavery.

45:2 – וַיִּשְׁמְעוּ מִצְרַיִם . . . בֵּית פַּרְעֹה

"And Egypt will hear ... and the House of Par'oh"

From this we can understand that the *Mitsrayim* (Egypt) and the House of *Par'oh* are written as if they are two separate entities. We see a similar distinction sometimes within the 'People of Yisrael,' which is a term that includes those from the other nations of the world who joined and cast their lot with the House of Yisrael. This would include the 'mixed multitude' that leaves Egypt with Yisrael, and those *ger'im* (converts) who will later cling to the God of Yisrael. This seems to be the meaning of Rashi's interpretation of the verse. It seems that in *Mitsray'im* there was a class of landowners, which were the ruling class, and the people of *Mitsray'im*, which included a broad spectrum of statuses. So too, in Yisrael, where there exists the Children of Yisrael, each of whom have a an ancestral holding as an inheritance, and the rest of the People, which included converts, residents, and others. In this we can better understand the important *mitswah* of loving the *ger*, a term that we usually translate as convert, but whose root comes from that of resident. That is to say, an outsider who becomes a resident of Yisrael. We are commanded to "love" the *ger*, as we are to love the orphan and the widow, because these statuses haven't and source of support and livelihood (they don't have an ancestral plot of land as an inheritance), like *Bney* (the Children of) Yisrael. This is elucidated further when we understand the root the word for 'love' (*ahavah*) comes from the root *hav*, meaning "to give". The essential aspect of loving the *ger*, is to sustain him or her, providing sustenance. This helps us to understand the Torah's continual reminder of this important *mitswah*, and that we, Yisrael, were not citizens, but *ger'im* in *Mitsray'im*, relying on the benevolence of the ruling class the House of *Par'oh*, which was severely lacking.

45:3 – הַעוֹד אָבִי חָי

"...does my father still live?"

This seems to me be a very curious question, considering that throughout the episode, the brothers have continually told *Yosef* of their elderly father. Sforno suggests that *Yosef* is asking how his father did not die from worry over *Yosef*'s well being. Kli Yaqar teaches that one possibility for the question is that *Yosef* thought they might have evoked the "elderly father" to gain sympathy from him.

Neither of these explanations satisfies me. It might be that instead of asking if his father is still alive, *Yosef* is declaring that his father "will yet live." This in itself can have a number of meanings. The literal meaning would suggest that because, I am *Yosef* and I am in charge of the food distribution you needn't worry about survival — my father will yet live. Another possibility is that it might be a reflection of *Ya`aqov*'s descent into depression, and spiritual/emotional death. Now that *Yosef* has revealed himself, he tells the brothers, my father can live again.

Another possibility might be a reflection of Ya'aqov descent into sadness, and his concern of Sheol. Now, that Yosef revealed himself, he tells his brothers, "My father can live again." This seems to be the understanding of my great great grandfather, Hakham Avraham Dayan, z"l, who writes, that the entire time that Yosef was lost and missing, Ya'aqov mourned him, and therefore was unable to receive *RuaH haQodesh* (prophetic insight). But, now, says Yosef, his spirit will return and the Holy Presence will once again rest upon him.

This follows the Holy Zohar [Parshat *WayHi*, page 216b] which states that it is written 'all his days,' and not his life, because when he saw his son as a king, and his sons pure and righteous, everyone enjoying the delicacies of the world, with him sitting among them like a good wine sits among guardians. Only then do we read "*WayiHi* Ya'aqov." Because only then does "My father yet live."

Yosef uses the personal pronoun "my" in describing their father, and not "our." This might be another clue into the verse's meaning. If we assume, as is logical, that *Yosef* did not know how his father related to his disappearance, the question takes on an atmosphere of renewed hope. *Yosef* exclaims, "Does *my* father still live?" That is, does he still relate to me as a father. In other words, *Yosef* gives voice to the anxiety that he has felt over the last twenty-two years that it seemed to him that his father had at best abandoned him or, at worst, was a part of the conspiracy that sold him into slavery.

45:3 – נִבְהֲלוּ מִפָּנָיו

"...they were afraid before him/it..."

Rashi teaches that this is due to their shame. However, I think that there are other possible meanings as well. They may have been afraid of him (*Yosef*), and what his reaction might be, and what his motivations were for revealing the matter. Also one could understand the verse that they were afraid of it, that is there past actions. It was now coming back to haunt them, so to speak.

45:4 – גְּשׁוּ־נָא אֵלַי

"...come near..."

This is the same word used to describe *Yehudah*'s action in the beginning of the parsha. There it was ambiguous, meaning possibly three different actions (or the potential for all three). Here, it clearly is used in the context of conciliation and rapprochement.

45:5 – שְׁלָחַנִי אֱלֹהִים לִפְנֵיכֶם

"...God sent me before you."

Yosef recognizes, again, that all solutions belong to HaShem, and that upon reflection, everything that happened had to happen the way it happened.

45:7 – לִפְלֵיטָה גְּדֹלָה

"...for a greater deliverance."

That is the exodus from *Mitsrayim* [Egypt] in the time of *Moshe Rabbeinu*. Just as *Yosef* recognizes that his enslavement was necessary in order to sustain and deliver his family from the famine, so to is *Yisrael*'s enslavement in *Mitsrayim* necessary for them to develop into a nation, which will become a light unto the entire world, sustaining and delivering it.

45:8 – לְאָב לְפַרְעֹה

"...a father to *Par'oh*..."

As in, an adviser or a teacher. This term is used often for prophets in the latter books, and the sages are also called "father" by their students and followers.

45:12 – כִּי־פִי הַמְדַבֵּר אֲלֵיכֶם

"…that my mouth speaks to you…"

Yosef was speaking in the Holy language of Hebrew according to *Bereshith Rabba*.

45:18 – אֶת־טוּב אֶרֶץ מִצְרַיִם

"…the good of the land of *Mitsrayim*…"

Rashi teaches that this is referrring to the region *Goshen*. Yet, without realizing it, *Par`oh* prophesized that *Yisrael* will eventually carry away the best of the land when they are redeemed from *Mitsrayim*.

45:27 – אֵת כָּל־דִּבְרֵי יוֹסֵף

"…all the words of *Yosef*…"

We learn that *Yosef* gave them a sign concerning the last subject that he had learned with his father before his disappearance.

45:28 – רַב עוֹד

"…it is enough…"

Rashi teaches that this means he had much joy, and happiness left in him, for now he could rejoice. However, it seems to me that there is another possibility. *Ya`aqov* might be saying, that despite all the unanswered questions this causes, he will not investigate what occurred in the past, but will be satisfied that his son, *Yosef*, is alive.

46:1 – לֵאלֹהֵי אָבִיו יִצְחָק

"…God of *YitsHaq* …"

It is note worthy that only *YitsHaq* is mentioned and not Abraham. There are several possibilities. First, *Ya`aqov* might be using the very altar in which his father, *YitsHaq* erected. Alternatively, this might be addressing the fact that God categorically forbid *YitsHaq* from going down to *Mitsrayim*.

Rashi explains, simply, that one is obligated to honor his father more than his grandfather. Ramban, however, argues that Rashi's explanation is not sufficient. He points out several factors, which point to the idea that *Ya`aqov* needed to invoke the merit of the *Aqeidah* (the Binding of *YitsHaq*) and offer special sacrifices to insure the eventual exodus from *Mitsrayim*.

Be'er Sheva is a crucial place where both his father and grandfather had built alters and made offerings to HaShem. It is also the place where Abraham left *Erets Yisrael* to descend into *Mitsrayim* and where HaShem told *YitsHaq* not to go down to *Mitsrayim*. *Ya`aqov* needed to be assured that the Presence of God would be with them in *Mitsrayim*.

46:2 – יַעֲקֹב | יַעֲקֹב
"...Ya `aqov, Ya `aqov..."

Rashi tells us simply that the doubling of the name is a sign of endearment.

However, considering the context, I am immediately reminded of the Aqeidath *YitsHaq*, and the *malakh* [angel] calling to Abraham in the same manner. It is interesting to note that the *ta'amei-hamiqra* [the trope or musical notation that indicates how a verse is meant to be read] is the exact same as that of the *Aqeidah*. It seems to me that the text is calling our attention to that earlier incident. HaShem reminds *Ya`aqov* that He promised to make Abraham's seed a great nation, and even though he commanded him to do something contrary to the logic of the promise, it was for Abraham's merit that the command was made.

Here too, despite the fact that the family's descent into *Mitsrayim* seems contrary to the logic of establishing them as the possessors of *Erets Yisrael* (Canaan), it is a necessary step for the fulfillment of that promise.

46:4 – וְאָנֹכִי אַעַלְךָ גַם־עָלֹה
"...I will bring you up..."

This could be referring to *Ya`aqov*'s burial in *Erets Yisrael* as Rashi suggests. To me, however, it seems to be referring to the redemption from *Mitsrayim* through *Moshe*.

46:4 – וְיוֹסֵף יָשִׁית יָדוֹ עַל־עֵינֶיךָ
"...Yosef will place his hand on your eyes."

Ibn Ezra teaches that this is referring to *Ya`aqov*'s death (which might lend support too Rashi's understanding of the earlier phrase), for that it was the custom, and still is, for the survivor to close the eyes of the deceased.

Or HaHayyim suggests that this was a way of promising *Ya`aqov* that *Yosef* would not die during *Ya`aqov*'s lifetime. Also, *Or HaHayyim* says that this implies that *Ya`aqov* will not leave *Mitsrayim* and return to *Erets Yisrael* in his lifetime, but only after his death.

46:6 – אֲשֶׁ֥ר רָכְשׁ֖וּ בְּאֶ֥רֶץ כְּנַ֑עַן
"...which they had acquired in the land of Canaan ..."

This is specifically not the property that they had acquired from *Lavan*. That property, according to the Midrash, *Ya`aqov* used to purchase `*Esaw*'s portion of the burial Cave of the *Makhpelah*.

46:8 – הַבָּאִ֥ים מִצְרַ֖יְמָה
"...who come into *Mitsrayim*..."

Rashi notes that the verb is in the present tense. He suggests that it is because Torah is speaking from the point of time when they actually descended to *Mitsrayim*. *S'ftei Hakhamim* points out a difficulty with this saying that the Torah was written down by *Moshe Rabbeinu*, and at that time, it was already past.

It seems to me that in a metaphorical sense, we are always in a continual process of going "down to *Mitsrayim*," literally to a "narrow place," and then, God Willing, being redeemed from that place. Our lives of full of spiritual lows and peaks, descents that give us the impetus to rise even higher. As our sages say, a righteous one falls seven times, only in order to rise.

46:10 – וְשָׁא֖וּל בֶּן־הַֽכְּנַעֲנִֽית
"...Sha'ul the son of the *K'na'anith* ..."

Why does the Torah call him the son of the *K'na'anith* (Canaanite)? Rashi has difficulty with this, himself, so he brings the Midrash [B'reshith Raba 80:11], which teaches that he is the son of *Dina*, the daughter of *Ya'aqov*, who was raped by *Sh'khem*, who a *K'nanni*. After *Sh'khem* was killed and *Dina* liberated, she didn't want to leave the city until *Shim'on* swore an oath that he would marry her. Therefore, the isn't actually *Shim'on* real son.

This Midrash is difficult on several levels. First, if he's *Dina*'s son, why would he be called the son of the *K'na'anith* which refers to the female

K'na'ani. Rather he should be called the son of the *K'na'ani* (male Canaanite), because *Dina* isn't the *K'na'anith* in the story, but *Shkhem* is. One can resolve this, based on the general rule that the wife goes after her husband's tribe and custom. This is the way we do practice today, but only during the lifetime (or duration of the marriage) of the husband. However, the moment she returns to her father's house, she returns to her father's custom. Even more so here, if *Shim'on* married her. (Of course, this theoretical supposition wouldn't apply, in reality to our case, because *Dina* was taken by force, and more so by a Pagan. And if we want to content that *Sh'khem* converted, and legally married *Dina* per the agreement with the brothers, then he would have left the designation as a *K'na'ani*, becoming a member of Ya'aqov's household as a *ger* (convert).

Of course this begs the question, as to how *Shim'on* could have married *Dina*, since she is his sister both from their mother and their father, a relationship that is forbidden even to *Beney NoaH*. (all the decedents of Noah are forbidden to marry their maternal sister).

Further, this contradicts another Midrash which teaches that *Osnath* the daughter of *Poti Par'a*, whom Yosef marries, is in fact Dina. After she was liberated from *Shkhem* she left and went down to *Mitsrayim*. and was adopted by *Poti Par'a* [Perqe d' Ribi Eli'ezer, Chapter 38, Masekhet Sofrim 21:9, and also see Rabeinu *BaH'ye* and *Hisquni*, who bring this story i the name of the Midrash].

In short, this explanation is difficult.

It seems to me, that we might be able to understand that he really was the son if of a *K'na'anith*. For, did we not in fact, we see that Yehudah married the daughter of a *K'na'an* [38:2]. It might be that before the receiving of the Torah at Sinai, there wasn't a prohibition to marry the daughters of the *K'na'anim*, even for those who hold that the descendents of *Avraham Avinu* already left the status of *Bney NoaH*, from the time that he underwent circumcision. Further proof of this, comes from *Avraham* himself, who, albeit preferred to marry his son to a woman from the family in Haran, if the woman was not willing to follow *Eli'ezer* to the Land of Yisrael, he would be free from the oath, and presumably, *YitsHaq* would marry a *K'na'anit* [24:2-8]. It also seems to me that at that time, there wasn't any prohibition to receive *gerim* (converts) before *Y'hoshu'a*'s conquest. All of this demands further study.

46:15 – כָּל־נֶפֶשׁ בָּנָיו וּבְנוֹתָיו שְׁלֹשִׁים וְשָׁלֹשׁ

"...all the souls of his sons and daughters were thirty-three ..."

Yet, as Rashi points out, upon counting, we arrive at the number thirty-two. The Midrash explains that *Yokheved* (*Moshe*'s mother) was born to *Lewi* between the ramparts as they entered the city.

Ibn Ezra suggests another solution, that *Ya`aqov* is the thirty-third individual in the counting. Rashi's apparent difficulty with this is that this was only a listing of those children descended from *Leah*.

It is clear from verse ten, that only the males are mentioned, with the exception of *Dinah*, and *SeraH*, the daughter of *Asher*. These were exceptional women, whose personal story contributed to the story of the nation. *Dinah* is mentioned, as she is the sole daughter of *Ya`aqov*. Also her story was crucial in the unfolding saga of the *Ya`aqov*'s journey. *SeraH*, according to the Midrash, lived an extraordinarily long life (well into the time of *Dawidh HaMelekh*). She is also the one who showed *Moshe Rabbeinu* where the bones of *Yosef* lay.

It is interesting to note that King *Dawid*'s rule lasted forty years, thirty-three of those in *Yerushalayim*.

46:27 – כָּל־הַנֶּפֶשׁ לְבֵית־יַעֲקֹב

"...and all the soul(s) [*nefesh*] of the House of *Ya`aqov* ..."

Vayikra Rabba notes that regarding `*Esaw*, his descendents are referred to as "souls," using the plural, while *Ya`aqov*'s household is called "soul" in the singular. This tells us that those that descended from `*Esaw* worshipped many gods, but for the House of *Ya`aqov*, they all worshiped the One True God.

Another explanation, implicit in the first, might be that the Children of *Ya`aqov* had one purpose, and therefore, despite that there were seventy faces, they were one "soul."

There is a *sod* [a hidden message] I learned from my teacher concerning the "*sh'm`a Yisrael*" [the section of Torah which is repeated twice a day – the most well known "prayer" of even the most distant Jew from his tradition]. The word *sh'm`a* can be broken up into two words to say the "The name of the Seventy is Israel. *Shem* [the first two letters of the word] means 'name,' and the last letter, the final letter "*ayin*" of the word "*sh'm`a*" is the numerical representation of 70. It should be noted that seventy is ten times the number seven, representing completeness (refer to the Creation story).

46:28 – וְאֶת־יְהוּדָ֞ה שָׁלַ֤ח לְפָנָיו֙ אֶל־יוֹסֵ֔ף לְהוֹרֹ֥ת לְפָנָ֖יו

Yehudah was sent before him to _Yosef_ to show [_l'horoth_] (the way) before him..."

The plain meaning is that he went ahead to know where the entourage of _Ya`aqov_ should go once they entered _Mitsrayim_. According to the Midrash, however, _Yehudah_ went ahead to establish a House of Torah Study from where learning [_hora'ah_ - note the similarity of the words] would issue forth.

This is a further hint at the roles of their descendents, the future redeemers of _Yisrael_. As noted earlier, in the End of Days, after the _MashiaH ben Yosef_ make us aware of the problems facing us, _MashiaH ben Dawidh_ (who comes from _Yehudah_) will come to teach us how to fix those problems.

46:29 – וַיִּפֹּ֥ל עַל־צַוָּארָ֖יו וַיֵּ֥בְךְּ עַל־צַוָּארָ֖יו עֽוֹד

"...and he wept on his neck..."

This is _Yosef_ weeping on his father's neck. We are reminded of another scene that is both similar and inherently dissimilar, with `_Esaw_ weeping on _Ya`aqov_'s neck. There, _Ya`aqov_ is meeting his brother whom he suspects still wants to kill him; here, he is meeting his son, whom he thought was killed. There, he was returning home to the Land; here, he is going into exile. Yet, both times, _Ya`aqov_ is not the one crying, but instead, receiver of the emotional expression.

46:34 – כִּי־תוֹעֲבַ֥ת מִצְרַ֖יִם כָּל־רֹ֥עֵה צֹֽאן

"...for all shepherds are an abomination for _Mitsrayim_."

This is because, Rashi teaches, the flock animals are gods to the people of _Mitsrayim_.

47:2 – לָקַ֖ח חֲמִשָּׁ֣ה אֲנָשִׁ֑ים

"...he took five men ..."

We learn from _Bereshit Rabba_ that these were the weaker looking brothers, for he did not want _Par`oh_ to impress them into his army, or to be intimidated by their strength.

47:8 – וַיֹּאמֶר פַּרְעֹה אֶל־יַעֲקֹב כַּמָּה יְמֵי שְׁנֵי חַיֶּיךָ
***Par`oh* said to *Ya`aqov*, 'How old are you?'"**

One interpretation is that *Par`oh* though that this was Abraham, who had come to *Mitsrayim* previously. Sforno suggests that he asked because it was not common in *Mitsrayim* for one to live as old as *Ya`aqov*, and still be so active. However, *Kli Yakar* suggests that it is because *Ya`aqov* looked so old he thought he would die in a day or two.

47:9 – יְמֵי שְׁנֵי מְגוּרַי שְׁלֹשִׁים וּמְאַת שָׁנָה מְעַט וְרָעִים הָיוּ יְמֵי שְׁנֵי חַיַּי וְלֹא הִשִּׂיגוּ אֶת־יְמֵי שְׁנֵי חַיֵּי אֲבֹתַי בִּימֵי מְגוּרֵיהֶם
"…The span of my years of travels is one hundred and thirty years; few and evil have been the span of years of my life …"

I learned from my teacher that *Ya`aqov* was punished for this statement. We learn that one could expect to live, naturally, about as long as one's parents. This is why *YitsHaq* made preparations for his death, when he approached the age of his mother at the time of her death.

He, however, lived to one hundred and eighty. This is also the age that Abraham was supposed to live to, however, our sages teach that he died five years prematurely so that he would not suffer by seeing his grandson, *`Esaw*, as a "*rash`a*" [evil person] at the age of thirteen.

Ya`aqov*, thus, could have reasonably expected to live to the age of one hundred and eighty. However, *Ya`aqov lost one year for each of the words (in Hebrew) of his answer to *Par`oh*. In addition he lost a year for each one of the words of *Par`oh*'s question, for it is assumed that he asked it, because *Ya`aqov* looked and acted old. Thus *Ya`aqov* lived to only one hundred and forty, as we will see in next week's parsha.

Overview

The last parsha of the Book of *Bereshith* begins with *Ya`aqov* making prepartions before his death. He extracts a promise from his son *Yosef* to bring him to *Hebron*, to be buried in the Cave of the *Makhpela* with his fathers, Abraham and *YitsHaq.*

Ya`aqov* becomes ill and *Yosef* is informed. *Yosef* brings his two sons to visit their grandfather. *Ya`aqov gives *Yosef* a double portion by making his two sons as his own, and thus each earning an equal portion of the inheritance. *Ya`aqov* also explains to *Yosef* the circumstances behind his mother, *RaHel,* not being buried with the rest of the family in *Hebron* (*RaHel* is buried in *BethleHem*).

Ya`aqov then calls all of his sons. They gather around their father and he blesses each one of them, a blessing that carries the weight of prophecy. *Reu'ven* loses the birthright, which seems, in part to be given to *Yehudah,* while the double portion is given, creatively, to *Yosef.*

Ya`aqov dies at the age of one hundred and forty seven. All of *Mitsrayim* mourns him. *Yosef* has his father embalmed, and the brothers bring him to *Erets Yisrael* where he is buried.

Upon returning to *Mitsrayim,* the brothers, fearing a reprisal from *Yosef,* now that their father has passed away, send messages to him. This of course is an interesting parallel to the story of an enraged *`Esaw* declaring he will withhold revenge on *Ya`aqov* until after their father passes away. The message stated that it was *Ya`aqov*'s will that *Yosef* forgive the brothers. *Yosef* reassures them, and they are satisfied.

Yosef is the first brother to die. Upon his death, he tells the Children of *Yisrael* that HaShem will remember them, and return them to *Erets Yisrael.* When that occurs, *Yosef* makes them promise that they will take his bones along with them. *Yosef* then dies and is placed in a coffin in *Mitsrayim.*

In Detail: *A selection of some verses of interest:*

47:28 – וַיְחִי יַעֲקֹב

"*Ya`aqov* lived ..."

Rashi, and nearly every other commentator, asks why this parsha is completely closed -- that is why isn't there a paragraph break, as is normally the case, between this parsha and the preceding one?

We can also ask why here, after the Torah tells us that *Ya'aqov* lived it doesn't immediately follow with the number of years which he lived, as the Torah did with *Sarah* [Bereshit 23:1], or *Abraham* [25:7], or even with *YitsHaq* [35:28], writing "Theese are the days of the life of *YitsHaq.*" In fact the Torah is replete with examples. Yet, here, instead, the Torah tells us the nimber of years that *Ya'aqov* lived in *Mitsrayim* and only later, using different language concerning the approaching days of mourning for *Ya'aqov,* wherein his actual passing is much later. All of this demands an interpretation.

To our first question, that of the closed parshas, several answers are offered. *Bereshit Rabba* teaches that *Ya`aqov,* through prophesy learned when the final Redemption, that is the End of Days, would be, and desired to reveal it to his sons. HaShem, however, "closed" this to him and forbid him to reveal it. Another explanation is that when *Ya`aqov* died, the eyes and hearts of *Yisrael* were "closed" due to the beginning of the bondage which was to afflict them.

And, according to the Holy Zohar [parshath *Way'Hi* page 216b] "All of his days were not call "he lived" because all his days were filled with sorrow and distress, until he went down to *Mitsrayim,* when it says he lived, because he saw his son as a king, and his children pure and righteous, and all of them enjoying the delicacies of the world, and he was sitting among them like good wine poured on its fermentation. Then it states, "And *Ya'aqov* lived. For, indeed his father lived again.

Therefore, it seems that one way of understanding the closed nature of the parsha, is in order to connect the expression "he lived" with the seventy souls from *Ya'aqov*'s loins, because life is through one's descendents.

Also, it seems to me, another hint through the "closing" of the parsha. When the parsha is closed, the reader has difficulty finding the beginning. This act reflects, it seems to me, that parsha contains many hints about the future redemption and other hidden things, for which the careful reader must scrutinize the text.

47:28 – וַיְחִי יַעֲקֹב בְּאֶרֶץ מִצְרַיִם שְׁבַע עֶשְׂרֵה שָׁנָה
"*Ya`aqov* lived ...seventeen years..."

It is interesting to note that *Ya`aqov* lived in *Mitsrayim* [Egypt] exactly the same number of years that passed before *Yosef*, his favorite, disappeared. Seventeen is the *gematria* [numerical equivalent] of word "*tov*," meaning "good." *Ya`aqov* complained at the end of last week's parsha to *Par`oh* that his life was difficult and evil, but here we see that these difficult times were framed with goodness: Seventeen, "*tov*," years living with *Yosef* in the beginning and seventeen, "*tov*," in the end. There is a subtle message here that all life is a mixture of good and ill and only one's perspective determines it actual quality.

47:28 – וַיְהִי יְמֵי־יַעֲקֹב שְׁנֵי חַיָּיו שֶׁבַע שָׁנִים וְאַרְבָּעִים וּמְאַת שָׁנָה
"...the years of his life were seven years and one hundred and forty years ..."

We already discussed in last week's study how this was thirty three years shorter than his father's life as punishment for his words to *Par`oh*.

47:29 – שִׂים־נָא יָדְךָ תַּחַת יְרֵכִי
"...place your hand beneath my thigh ..."

As we discussed when Abraham made *Eli`ezer* swear to him, this was the manner in which oaths were taken. In lieu of the Torah, which had not yet been given (after which one would hold a Torah Scroll to make an oath), one took hold of the holy *brith milah*, and swore by it. It should be noted that the words "testify," and "testes" in English both come from the same root.

47:29 – חֶסֶד וֶאֱמֶת

"...with *Hesed w' emeth* [kindness and truth] ..."

We learn that the *Hesed* [literally nonreciprocating kindness] one shows the dead is the truest form of kindness, because one cannot gain any recompense for such service in this world.

47:29 – אַל־נָא תִקְבְּרֵנִי בְּמִצְרָיִם

"...do not bury me in *Mitsrayim* ..."

There are those that argue that since they worship the dead in *Mitsrayim*, *Ya`aqov* feared that he would be turned into an idol, especially because, as is known,the corpses of *Tsadiqim* (Righteous ones) do not decay. However, this difficult for me, because we see that Yosef performed several acts to prevent the populace from turning *Ya'aqov* into an object of worship. He even embalmed his father, knowing that he wouldn't be buried immediately. And, if this was *Ya'aqov*'s only concern, all of Yosef's efforts were sufficient. Further, at the end of the parsha, we see that Yosef himself has his brothers swear an oath that they will bring him up to Yisrael, when the nation is liberated from *Mitsrayim*.

There is special merit to being buried in *Erets Yisrael*. Those that are buried there are saved from many of the agonies of resurrection in the End of Days.

In fact, even people that do not merit living in *Yisrael*, try and make arrangements that they be buried there. Those that can't, are often buried with earth from *Erets Yisrael* to ease their return at the time of *MeHiyath hametim*, the resurrection of the dead in the final days.

Because, as the Even Ezra write: "The parsha reminds us of the superior status of the Land of *Yisrael* over all the other lands for both the living and the dead." The Gemara [Bavli, *Ketuboth* folio 111a] writes all those who are buried in the Land of *Yisrael*, it is as if they were buried under the altar, as it is written, "make for me an altar of earth." Written adjacent to this, it says: "And the earth will be atoned with him." And, in the Midrash [PesaHim A] tells us that *Ya'aqov* even used all of the property that he acquired from *Lavan* to pay *'Esaw* for his space in the *Ma'arat Makhpalah*, to insure that he would be buried in the Land of *Yisrael*.

The Virtue of Burial in the Land of Yisrael

The Midrash [Bereshit Raba 96:5] brings a disagreement between Ribbi Yehudah and the Rabbis, as to whether it is good for a resident outside the Land of *Yisrael* to be buried in the Land of *Yisrael*. It states: "In another matter: *Ya'akov* said, "The *Mitsr'im* will not redeem me. They worship the Lamb, and I ruled over the Lamb, as it says [*Yermiyahu* 50:17] *Yisrael* is a scattered sheep, and of *Mitsrayim* it says [*YeHezgel* 23:20]: "Whose whose flesh is the flesh of donkeys." And it is written [*Sh'moth* 34:20]: "The firstling of the donkey, you will redeem with a lamb."

"Please don't bury me in *Mitsrayim*. Why do all the patriarchs demand and favor being burial in the Land of *Yisrael?* Ribbi *El'Azar* say, 'things within.' Ribbi *Y'hoshu'a ben Lewi* says, 'What is 'things within?' (*Tehillim* 116:9): I will walk before HaShem in the Land of the Living. Our rabbis said two things in the name of Ribbi *Helbo*, 'Why the patriarchs favor being buried in the Land *Yisrael?* Because the dead of the Land of *Yisrael* come back to life first (the resurrection of the dead) in the days of the *MashiaH*, and eat (the fruits) in the years of the *MashiaH*."

"Ribbi Hanina says, 'One who dies outside the Land (of *Yisrael*), and is buried there, essentially goes through two deaths, as it is written [*Yermiyahu* 20:6]: 'And you, PashHur and all that live in your house, will go into captivity, and there you will die, and there you will be buried.' Woe to those that suffer two deaths. Therefore *Ya'aqov* said to *Yosef* 'Please, don't bury me in *Mitsray'm*.'"

"Ribbi Simon says, 'If so the Righteous lose out when they are buried outside the Land (of *Yisrael*). So, what does the Holy One do? He makes bulwarks in the land, and makes them like tunnels, and then they tumble through them and come until they arrive in the Land of *Yisrael*, and the Holy One restores to them a spirit of life, and they stand up. In this it is written [*Y'Hezqel* 37:12] "Behold, I open up your graves, and bring you up from the your graves, My People, and will bring you to the ground of *Yisrael*. After this [*Y'Hezqel* 37:14]: 'I will impart my Spirit in all of you, and bring you back to life.' Resh Laqish says, the text is replete with the concept that when they arrive to the Land of *Yisrael*, the Holy One bestow upon the a soul. As it says [*Y'sh'ayahu* 42:5], 'He that gives *n'shamah* (literally: breath, but also soul] to the people on it.'"

"There was an occurrence with Ribbi and Ribbi Eli'ezer when they went to Pili that is outside T'ver'ya (Tiberius), and saw a deceased person's casket. Ribbi said to Ribbi Eli'ezer, 'What is the benefit for that person, whose soul departed outside the Land (of *Yisrael*), and they bring him to be buried in the Land of *Yisrael*?' I apply to him the verse [*Yermiyahu* 2:7] 'You made my heritage an abomination' - in your lifetimes. And, 'You defiled my land' – in your deaths. He said to him, Because he will be buried in the Land of *Yisrael*, the Holy One atones for him, as it is written [*D'varim* 32:43] 'He will forgive His land and His people.'"

Rabbeinu *B'Haay* [*Beresheet* Chapter 47] explains that there are three reason why it there is virtue in being buried in the Land of *Yisrael*: 1.) The Land of *Yisrael* is holy, and atones for one's sins, as is written [*Y'sh'ayahu* 33:24]: 'The people that dwell in it, shall be forgiving their iniquity,' and it's written [*D'varim* 32:43]: 'He will forgive His land and His people.' 2.) The Land of *Yisrael* is close to Gates of Heaven, therefore there is less need or bother, and to emerge in order to return to their roots. 3.) The dead of the Land of *Yisrael* are resurrected first at the time in the Days of the *MashiaH*, but the dead of outside the land (of *Yisrael*) do not live (are not resurrected), and only th Righteous will merit to come to the Land (of *Yisrael*) through the distress of trundling through tunnels and then will rise in the resurrection as elucidated in the *Gemara* [*Ketuboth* 111a].

Due to protecting the dignity of the deceased, the opening of graves was forbidden for the purpose of transferring the bones of the deceased from place to place. Thus, it is brought in the Jerusalem Talmud: "The dead, nor the bone of the deceased, are not evacuated from a dignified grave to another disgraceful grave, nor from a disgraceful grave to a different disgraceful one, nor from a disgraceful grave to a respectable grave; And there is no need to say from the respectable grave to the disgraceful one." (Talmud *Yerushalmi*, Tractate *Mo'ed Qatan*, Chapter 2, Law 4) The commentators explain the reason for this law in two different ways: First – To prevent the degradation of the dead, that is, an injury to his dignity by being seen in a state of decay or as a skeleton and bones [*Bavli*, Tractate *Baba Batra*, foli 154b]. And the second reason is from a spiritual perspective - because moving the remains pf the dead troubles their souls, who fear the coming of the great Day of Judgment [*Kolbo*, The Laws of Mourning, as quoted in the *Beth Yosef*, *Yoreh D'eah*, *Siman* 363].

There are two situation in which it's permitted vacate the dead from their graves, as is brought in a *Barayta* [in *Bavli*, *Sanhedrin*, folio 47b]: "There are three (types of) graves: a found grave, a known grave, and a grave that causes damage to public. A found grave – can be vacated; a known grave – forbidden to vacate; and a grave which causes damage to the public – permitted to vacate." The commentators explain that a "found grave," that becomes discovered on a private field, wherein the dead was buried there without permission of the field's owner. This grave was created as an act of theft, and therefore it's permitted to vacate it. "A known grave", is defined as a grave that was established with the permission of the field's owner, and therefore it's forbidden to vacate it, even when the field changes owners. A grave that causes damage to the public is a grave that graves that creates any amount of public hazard. An example of a gave that causes public damage would be grave that is adjacent to a public thoroughfare, that passersby are apt to become *tamey* (ritual impurity) from the *tumath* (ritual impurity)of the dead due to the location of the grave. This type of grave is permitted to vacate in order to prevent the damage to the public. These laws are also established in the *ShulHan Arukh* [*ShulHan Arukh, Yoreh D'eyah,* Section 363:1; and section 364:2; and 364:5].

The *Tosefta* brings that it's permitted to vacate a grave when a city expands, and the residential area of the city encroaches and surrounds it: "a grave that becomes surrounded by city, whether all four directions, whether three directions, or two directions each facing the other: a distance of more that fifty *amah* (an *amah* is approximately a half a meter, so fifty would equal slightly less than twenty-five meters), to here and from fifty *amah* to here – we do not vacate it. Less than this, we vacate it. All the graves except for the grave of the king, and the grave of a Prophet. Ribbi Aqiva says, even te grave of the king, and the grave of a Prophet are vacated." [*Tosefta,* Tractate *Baba Batra* 1, 7].

The *Rashb"a* (Ribbi *Shlomo ben Avraham Ibn Aderet,* Sefardi *Rishon* 4995-5070; a student of Rabbenu Yonah Gerondi and the Ramban) permits the removal of the deceased from his grave in order to transfer him to a family plot, which is considered a more respectable grave, and thus wrote the *Arukh HaShulHan*: "We don't bring the deceased from a city that has graves to another city, except from outside the Land (of *Yisrael*) to the Land (of *Yisrael*), or to bring him to the place of his ancestor's graves. And if his Will mandates to bring him from one place to another, or his Will mandates to bury him in his home, and not in the cemetery – we listen to him. And, it's permitted to place limestone on him, so as to cause the body to decompose faster, and to bring him to a place that he designates in his Will [*Yoreh De'ah* 363]".

The *ShulHan Arukh* the prohibition of vacated is reserved in two cases: The deceased and bones are not vacated; not from a respectable grave to a respectable grave, and not from a disgraceful grave to another disgraceful grave, and not from a disgraceful grave to a respectable grave; And there is no need to say from the respectable grave to the disgraceful one. But, within his own — even from a respectable grave to a disgraceful grave is permitted, that person is guaranteed to be able to rest with his ancestors. And also, in order to bury him in the Land of *Yisrael.*" [*ShulHan Arukh, Yoreh De'ah*, Section 363:1]

However, in the *Yerushalmi* [Tractate *Ketuboth*, Chapter 12:3] they say about bringing the bodies of the deceased to the Land of *Yisrael* - "They come and defile my Land."

Ribbi Yehudah said: *Ya'aqov* said, "And, I will lie with my ancestors, you should bring me up from *Mitsrayim*, and bury me in their graves." There, we learn, one whose soul departs in the domain of the other, and his body is buried in the holy land, on this it is written: "And they will and defile my land and my inheritance is made an abomination," and *Ya'aqov* says, "bury me in their graves," but his sould departed in another domain. Ribbi Yehudah says: *Ya'aqov* is different, because the Holy Presence clung to him and cleaved to him, as it states[*Bereshit* 46:4]: "I will go down with you to Mitsrayim" and I will dwell with him in the Exile, and I will surely bring you back up, to join with your soul, and bury your body in the graves of your ancestors. What is the intention? Even though his soul departed in the domain of another. "And Yosef will place his hands on your eyes," -- of course Yosef, because he is the firstborn according to the desire of the heart; the firstborn of the first drop, as it has been said. Because the Holy One knew, and to him it was hidden, I will inform him of Yosef, because upon him, all of his love is dependent. [the Holy Zohar, page 226a]

Maran *Hakham* Rabbi Ovadiah Yosef, of blessed memory, refers to this when he writes, "It is only permitted to bring the Righteous Yosef and Ya'aqov, because they were forced to live outside the Land." In his respona he continues to weigh the issue, stating that even the Holy Zohar [Section 1, page 266a] is very strict in this regard. Further, he adds, there are those who contend that in our time, when it is relatively simple to go up (immigrate) to the Land of *Yisrael,* and yet someone refuse to go up (and live in Israel), only wishing to be brought up for burial, after he pass away – this might be such case as discussed in the Zohar, in which the deceased being brought for burial in Israel, might be bring about a Heavenly indictment, G-d Forbid. However, Maran *Hakham* Ovadiah points out that the individual who truly desires to come up to the Land of *Yisrael* (but was unable), or he was engaged in spreading the teaching of Torah abroad, certainly it is good for that person's soul to be buried in the Holy Land, and it is concerning this, that it say the land will atone for him. In his Responsa, Maran *Hakham* Ovadiah cites the example of the funeral of Rabbi Moshe Feinstein, who passed away in the United States, and was buried in *Har MenuHoth* in *Yerushalayim* [See further: Responsa *Y'bi'a Omer*, Volume 7, *Yoreh De'ah*, Section 39, and Responsa *Tshuvoth* and *Hanhagoth* Volume 1, Section 707].

Sometimes, a long time passes before bones of the deceased are brought up, ieither due to their specific request, or do to a decision of their descendents. Thus, for example, our ancestor *Ya'aqov* asked *Yosef* to take care of burying him in the Land of *Yisrael*: "And I will lay with my fathers, Carry me out of *Mitsrayim* and bury me in their graves." *Yosef*'s bones were brought for burial in the Land of *Yisrael* by the *B'ney Yisrael* when they left *Mitsrayim* at his request before his death (*Sh'moth* 13:19), and at the time of the Exodus *Moshe Rabbenu* himself carried with him *Yosef*'s coffin. Examples from our own time include the the bringing the remains of the holy rabbi *Hayyim David Azuli* (the *Hida*), Rabbi Meir Shapira, and others.

When the subject was raised to bring the remains of Moshe Montefiore for burial in the Land of *Yisrael*, there was disagreement amont the *posqim*. According to one opinion, the *Halakhah* seems to be indicated in the *ShulHan Arukh* that all remains can be brought to the Land of *Yisrael*, and yhis is the way that Maran *Hakham* Ovadiah Yosef, *z"l*, ruled [Responsa *Yalqut Yosef*, volume 7, Section 32, note 5, page 269]. On the other hand, Rabbi Moshe Feinstein restricts this, claiming that it is only permitted "sons who want the good of their father, but not to others." In other words, according to his opinion, there is no blanket permission to bring all the deceased to the Land of *Yisrael*, but only when special circumstances apply [Responsa *Igroth Moshe*, on *Yoreh De'ah*, Volume 3, Section, 153] . It It should be noted that Rabbi Feinstein's prohibition was specifically for the burial of a body that had already been buried, but a body that has not yet been buried, he permitted to be brought to the Land of *Yisrael*, as was done after his own passing, wherein Rabbi Moshe Feinstein, who was brought to the Land of *Yisrael* for burial.

My own Rabbi, *Hakham* Ya'aqov Kassin, *tsz"l*, who was certainly familiar with the Zohar, requested to be buried in Israel. He was of the opinion, similar to that of Maran *Hakahm* Ovadia Yosef, that one who traveled abroad to serve the Jewish community there, was still connected to the Holy Land, as a traveler who happens to be abroad at the time of his passing, and certainly can be brought to *Yisrael* for burial.

47:30 – וְשָׁכַבְתִּי עִם־אֲבֹתַי
"But when I sleep with my fathers..."

Rashi teaches that this expression refers exclusively to one's death and not to burial. He brings several verses throughout the *Tanakh* in support.

Our tradition teaches that sleep is one sixtieth of death and that aspects of the soul actually leave the body during sleep. When one sleeps with one's fathers, the soul completely leaves and does not return, until the great awakening of the Resurrection of the Dead in the End of Days.

47:31 – וַיִּשְׁתַּחוּ יִשְׂרָאֵל
"...*Yisrael* bowed down ..."

This fulfilling the dream of *Yosef*, that even his father would bow down to him. Rashi teaches that "The fox in his time — bow down to him." That is, that even the lion (*Yisrael*), must bow down to the fox (*Yosef*, his son), when the latter is king. Ibn Ezra, however, teaches that *Yisrael* is bowing down to HaShem here.

48:2 – וַיִּתְחַזֵּק יִשְׂרָאֵל
" ...*Yisrael* strengthened himself..."

Rashi explains that even though *Yosef* was his son, *Ya`aqov* saw it appropriate to extend him the honor due to a ruler, for *Yosef* was "as a king in *Mitsrayim*." We learn throughout *Tanakh* [Bible] that it is incumbent upon one to extend honor to royalty, even if they are evil. For instance, we see *Moshe Rabbeinu* giving honor to *Par`oh* and the Prophet *Eliyahu* extending honor to *Ahab* (though in the latter case we only see this when the errant king of *Yisrael* repented of his evil ways, albeit, this too, only lasted briefly).

48:3 – וַיֹּאמֶר יַעֲקֹב אֶל־יוֹסֵף
"Ya`aqov says to *Yosef ..."*

Ya`aqov* explains to *Yosef* the prophesy he received from HaShem in *Luz*. There, God promises him that from him will issue "a nation" and "an assembly of nations." "A nation," refers to *Binyamin*, and "an assembly of nations," teaches that one of the tribes is to be divided into two. This gift, *Ya`aqov tells *Yosef*, he decides to bestow upon him. In this way, *Ya`aqov* was able to bestow the firstborn portion on *Yosef* without causing conflict amongst the brothers.

I find it interesting that there is no tribe of *Yosef*. It is as if when he was sold, and taken from *Ya`aqov*, he was removed, so to speak, from the 'children of Yisrael,' only to be restored through his children. To me this resonates with the many cases of *ba`al tshuva* [returnees to traditional Judaism] in our time. Many are the children and grandchildren of those that were taken, or turned their back on Judaism. Yet, their descendents felt a spark, or a pull, and chose to come home.

I am reminded of the true story of a friend of mine in yeshiva. He was a convert to Judaism from South America. He described how he always felt drawn to Judaism, even though he was raised Catholic. What is fascinating, however, is that after his parents passed away, he inherited a roomful of family artifacts. Among the artifacts was a small figure of Jesus that had been in the family for generations. As a convert to Judaism, he didn't know what to with it, and thought to donate it to a museum.

In the process of moving it, the small statue fell, and broke open, revealing a hidden scroll inside. The scroll was a *mezuzah*, the parchment that all Jews are commanded to place upon their doorposts.

Upon research, he discovered that he was descended from the *Anusim*, those Jews that had been forcibly converted in Spain and Portugal. Many of whom later left for the New World, to start a new life. It seems that his ancestors had been secret Jews, hiding their Judaism from their children. Eventually, however, their souls found their way home.

His story is unique, but not singular. I have met many converts to Judaism, who later discovered a Jewish ancestor in their family tree.

48:3 – אֵל שַׁדַּי נִרְאָה־אֵלַי

"...*E-l Shadday* appeared to me ..."

According to the Ar"i *z"l* [*Shaar HaPasuqim*, parshat *Way'Hi*], this is a beautiful hint at the future redemption throughthe agency of *Moshe* and *Aharon*, because "*E-l Shadday*" is the gematria of *Moshe*, and the word *nereh* (appeared) has the same letters as *Aharon*.

48:5 – לִי־הֵם

"...are mine ..."

That is they will be counted as *Ya`aqov's* own sons in every regard, and that each will be considered a full tribe, and will receive a tribal portion of land.

48:5 – אֶפְרַיִם וּמְנַשֶּׁה כִּרְאוּבֵן וְשִׁמְעוֹן

"*Efra'im* and *M'nasheh* is as *Reuven* and *Shim'on*"

The gematria of *Efra'im* and *M'nasheh* is equivalent (together) to the gematria of *Reuven* and *Shim'on* (together, with a *kollel*). Further, this is the gematria of the verse: "*Wayihi b'shalaH Par'oh*" "And *Par'oh* sent them". This seems extremmly appropriate, because it is true, that at the time of the Exodus, when the Children of *Yisrael* left *Mitsrayim*, the tribes of *Efra'im* and *M'nasheh* left exactly the same as the tribes of *Reuven*, and *Shim'on*. Further, it is also intersting to note that this is the same gematria for the verse: קוֹל דְּמֵי אָחִיךָ צֹעֲקִים אֵלַי מִן הָאֲדָמָה, "The voice of your brother's blood cries out to me from the earth." In other words, this seems to be a rectification, of *Kayan's* killing of *Hevel*.

48:6 – יִקָּרְאוּ בְּנַחֲלָתָם

"...and they shall be called in their inheritance."

In this way, *Ya`aqov* was able to give a double portion to *Yosef* without usurping the birthright of the eldest.

48:7 – וַאֲנִי בְּבֹאִי מִפַּדָּן מֵתָה עָלַי רָחֵל

"As for me, when I came from *Padan*, *RaHel* died ..."

Ya`aqov* explains to *Yosef*, why he is troubling his son to carry him to *Hebron* when *Ya`aqov did not do the same for *Yosef's* mother, but rather buried her where she died. We learn from the *Midrash* that

Ya`aqov was commanded to bury *RaHel* there, so that when the Children of *Yisrael* would be exiled from the land, she would be able to beseech mercy from HaShem, at the border of the Land.

48:8 – וַיֹּאמֶר מִי־אֵלֶּה

"…and said, 'Who are these?'"

It seems strange that *Ya`aqov* doesn't seem to recognize his grandchildren. The Torah seems to be hinting to the time when *Ya`aqov* came before his father for a blessing, and was asked who he was. Moreover, by asking who they were, we understand the significance of the their names. This is the hint that helps us understand why *Ya`aqov* switches his hands on the two boys, blessing the younger with his right, and the older with is left. It seems to me that the significance of their names and the reason they received those names plays a vital role in this decision.

48:10 – וְעֵינֵי יִשְׂרָאֵל כָּבְדוּ מִזֹּקֶן

"The eyes of *Ya `aqov* were *kaved* [literally "heavy though often translated as dim] from age …"

Throughout this section we are reminded, through many parallels of the blessing that *Ya`aqov* received from his father. As such, we must pay close attention to the various similarities, and differences that resonate throughout.

One significant difference is that, as opposed to the time when he received the blessing from *YitsHaq*, *Ya`aqov* is fully in charge of the situation, and everything is done out in the open, in full view, as it were. It seems to me that the expression, "his eyes were heavy with age," according to this understanding, may indicate that they contained the wisdom of age. It should be noted that in reference to *YitsHaq*'s sight, the word used is "*kh'hey*" (meaning weak, the same word used for *Leah*'s eyes), not "*kavod*."

48:16 – הַמַּלְאָךְ הַגֹּאֵל אֹתִי מִכָּל־רָע

"The *malakh* [angel] who redeemed me from evil …"

Rashi tells us that is the *malakh* who came to *Ya`aqov* while he was working for *Lavan* [*Bereshith* 31:11].

It seems to me, however, that this might also be the one who he wrestled with and changed his name to *Yisrael*, or that went before him to confront `*Esaw.*

Or, more precisely, the *malakh* an the aspect of the Holy One's Presence, which interacts with us in this world, and even though he may possess several names, he is ultimately the same servant serving faithfully in the role of messenger of the Most High.

48:16 – וְיִדְגּוּ
"...*w'yidgu* ..."

The word is translated as "let them grow." It's similarity to the word for fish, "*dag*," compels Rashi to explain the meaning as "to multiply and increase like fish."

It should be noted that there is a special relationship between this and HaShem's Name *Shadday,* when it is written out in full (each letter is written out in the full name of the letter. The equivalent in English would be akin to writing out the letter 'B', as 'Bee', 'F' as 'ef'' or 'W' as 'double yoo.''). For *Shadday,* it would be written out שין דלת יוד (*Shin, Daleth, Yod*), the filler letters are the gematria for פר"ו ורב"ו (*p'ru w'rabu*) meaning "to be fruitful and multiply." And this a further hint that the *malakh* simply represents the hidden Hand of HaShem.

48:19 – יָדַעְתִּי בְנִי יָדַעְתִּי
"...I knew, my son, I knew ..."

Rashi states simply that the *Ya`aqov* knows that he is the first born, yet this neither addresses the repetition of the verb, nor it being written in the past tense.

Ba`Al HaTurim tells us that the *gematria* of the word for "I knew" is equal to that of the words, "five kings," for from *Menasheh* will come five kings.

Or HaHayyim suggest that the verb is repeated because *Ya`aqov* is answering two questions of *Yosef.* The first being that *Ya`aqov* was not confused, and knew which boy was which, and the second that he understood who should be given the favored blessing for he knows the future through prophecy.

It seems to me that there may be another explanation for these phrases. When *Ya`aqov* heard the dreams of *Yosef,* we are told that he decided to guard the matter, which Rashi suggested meant that he understood its truth, and would wait for its fulfillment. One of the phrases might be a confession that he knew the truth of the dream, and now was witnessing its fulfillment.

It is also possible that the repetition of the phrase indicates that, on some level, he knew what had transpired between *Yosef* and the brothers. It seems significant to me that *Yosef* avoided any long personal contact with his father until this time. It might be, now that he was reconciled with his brothers, that he was avoiding the inevitable questions of such an encounter, which might incriminate his brothers, and cause a rift between them and their father.

48:19 – וְאוּלָם אָחִיו הַקָּטֹן יִגְדַּל מִמֶּנּוּ

"...however, the younger brother will be greater than he..."

This can be understood as, "I have chosen to make the younger brother greater." However, Rashi renders it that he is greater, because from him comes *Yehoshuah*, who will lead the conquest of *Yisrael* and teach Torah to the nation.

This is also a reflection of his name, *Ephraim*, which implies the blessing of fruitfulness. The name of his brother, *Menashe*, however, reflects being forgotten. The blessings *Ya`aqov* bestows is one of growth and remembrance.

48:20 – בְּךָ יְבָרֵךְ יִשְׂרָאֵל

"...by these shall *Yisrael* bless, saying ..."

And this is so, for every *Erev Shabbath*, Jewish parents bless their children with these very words. One explanation for this tradition, is that even under the most adverse of circumstances, *Ephraim* and *Menashe* maintained their Jewish identity. They grew up as Jews amidst a hostile gentile environment, of a corruptive culture, and assimilation. This is something that their descendents will need to do both in their continued exile in *Mitsrayim*, and in the later exiles. The last of which, we are still in its midst.

48:22 – שְׁכֶם אַחַד

"...*Shkhem aHad* [literally one shoulder, but rendered one portion]..."

Yosef will receive his own portion as well, according to Rashi, and this is the city of *Shkhem*, where he will be buried. His grave site is visited there to this day.

Another possibility is that the "one portion more" refers to the two portions given to *Yosef's* sons.

Another interesting comparison is a verse in *Zephania* [3:9]: "For then will I turn to the people a pure language, that they may all call upon the name of the HaShem, to serve Him as one [*Shkhem aHad*]" which gives resonation to other "End of Days" prophecies of *Ya`aqov*.

49:1 – וְאַגִּידָה לָכֶם אֵת אֲשֶׁר־יִקְרָא אֶתְכֶם בְּאַחֲרִית הַיָּמִים
"...that I may tell you...that which will occur in the End of Days."

While the words can also be translated "in the latter days," that is in the near (or distant) future, Rashi explains that he wanted to reveal the end, but at that moment the Divine Presence withdrew from him, and he began to discuss other things.

This is further supported by a careful reading of the text. *Ya`aqov* tells the sons to gather together, and then he will literally "call to them" about the End. The sons are told to gather together and heed the words of their father. It seems to me this is an allusion to the time when *Yisrael* will begin to gather together (*kibuts galioth*), and then HaShem will bring them the rest of the way home. This occurs when we heed our Father in Heaven. Further, each blessing is a prophecy of the role that they will bring to the future redemption.

And this seems to be the explanation of Rashi and the Ramban on the verse in *D'varim* [33:5], that "They gathered together in one bunch, and there was *shalom* among them – He is their King, and not as when there is disagreement among them" (Rashi). And "they make one collective bunch, and not as when they make several groups .. and the King is the Holy One. And, also it is the custom of the House of Rav to say this at the time of the blowing of the shofar." [See the Ramban, and the *Yerushalmi*, Tractate *Rosh Hashanah* 1:3]

If this is the message, then the key to redemption is the ability of the Children of *Yisrael* to gather together, to unify. When we become one, HaShem's Name becomes one. Yet just as there are twelve sons – and twelve tribes – unity does not mean sameness, as too many people think today. Rather, variety is desirable, even necessary, as long as everyone is unity in the goal of bringing HaShem's Light into the world, in accordance with His Will.

49:3 – רְאוּבֵן בְּכֹרִי אַתָּה כֹּחִי וְרֵאשִׁית אוֹנִי יֶתֶר שְׂאֵת וְיֶתֶר עָז

"Reu'ven, you are the first-born...crown of dignity...crown of power ..."

Rashi teaches that *Reu'ven* could have merited all three, namely the rights (and double portion) of the first born, the crown of the priesthood, and the crown of the kingship. However, due to his actions, he lost all of them.

This is a common theme in Torah. We do receive certain merits, or at least the potential fro them, based on inheritance. Everyone may have a different starting point. Even leadership positions have a certain level of inheritance to them, according to the Torah. However, this is not a fixed caste system, far from it. And, even the most lowly of birth can rise to the highest level of leadership and respect. For instance, it is known that some of the greatest sages came from very humble beginnings. Rabbi Akiva and Rabbi Meir, considered two of the greatest sages, were both descended from converts, for example.

Further, we are taught that everyone is judged in Heaven, at the End of Days, on his merits alone. No one is judged according to Rabbi Akiva's scale, for instance. The Sages teach that everyone is only expected to realize their own potential, not someone else's. Likewise, no one has an excuse for not realizing their full potential. Even if they achieved more than their neighbor, but fell short of what they themselves could accomplish, they will be considered deficient. As well, even if someone's achievements don't reach the level of others, but he exerted maximum effort, he will be considered meritorious.

49:4 – פַּחַז כַּמַּיִם

"Unstable as water ..."

That is he acted with recklessness and haste. HaRav Ya`aqov Peretz, *shlit"a*, teaches that the most important characteristic a person can have is that of a "restful soul." A person should take everything in stride, and be in control of himself to the point where he is able to respond with wisdom and patience to every situation. This quality, he teaches, will lead one to conquer other character flaws, such as anger and the like. When one is at peace with himself, he will not lose, as *Reu'ven* did, all that he deserves, but be able to examine the future and the impact his actions will have on it.

HaRav Peretz recommends that everyone train himself to be of restful spirit. That is they should not rush, but allow time to arrive where they need to be. They should take their meals slowly and deliberately, and perform other similar actions, in order to train themselves to be more relaxed. This, he teaches, is the secret to success. He relates that he had known several great men, such as the Hazon Ish and Rabbi Eliyahu Dessler, and both of them were expert in this characteristic. So too, did *Ya`aqov* operate, as when he "guarded the matter" of the dreams, and the incident of *Dinah*, until something could be done.

49:6 – אַל־תֵּחַד כְּבֹדְי

"...let my glory not be united ..."

That is, *Ya`aqov* is saying that he does not want his name linked with theirs, as is the case with the rebellions of *Zimri* (from *Shim`on*) and *QoraH* [from *Lewi*], where the Torah did not include, "the son of *Yisrael*" when it brought their lineage.

49:6 – בְּאַפָּם הָרְגוּ אִישׁ

"...for in their anger they slew men ..."

This refers to the destruction of *Shkhem* in anger. They were not punished for its destruction, and it seems from the blessing of *Moshe* that it was HaShem's Will, however, their motivation was less than pure.

However, it seems to me that this might also be referring of *PinHas's* (*Lewi*) killing of *Zimri* (*Shim`on*).

49:6 – וּבִרְצֹנָם עִקְּרוּ־שׁוֹר

"...and in their self-will they uprooted an ox."

This refers to their desire to lame *Yosef*, teaches Rashi. *Yosef* is referred to as an ox by *Moshe Rabbeinu*, when he blesses the tribes [*D'varim* 33:17].

49:8 – יְהוּדָה

"Yehudah ..."

The name is very significant, for the first [*yod*] and last [*hey*] letters spell one of the names of God, and the remainder is the word for glory [*hey-waw-daleth*]. Also, the name is HaShem's explicit name with an additional letter *daleth*. It is through the tribe of *Yehudah* that HaShem's name will be glorified, namely through *Dawidh HaMelekh* [King David] and the future *MashiaH*.

49:10 – לֹא־יָסוּר שֵׁבֶט מִיהוּדָה
"The scepter shall never depart from *Yehudah*..."

The kingship will be given to *Dawidh*, and his seed for eternity. It is from *Dawidh*, who is from the tribe of *Yehudah*, whom the *MashiaH* will descend.

49:11 – אֹסְרִי לַגֶּפֶן עִירֹה
"Binding to the vine, his foal ..."

Targum Onkelos renders the entire passage as referring to the time of Melekh Ha*MashiaH*. "The vine" is *Yisrael*; "his foal" is *Yerushalayim*. He then translates the rest of the verse as, "They will build His Temple."

49:13 – זְבוּלֻן לְחוֹף יַמִּים יִשְׁכֹּן
"*Zebulun* will live on the shore of the sea ..."

His possession will border the sea, for he will be engaged in trade.

49:14 – יִשָּׂשׂכָר חֲמֹר גָּרֶם רֹבֵץ בֵּין הַמִּשְׁפְּתָיִם
"*Yissakhar* is a large-boned ass..."

One that is able to bear a heavy burden, namely the yoke of the Torah.

49:16 – דָּן יָדִין עַמּוֹ כְּאַחַד שִׁבְטֵי יִשְׂרָאֵל
"*Dan* ..."

Rashi understands this passage to be referring to *Shim'shon* [Samson].

I learned from my teacher that *Shim'shon* is called, "the eyes of the *MashiaH*. Aside from the *MashiaH ben Yosef* and *MashiaH ben Dawidh*, there is also a *MashiaH ben Dan*, whose role is that of the warrior of *Yisrael*, the shield bearer of *MashiaH ben Dawidh*.

49:22 – בֵּן פֹּרָת יוֹסֵף בֵּן פֹּרָת עֲלֵי־עָיִן
"Ben Porath ..."

Literally: *Yosef* is a fruitful bough. The gematria of '*Porath*,' is equal to the four permutations of the name of HaShem יהו"ה (meaning the four different ways the Name can be written out in full -A"B S"G M"H and B"N), along with the four permutations of the Name אהי"ה [QS"A, QM"G and QN"A] together with the *kollel*. Also, the letters of the word *Porath*, can be rearranged to spell the word, *Potar* which means to solve or interpret, because *Yosef* is the interpreter of dreams.

49:23 – בַּעֲלֵי חִצִּים
"...the archers ..."

So called, because their tongues were like arrows, according to the Midrash, but Onkelos interprets these words to mean, "those who were divided," that is, those where were designated to divide the inheritance with him.

49:24 – אֶבֶן יִשְׂרָאֵל
"...the Stone of *Yisrael* ..."

Rashi teaches that the word for stone, "*even*," denotes "*av*" [father] and "*ben*" [son], meaning that *Yosef* was able to sustain *Ya`aqov* and his sons during the famine.

49:27 – יִטְרָף בַּבֹּקֶר יֹאכַל עַד
"...in the morning he devours the prey ..."

This refers to *Sha'ul* who was the first king, and is called morning.

49:27 – וְלָעֶרֶב יְחַלֵּק שָׁלָל
"...and at evening time he divides the spoils."

This refers to *Mor'dikhai* and *Esther* who divide the spoils of *Haman* in the evening, which is the exile.

49:28 – וַיְבָרֶךְ אוֹתָם

"...and blessed them ..."

Rashi teaches that from this, we see that every one of the sons received a blessing, even though it might not seem so from that which was written.

49:33 - וַיְכַל יַעֲקֹב לְצַוֹּת אֶת־בָּנָיו וַיֶּאֱסֹף רַגְלָיו אֶל־הַמִּטָּה וַיִּגְוַע וַיֵּאָסֶף אֶל־עַמָּיו

"*Ya`aqov* finished charging his sons; he gathered up his feet and passed away..."

This is the way in which the truly righteous die. My wife's mother tells of her father, *z"l*, who lived to be over a hundred years old. One day, he was feeling "under the weather," so the entire family gathered to see him. He blessed all of the children and grandchildren, charged them and then recited the *Sh'ma`*. At that point, he simply closed his eyes and passed away.

It is taught that the soul begins to tear away from the body forty days before one dies, and the righteous are sensitive to this, allowing them to make the necessary preparations.

50:2 – לַחֲנֹט אֶת־אָבִיו

"...to embalm his father ..."

This seems strange, for this is contrary to Jewish practice. Ribbi *Yehudah HaNasi*, cited in *Bereshit Rabbah*, suggests that this is one reason why *Yosef* died before his brothers. However, other rabbis are cited as saying it was *Ya`aqov* who requested this, for it states that "his sons did as he had commanded them" [*Bereshith* 50:12].

It is suggested that this was done, so that it would not arouse suspicions amongst the Egyptians. It is taught that the bodies of the righteous do not rot. Therefore, in order that Egyptians did not witness *Ya`aqov*'s body being preserved, without being embalmed, *Yosef* had him embalmed. In this way, he also insured that *Ya`aqov* would not become the object of worship when the people witnessed the miracle.

50:3 – וַיִּבְכּוּ אֹתוֹ מִצְרַיִם

"...and the Egyptians wept ..."

Because *Mitsrayim* was filled with blessings when *Ya`aqov* arrived.

50:6 – כַּאֲשֶׁר הִשְׁבִּיעֶךָ

"...as he made you swear ..."

Rashi teaches that *Par`oh* only allowed *Yosef* to go because of the oath.

50:10 – גֹּרֶן הָאָטָד

"...the threshing floor of *Atad* ..."

According to *Masekhet Sota*, all the kings of Canaan, and the chiefs of *Yishmael* came out to battle, but when they saw the crown of *Yosef* on *Ya`aqov*'s bier, they all rose and hung their own crowns on it as well, surrounding it with crowns, like a threshing floor surrounded by a fence of thorns.

50:15 – וַיִּרְאוּ אֲחֵי־יוֹסֵף

"When the brothers of *Yosef* saw ..."

That is to say, they realized the possible implications. There seems to be a hint to their father's relationship with *`Esaw* who vowed to destroy *Ya`aqov* after his father died.

50:16 – אָבִיךָ צִוָּה

"...your father commanded ..."

Masekhet Yebamot states that they modified the words of their father in the interest of peace, for *Ya`aqov* did not make this commandment, for he did not suspect *Yosef*.

50:21 – וַיְדַבֵּר עַל־לִבָּם

"...spoke to the heart ..."

His words were spoken in a way that they could accept them. It is these traits of the sons of *Ya`aqov* — forgiveness, trust, and reconciliation, which will allow us to merit the blessings of *Yisrael* and witness the End of Days.

APPENDIX

For Sending a Friend Off on a Long Journey

<u>E</u>scort:

לִישׁוּעָתְךָ קִוִּיתִי יְהֹוָה: קִוִּיתִי יְהֹוָה לִישׁוּעָתֶךָ (בראשית מט:יח)

Lishu`athekha qwithi adonai; qwithi adonai lishu`athekha

Your salvation, I hope for HaShem; I hope for HaShem, your salvation.

(repeat 30 times)

וַיְהִי בִּנְסֹעַ הָאָרֹן וַיֹּאמֶר מֹשֶׁה קוּמָה יְהֹוָה וְיָפֻצוּ אֹיְבֶיךָ וְיָנֻסוּ מְשַׂנְאֶיךָ
מִפָּנֶיךָ: וּבְנֻחֹה יֹאמַר שׁוּבָה יְהֹוָה רִבְבוֹת אַלְפֵי יִשְׂרָאֵל: (במדבר י:לה-לו)

*Way'hi binso`a ha-aron wayomer Moshe quma adonai w'yafutsu
oyvekha wyanusu m'sanekha mipanekha. Uv'nuHo yomar shuvah
adonai r'vavoth alfey Yisrael.*

When the ark went for *Moshe* said, "Arise HaShem and scatter
Your enemies, cause those who despise You to flee before
You." And when it rested, he said, "Return HaShem the
thousands of myriad of Israel."

(repeat 6 times)

240

יְבָרֶכְךָ יְהוָה וְיִשְׁמְרֶךָ: יָאֵר יְהוָה פָּנָיו אֵלֶיךָ וִיחֻנֶּךָּ:

יִשָּׂא יְהוָה פָּנָיו אֵלֶיךָ וְיָשֵׂם לְךָ שָׁלוֹם: (במדבר ו:כד-כו)

*Yivarekh'kha adonai w'yishm'rekha: ya'er adonai panaw elekha
wiHuneka: yisa adonai panaw elekha w'ysem lkha shalom:*

May HaShem bless you and guard you. May HaShem shine
His Countenance upon you and be gracious to you. May
HaShem rest His countenance upon you and rest upon you
peace.

(repeat 10 times)

הַמַּלְאָךְ הַגֹּאֵל אֹתִי מִכָּל רָע יְבָרֵךְ אֶת הַנְּעָרִים וְיִקָּרֵא בָהֶם שְׁמִי וְשֵׁם
אֲבֹתַי אַבְרָהָם וְיִצְחָק וְיִדְגּוּ לָרֹב בְּקֶרֶב הָאָרֶץ: (בראשית מח:טז)

*Hamal'akh hagoel othi mikol ra` yivarekh eth han'`arim w'yiqare
vahem sh'mi w'shem avothay abraham w'YitsHaq wyidhgo larov
b'qErev haarets:*

The angel that redeemed me from all evil, may he bless the
youths and call them in my name and the name of my
fathers, Abraham and *YitsHaq*, and may the increase in the
bosom of the Land.

(repeat 5 times)

****

Traveler:

וִיהִי נֹעַם אֲדֹנָי אֱלֹ'הֵינוּ עָלֵינוּ וּמַעֲשֵׂה יָדֵינוּ כּוֹנְנָה עָלֵינוּ וּמַעֲשֵׂה יָדֵינוּ
כּוֹנְנֵהוּ: (תהילים צ':יז)

תְּפִלָּה לְמֹשֶׁה אִישׁ הָאֱלֹהִים אֲדֹנָי מָעוֹן אַתָּה הָיִיתָ לָּנוּ בְּדֹר וָדֹר:
בְּטֶרֶם הָרִים יֻלָּדוּ וַתְּחוֹלֵל אֶרֶץ וְתֵבֵל וּמֵעוֹלָם עַד עוֹלָם אַתָּה אֵל:
(תהילים צ':א-ב)

*Wihi no`am adonai elohenu `alenu uma`ase yadenu kon'nah `alenu
uma`aseh yadenu kon'nehu: t'filah l'Moshe ish ha-elohim adonai
ma`on atah hayitha lanu b'dor wador: b'Terem harim yuladu
wat'Hilel Erets w'thevel ume`olam `ad `olam atah el:*

Let the pleasantness of the Lord our G-d be upon us, may
the activities of our hands be prepared for us, and may the
deeds of our hands be prosperous.

(repeat 7 times)

Escort:

כִּי הוּא יַצִּילְךָ מִפַּח יָקוּשׁ מִדֶּבֶר הַוּוֹת: בְּאֶבְרָתוֹ יָסֶךְ לָךְ וְתַחַת כְּנָפָיו
תֶּחְסֶה צִנָּה וְסֹחֵרָה אֲמִתּוֹ: לֹא תִירָא מִפַּחַד לָיְלָה מֵחֵץ יָעוּף יוֹמָם:
מִדֶּבֶר בָּאֹפֶל יַהֲלֹךְ מִקֶּטֶב יָשׁוּד צָהֳרָיִם: יִפֹּל מִצִּדְּךָ אֶלֶף וּרְבָבָה
מִימִינֶךָ אֵלֶיךָ לֹא יִגָּשׁ: רַק בְּעֵינֶיךָ תַבִּיט וְשִׁלֻּמַת רְשָׁעִים תִּרְאֶה: (תהילים
צא:ג-ח)

*ki hu yatslikha mipaH yaqush midever hawoth. b'ev'ratho yasekh lkh
wthaHath k'nafaw teHseh tsinah w'soHerah amito. lo thira
mipaHadh laylah meHets ya`Uf yomam. medever ba-ofel yahalokh*

miqTev yashur tsohorayim yapol mitsid'kha elef urr'vavah miminekha elekha lo yanosh. raq b''enekha thabiT w'shilumath r'sha`im tir'-eh.

He will deliver you from the hunter's snare and from the pestilence He shall cover you with his pinions and under his wings shall you find refuge His truth will be your shield and buckler you shall not be afraid of the terror of the night nor of the arrow that flies by day nor of the pestilence that walks in the darkness nor of the destruction that wastes at noonday a thousand shall fall at your side and ten thousand at your right hand but it shall not come near you Only with your eye that hall behold and see the recompense of the of the wicked

****

Traveler:

כִּי אַתָּה יְהֹוָה מַחְסִי עֶלְיוֹן שַׂמְתָּ מְעוֹנֶךָ: (תהילים צא:ט)

Ki atah adonai maHsi `elyon samta m''onekha

For You HaShem are my refuge. The Eternal is Your dwelling place

****

Escort:

כִּי אַתָּה יְהֹוָה מַחְסִי עֶלְיוֹן שַׂמְתָּ מְעוֹנֶךָ: לֹא תְאֻנֶּה אֵלֶיךָ רָעָה וְנֶגַע לֹא יִקְרַב בְּאָהֳלֶךָ: כִּי מַלְאָכָיו יְצַוֶּה לָּךְ לִשְׁמָרְךָ בְּכָל דְּרָכֶיךָ: עַל כַּפַּיִם יִשָּׂאוּנְךָ פֶּן תִּגֹּף בָּאֶבֶן רַגְלֶךָ: עַל שַׁחַל וָפֶתֶן תִּדְרֹךְ תִּרְמֹס כְּפִיר וְתַנִּין: כִּי בִי חָשַׁק וַאֲפַלְטֵהוּ אֲשַׂגְּבֵהוּ כִּי יָדַע שְׁמִי: יִקְרָאֵנִי וְאֶעֱנֵהוּ עִמּוֹ אָנֹכִי בְצָרָה אֲחַלְּצֵהוּ וַאֲכַבְּדֵהוּ: אֹרֶךְ יָמִים אַשְׂבִּיעֵהוּ וְאַרְאֵהוּ בִּישׁוּעָתִי:

(תהילים צא: ט: טז)

ki atah adonai maHsi `elyon samta m''`onekha. lo th'-uneh elekha ra`ah w'nena` lo yiqrav b'oholekha. ki mal'akhiw yatsaweh lakh lishmar'ekha b'khol d'rakhekha. `al kapayim yisa-unekha pen tinof ba-even ragh-lekha. `al shaHal wafethen tidh-rokh tirmos k'fir w'thanin. Ki vi Hashaq wa-afaltehu asanvehu ki yadha` sh'mi. yiq'ra-eni w'e`enehu `imo anokhi v'tsarah aHal'tsehu wa-akhab'dhehu. orekh yamim asbiy`ehu w'arehu bishu`athi.

Because you HaShem are my refuge. The Eternal is Your dwelling place. no evil shall befall you nor shall any plague come near your dwelling for he shall give hs angels charge over you to keep you in all your ways. They shall bear you upon their hands lest you dash your foot against a stone you shall tread upon the lion and the adder the young lion and the crocodile you shall trample under foot because he has set his delight upon me therefore will I deliver him I will set him on high because he has known my name he shall call upon me and I will answer him I will be with him in trouble and I will deliver him and honor him with long life I will satisfy him and show him my salvation.

בִּטְחוּ בַיהֹוָה עֲדֵי עַד כִּי בְּיָהּ יְהֹוָה צוּר עוֹלָמִים: (ישעיה כו:ד)

עוֹלָמִים צוּר יְהֹוָה בְּיָהּ כִּי עַד עֲדֵי בַיהֹוָה בִּטְחוּ:

bitHu va-donai `adey `ad ki b'yah adonai tsur `olamim.

`olamim tsur adonai b'yah ki `ad `adey va-donai bitHu.

Trust in HaShem forever more, for HaShem God is an
Eternal Rock

Rock Eternal an is God HaShem for, more forever HaShem
in trust

(repeat 3 times)

יְהֹוָה עֹז לְעַמּוֹ יִתֵּן יְהֹוָה יְבָרֵךְ אֶת עַמּוֹ בַשָּׁלוֹם: (תהילים כט:יא)

בַשָּׁלוֹם עַמּוֹ אֶת יְבָרֵךְ יְהֹוָה יִתֵּן לְעַמּוֹ עֹז יְהֹוָה:

adonai `oz li`amo yiten adonai y'varekh eth `amo vashalom
vashalom `amo eth y'varekh adonai yiten li`amo `oz adonai

HaShem will give strength to His People, HaShem will bless
His people with Shalom

Shalom with people His bless will HaShem, people His to
strength give will HaShem

(Repeat 3 times)

יְהֹוָה צְבָאוֹת עִמָּנוּ מִשְׂגָּב לָנוּ אֱלֹהֵי יַעֲקֹב סֶלָה: (תהילים מו:ח)

Adonai ts'va-oth `imanu misgav lanu elohey Ya`aqov selah

HaShem of the Hosts in with us, the God of *Ya`aqov* is a fortress for us, forever.

(Repeat 3 times)

יְהֹוָה צְבָאוֹת אַשְׁרֵי אָדָם בֹּטֵחַ בָּךְ׃ (תהילים פג:יג)

Adonai ts'va-oth ashrey adham boTe-aH bakh

HaShem of the Hosts – content is the one who trusts in you.

(Repeat 3 times)

יְהֹוָה הוֹשִׁיעָה הַמֶּלֶךְ יַעֲנֵנוּ בְיוֹם קָרְאֵנוּ׃ (תהילים כ:י)

Adonai hoshi`ah HaMelekh ya`anenu v'yom qor-enu

HaShem save, the King will answer us on the day we call upon Him

(Repeat 3 times)

****

Traveler:

שִׁיר לַמַּעֲלוֹת אֶשָּׂא עֵינַי אֶל הֶהָרִים מֵאַיִן יָבֹא עֶזְרִי׃ עֶזְרִי מֵעִם יְהֹוָה עֹשֵׂה שָׁמַיִם וָאָרֶץ׃ (תהילים קכא:א-ב)

shir lama`aloth esa `eynay el heharim meayin yabo `ezri  `ezri me`im adonai `oseh shamayim wa-arets

A Song of Ascent. I lift up my eyes to the mountains; rom where with my help come? My help is from HaShem, Maker of the Heavens and the Earth.

****

Escort:

אַל יִתֵּן לַמּוֹט רַגְלֶךָ אַל יָנוּם שֹׁמְרֶךָ: הִנֵּה לֹא יָנוּם וְלֹא יִישָׁן שׁוֹמֵר יִשְׂרָאֵל: יְהֹוָה שֹׁמְרֶךָ יְהֹוָה צִלְּךָ עַל יַד יְמִינֶךָ: יוֹמָם הַשֶּׁמֶשׁ לֹא יַכֶּכָּה וְיָרֵחַ בַּלָּיְלָה: יְהֹוָה יִשְׁמָרְךָ מִכָּל רָע יִשְׁמֹר אֶת נַפְשֶׁךָ: יְהֹוָה יִשְׁמָר צֵאתְךָ וּבוֹאֶךָ מֵעַתָּה וְעַד עוֹלָם: (תהילים קכא:ג-ח)

al yaten lamoT raghlekha al tanum shomrekha. hineh lo yanum w'lo yishan somer Yisrael. adonai somrekha adonai tsil'kha `al yad y'minekha yomam hashemesh lo yakakah wyare-aH balaylah. adonai yishmar'kha mikol ra` yishmor eth nafshekha. adonai yishmor tse-th'kha uvo-ekha me`atah w''`ad `olam.

He will not let your foot falter; your Guardian does not slumber. Indeed, the Guardian of Yisrael neither slumbers nor sleeps. 6. HaShem is your Guardian; the HaShem is your protective shade at your right hand. The sun will not harm you by day, nor the moon by night. HaShem will guard you from all evil; He will guard your soul. HaShem will guard your leavings and your comings from now and for all time.

לֵךְ לְשָׁלוֹם

Lekh l'shalom

Go in Peace!

ABOUT THE AUTHOR

Rabbi Dov Abraham Ben-Shorr originally from Cleveland, Ohio lives with his family in Israel. He continues in the path of his teacher, one of the hidden greats of Israel.

Rabbi Ben-Shorr received his rabbinical training at Midrash Sephardi, before later becoming the school's Director of the English Language Program. He has also served as a community rabbi in the States, and currently lectures, teaches and learns at a variety of venues in Israel.

He also holds a B.A. in Linguistics and a M.A. in Bible.

He is the founder and Rosh Yeshiva of 'Beith David Yeshiva' and Yeshivat Shevet AHim.

Rabbi Ben-Shorr also wrote a weekly column for New York's Jewish Press.